"The missional church project endeavored to reconnect ecclesiology and missiology and identified the key convictions that undergirded the church in a post-Christendom, pluralistic world. In the years since, the term 'missional' has been adopted by a wide variety of traditions and attached to many add-on programs. This book brings much-needed clarity to a confused picture. It is no rehash of familiar material but rather breaks new ground and leaves the reader with an appetite for more!"—**Eddie Gibbs,** Fuller Theological Seminary

"*The Missional Church in Perspective* is the most precise, informed, and uncompromising parsing to date of the history of the concept of 'missional' both as a sensibility and as a form of praxis. Like all good historical analyses, this book provides not only a basis for understanding where we have been but also a well-honed tool for considering where we may need and want to go next."—**Phyllis Tickle,** author, *The Great Emergence*

"Concertgoers are familiar with the cacophonous roar that precedes great orchestral performances. Confusing and competing noises spill out of the orchestra pit as musicians tune and warm up their instruments. When the conductor takes the stand, however, these same instruments—now focused on a musical score—produce music. *The Missional Church in Perspective* provides sheet music for all those who want to participate in the missional symphony. The book's scholarship and synthesis qualify it to be a common score for us all."—**Reggie McNeal,** Leadership Network

"This book is a veritable morphology of the term 'missional.' As such it provides both conceptual tools with which to assess the impact of missional ideas on the Western church and a map that helps us chart possible future trajectories of what is clearly one of the most important movements in our times. Whether one fully agrees with the analysis or not, it certainly brings needed clarity to what is fast becoming a dangerously murky concept."—**Alan Hirsch,** Forge Mission Training Network

"*The Missional Church in Perspective* is a helpful and well-researched work that traces and evaluates streams within the missional church conversation, showing a wide awareness from evangelical, mainline, and historical sources. I have found a new required textbook for my missional church class."—**Ed Stetzer,** LifeWay Research; missiologist

"It is a rare book that can clearly and cogently describe a highly complex field while also setting a bold course for the future. *The Missional Church in Perspective* does precisely this. Making sense out of diverse and sometimes conflicting perspectives, it provides a brilliant historical analysis and useful categorization of the diverse voices in the missional conversation, offering a compelling vision for congregational renewal and transformation. I have little doubt that this book will serve as a centerpiece for the missional conversation for the next decade and beyond."—**Jack Reese,** Abilene Christian University

"I am among the many who have been deeply enriched by the missional church conversation, but I have been concerned lately that the term 'missional' has been losing potency even as it has been gaining popularity. This book comes along at just the right time to help participants in the missional conversation reconnect with the deeper theological themes that originally inspired Lesslie Newbigin and others. It is a fitting follow-up to *Missional Church*."—**Brian McLaren**, author and speaker

"The word 'missional' has been tossed around in so many different ways in recent discussions regarding the church that it is tempting to give up on it. But that would be a mistake; something of great importance has been associated with the term even amid all the confusion. This marvelous book helps us move beyond the confusion of tongues, while also pointing us in healthy new directions for a vital Christian presence in the world."—**Richard Mouw**, Fuller Theological Seminary

"Since the 1998 publication of *Missional Church*, 'missional' has become a buzzword in many church circles with too many church leaders picking up the language and attaching their own meanings to the term. The purpose of *The Missional Church in Perspective* is to restart and reshape the conversation—I expect it to succeed."—**George G. Hunter III**, Asbury Theological Seminary

"Dozens of books and articles have explored missional aspects of ecclesiology and church practice in the past decade and followers of the missional conversation have often found themselves confused by the elasticity of the word 'missional'—until now. This book examines the key voices in the missional conversation, plots its terrain, and then with sublime grace values and evaluates the contributions of numerous conversation partners. Don't buy another book on missional theology until you have read this one. It puts all others in perspective."—**Clayton J. Schmit**, Fuller Theological Seminary

"Van Gelder and Zscheile make 'missional' make sense. While many churches try to 'go missional' and many books on 'being missional' hit the market, this wise conversation guide sorts through the different uses of the term and points us toward a rich, hopeful future for God's people."—**M. Scott Boren**, pastor, consultant, and author, *Missional Small Groups*

"The missional conversation, which has experienced explosive growth over the last ten years, has been in sore need of a road map. *The Missional Church in Perspective* provides just that. In this scholarly and generous guide, Van Gelder and Zscheile clear away the confusion by providing a masterful, historical description of the various tracks of the missional church. Along the way, they tell the whole story of the movement, assessing its weaknesses and making counter proposals. In so doing, they have given us the book that can chart the course for the next era of the missional church, one of the most vital missionary movements in North America."—**David Fitch**, Northern Seminary

"The use of the term 'missional' has exploded in the last decade, taking on an extraordinary range of meaning. In the midst of this situation, Van Gelder and Zscheile perform two invaluable services: first, they provide a taxonomy of the various usages of the term that clarifies commonalities and differences; second, they set forth a compelling agenda for future reflection. As with any enterprise of this sort there will be disagreement concerning their judgments, but it is hard to imagine anyone interested in the missional conversation who would not find this to be an extremely helpful volume."—**John R. Franke**, First Presbyterian Church of Allentown, PA; Gospel and Our Culture Network

"This is one of those rare, paradigm-shifting books. More than a constructive synthesis of the various strands of the missional conversation, *The Missional Church in Perspective* provides a focused yet fluid and participatory approach that serves the church by addressing the future imaginatively and hopefully. This is an indispensable volume for academics, practitioners, and anyone whose heart is responsive to the mission of God in the world."—**Linda Bergquist**, Southern Baptist Convention California

"With anything outside the church's own walls now being labeled as 'missional,' the authors provide a healthy corrective. They do so not by throwing stones but by shaping content for the conversation, showing how missional is more than simply another strategy. The authors lay out how radically different and revolutionary it is for the church to be a missional people. This book not only adds to the conversation but also shapes and deepens it."—**Gary V. Nelson**, Tyndale University College and Seminary; author, *Borderland Churches*

"This is an important book. It represents the theological homework for those who want to take seriously the impulse toward a missional church by powerfully underscoring the vitality of trinitarian theology understood within a social and relational model. It offers a vibrant and relevant ecclesiology and invites a conversation about missiology that goes far deeper than mission studies and church growth strategies. It belongs on the reading list of anyone whose ecclesiological imagination is stirred by the promise of the reign of God."—**Paul K. Hooker**, Presbyterian Church (USA)—Presbytery of St. Augustine

"The missional conversation has for some time been in need of clarity. This book provides us with an understanding of this term and its origin while also offering helpful suggestions for extending the conversation. Using both biblical and theological resources, *The Missional Church in Perspective* clarifies and deepens the missional conversation. It is a welcome addition and should enhance our dialogue and work in the future."—**John M. Bailey**, Southern Baptist Convention

"'Missional' is a word everyone uses and few understand. It is a term that has been used, misused, and at times abused until it has lost its edge. The authors do a wonderful job in sharpening this dull edge so that it will serve the church well. This book provides both perspective and place—a perspective from which to understand the term 'missional' and a place to freshly engage it. Church leaders, pastors, church planters, and anyone seeking to understand God's mission are invited to join the conversation and engage the project."—**Jerry Dykstra**, Christian Reformed Church in North America

"Van Gelder and Zscheile make a most valuable contribution to the missional conversation. They offer a much-needed theological and missiological framework that invites ministers and congregations to inhabit the 'shalom space' of

God's reign coming on earth as it is in heaven."—**Terry Hamrick**, Cooperative Baptist Fellowship

"Over the last decade the missional church movement has proliferated with one casualty of this expansion being clarity about the key issues—biblical, theological, cultural, and ecclesiological—that initially informed and continue to shape the missional conversation. This book provides not only a definitive overview of the history of the movement but also points to a number of critical topics that must be explored as we move ahead."—**David Dunbar**, Biblical Seminary

"Finally, a book that untangles the web of ideas surrounding the 'missional' concept. Van Gelder and Zscheile provide a road map for the missional journey by sharing insights into its history, conception, and perspectives. With expertise, they engage us in theological thoughts and practical applications, taking readers on a virtual tour of all things missional."—**Bo Prosser**, Cooperative Baptist Fellowship

"Many say the term 'missional' has lost significance because of its wide use and diverse meanings. These authors take the opposite view, celebrating the elasticity of the term and offering an invitation for us to discover the powerful work of the Spirit within the missional conversation. This book challenges readers with its exploration of the intersection of contemporary theological thought and missional dialogue. It advocates a robust theological imagination, a posture of wonder regarding God's presence and work in the world today."—**Milfred Minatrea**, Missional Church Center

"If you are just starting to delve into all things missional, this is a great place to get the lay of the land. If you are a missional veteran, you simply must read this book in order to understand the history, where the discussion is now, and where we faithfully go from here."—**Teresa Lockhart Stricklen**, Presbyterian Church (USA)

"The missional church conversation has matured to the point that it is in need of curation, which is what this book provides in careful, faithful, and imaginative terms. But the book is also a call to remember (1) that 'missional church' is not a strategy or an approach but rather the taproot and (2) that mission is core to the church because mission is core to God, meaning that we must come together by the power of the Spirit to find a fruitful way forward. This book is a critical force in clarifying, deepening, and sustaining this important conversation."—**Nate Frambach**, Wartburg Theological Seminary

"The missional church conversation offers the most important and generative perspectives on theological praxis in a generation. Or the missional church conversation only repackages old habits and missteps in new language. Or the missional church conversation may engage some interesting theological matters, but it is not translated into praxis. With dozens of books claiming roles in this venture, how might we make sense of it all? Van Gelder and Zscheile walk us through these resources, provide historical and contextual perspectives, clarify the center and the fringes, offer connections and critiques, point toward the work ahead, and leave us all in their debt."—**Mark Lau Branson**, Fuller Theological Seminary

"This volume performs two essential tasks. First, it provides us with a way of understanding the missional conversation so that we can make sense of the many contributions to the debate. Second, it provides a theological framework that propels the conversation to a new level of debate. Van Gelder and Zscheile offer a work that is generous, balanced, and insightful."—**Martin Robinson**, Bible Society, United Kingdom

"Van Gelder and Zscheile have done a masterful job of unpacking the history, identifying the underlying assumptions, pointing out gaps in the theological discussion, and mapping out various streams of missional church theory and practice. Their emphasis upon the role of the Holy Spirit, within a relational trinitarian perspective, invites readers to envision a more biblically grounded and theologically relevant shape for a missional church. For anyone, lay or clergy, seeking to discern and participate in God's redemptive mission in the world, this book is a must-read."—**Inagrace Dietterich**, Center for Parish Development

"Van Gelder and Zscheile have succeeded in bringing clarity to the term 'missional' by providing the most rigorous and theologically astute treatment of the subject to date. Beginning with a thorough review of the history and development of the missional conversation, they graciously critique some of the inadequacies of how the term 'missional' has been defined, described, and applied, and they further articulate a clear theological basis for understanding the missional church."—**Ken Thiessen**, Power of One Consulting

"Why another book on the missional church? The answer is simple: these authors have captured the heart and substance of the conversation about living into God's vision for mission in a post-Christian culture. They offer a rich and powerful perspective about where and how God's Spirit is leading congregations to engage in the life of the world. For churches disconnected from their culture or those seeking to rediscover a sense of God's promised future, this book offers hope and expands our missional imagination."—**Rick Rouse**, Grand Canyon Synod, Evangelical Lutheran Church in America

"These authors provide us with the biblical and theological resources that have often been neglected in discussions around missional churches. This is essential reading for all leaders who seek to transform their churches from a maintenance mind-set to a missional one."—**Dennis Bickers**, American Baptist Churches of Indiana and Kentucky

"This book is the most comprehensive and clear analysis of the missional conversation to date, providing helpful historical perspective of the movement as well as needed clarity to the current use of missional language. It interacts with an extensive collection of missional literature, all carried out with great wisdom and grace, and advocates several important theological categories for strengthening and extending the missional conversation. Anyone serious about understanding and engaging the missional conversation will find this latest contribution to be invaluable."—**Brad Brisco**, church planting strategist

## THE MISSIONAL NETWORK

### CRAIG VAN GELDER

Editor, The Missional Network Series

The Missional Network series publishes books that contribute to the ongoing missional church discussion in light of biblical and theological perspectives. Books in the series seek to reclaim more fully the identity of the church in order to better inform its purpose and ministry and aid the church in participating more fully in God's mission within our dramatically changed context.

# The
# Missional Church
# in Perspective

## Mapping Trends and Shaping the Conversation

Craig Van Gelder
Dwight J. Zscheile

Foreword by Alan J. Roxburgh

Baker Academic
a division of Baker Publishing Group
Grand Rapids, Michigan

Published by Baker Academic
a division of Baker Publishing Group
P.O. Box 6287, Grand Rapids, MI 49516-6287
www.bakeracademic.com

Printed in the United States of America

Library of Congress Cataloging-in-Publication Data
Van Gelder, Craig.
    The missional church in perspective : mapping trends and shaping the conversation / Craig Van Gelder, Dwight J. Zscheile.
        p.   cm.
    Includes bibliographical references and index.
    ISBN 978-0-8010-3913-3 (pbk.)
    1. Mission of the Church. 2. Missional Church. I. Zscheile, Dwight J., 1973– II. Title.
BV601.8.V29 2011
262′.7—dc22                                                                2010048257

11   12   13   14   15   16   17        7   6   5   4   3   2   1

To the many church leaders
participating in the missional conversation
through whom the Spirit is innovating a
renewed vision for the church in our time

# Contents

# Foreword

ALAN J. ROXBURGH

During the last dozen years it's been my privilege to travel across North America and much of the world working with churches, leaders, schools, and denominational systems on questions of change, innovation, and missional transformation. In all these places the language shaping these engagements is *missional* language. Some ten years ago, when the book *Missional Church: A Vision for the Sending of the Church in North America* was published, "missional" was a little-known word buried in the deliberations of European missiologists. Today the word is so commonly used that hardly a month goes by without a book or two arriving at my door from one publisher or another with the word "missional" in its title. It is significant that in the brief space of a decade such an obscure word came into common use across all denominational systems and within a diverse set of Christian movements. And yet, despite such widespread usage, it is a word that is regularly misunderstood by the vast majority of people, be they clergy or laity. One of the first questions I am usually asked by clergy and church members alike is, can you give us a definition of "missional"?

I write this as a way of introducing this wonderful book by Craig Van Gelder and Dwight Zscheile. It addresses the issues around the word "missional" with clear analysis, a strong theological assessment, and a comprehensive understanding of the missiological issues at stake in both its history and current usage. At the same time, this book is not primarily an analysis of what has happened to this word; rather, it is a call to the church to embrace the mission of God in our strange new place. I confess that for the past several years I've been frustrated, angry, disillusioned, and disheartened at the ways the missional language has come to be used within the church. The metaphor that comes to mind is that of *after Babel*, when people use language to describe reality and yet the language seems to be so different it fails to communicate or connect.

Like me, you may have noticed the plethora of missional images presented in a wide variety of books and seminars these days (obviously, I have contributed to this Babel of proposals, so I count myself in the observations). We are told how to form a missional movement or create a missional renaissance or form missional leaders or find a missional Jesus and so on and so on. One reads these various books with a basic question: how can they use the same word but not seem to have much in common beyond that one point? No wonder people in our churches keep asking what the word means, and why they feel as if they have been propelled into a confusing world whose language sounds like a lot of "ba, ba, ba, ba, ba. . . ." In this context, this particular book is a welcome gift. Carefully, thoughtfully, and with incredible grace, Craig and Dwight seek to convene a table where we are able to listen to one another, discern our differences, understand what is at stake in terms of gospel issues, and so frame a new kind of conversation.

But this book also offers much more. It is a work of imagination; it wrestles with utterly critical, existential issues that are shaping the future of the church. These authors are convinced that missional language contains crucial ideas and themes essential for the future of the church. What they have undertaken is nothing less than an invitation to a divergent audience of church leaders and academics to enter a robust community of engagement, not to determine who is right or wrong about specific aspects of what "missional" means, but to recognize what is at stake right now: our very participation in the mission of God in North America.

Craig and Dwight are not asking us to agree on all the theological points they make; they're not assuming we will concur with everything about their assessment of some movements or, even, some theologian or missiologist. You may not agree with how they present certain facts, and you might parse details of twentieth-century missiology or discussions of the past decade differently, but this level of argument is really not their intention. They believe the missional language continues to offer us something really important; critical issues are at stake in its usage, and we have to engage them with as much theological vigor and wisdom as we can. This book grapples with the evangelical call of the church to be God's sign, witness, and foretaste in massively shifting, changing, morphing worlds.

What strikes me about this work of imagination is how Craig and Dwight have gone about constructing their book. As I read the emerging argument of these chapters, I was struck by the generosity that pervades every page. The pull of the book is to construct a welcoming table around which differing versions, visions, and views of missional might come together to ask new questions that are God-shaped, seeking to support one another and discern ways in which the theological and missiological implications of missional language during the past decade or more might support us all for the sake of the kingdom. This central motif of the book kept drawing me forward in following the unfolding of these two writers' carefully developed arguments and proposal.

This book is written by two people who love the church and who long for the gospel to be practiced in our strange times. It is unique, therefore, in its direct appeal to many, like me, who have shaped this missional conversation during the last decade. The book invites everyone to a table for engagement with one another because the authors believe we can't let the missional conversation slide into the oblivion of another Babel. As I read the manuscript and moved through its chapters, I was addressed by the Spirit of God at this very point. In my own work I talk a lot about creating safe spaces in which to call forth the voices and stories of God among the people. I provide others with the resources and skills to do this. And yet, to confess my own issues, I have also carried a critical spirit toward many of the ways that people use missional language in their work. This book offers me a different possibility, inviting me out of my sense of being right and calling me to a table of listening and dialogue with others for the sake of the kingdom. It challenges me to offer a welcoming, safe space in the midst of others with whom I disagree about how they use missional language. This book goes much deeper than argument; it is an invitation to all of us to enter the spaces of welcoming and dialogue where we might be read and transformed by the Spirit of God.

I am deeply grateful for this book and the two people who wrote it. In truth, it has changed my mind and attitudes. I have heard the Spirit of God in these pages and want to respond to the invitation I have received. And I want to invite others who write, teach, preach, consult, and seek to lead movements that are missional to read this book with an openness also to hear its invitation and come to the table. This will not be an easy table. Craig and Dwight have made it clear that there are hard questions and tough issues to engage, but this is the conversation we need now. We need the engagement, not the Babel and not the distance from one another.

Earlier this year I was in Marburg, Germany. I was taken on a brief but delightful tour of the old city with its wonderful streets and massive castle. It was pointed out to me that in one of the castle's rooms Luther and Zwingli met in the early days of the sixteenth-century European-Germanic Reformation to discuss their differences concerning the Eucharist. The details of the debate are not important here. I was struck by what it must have cost these men to make this journey in terms of the times and the terrain. The castle sits atop a high hill; reaching it today still requires a demanding walk. The tragedy of the image that came to me, as I stood by the castle on a cold March day and looked up at the window of the room where the two men met, is that they walked away from each other without ever coming to resolution. How different those European movements might have been had they stayed and reached a new understanding. I think we are in such a place today in the missional conversation. I read this book through the Spirit inviting us to come together for the sake of the church and its mission in our time, and I invite you to read it with openness to the possibility of the Spirit's invitation to you.

May 2010

# Series Preface

The missional church conversation is continuing to expand. Scores of books have come into print over the past decade that reference "missional" as a key concept for discussing the identity, purpose, and ministry of the church. Those of us working with The Missional Network (TMN) are especially committed to contributing to this conversation in three primary ways: (1) offering consulting and coaching services to churches; (2) providing tools and resources to help churches engage in adaptive change; and (3) publishing books that utilize missional theology to help churches engage in systemic transformation. Our focus in each of these ministry initiatives is to contribute to the ongoing missional discussion in light of biblical and theological perspectives. We believe that reclaiming more fully the identity of the church is basic for informing its purpose and ministry.

The church's identity has to do with its very nature, what the church *is* in light of its being created by the Spirit. Much of current missional church literature assumes the church's identity is self-evident and moves all too quickly to focusing on what the church is to *do* on behalf of God in the world or how the church should organize itself for this work. These approaches, however, shift the focus too quickly away from the agency of the Spirit in the midst of the church and redirect it to the primacy of human agency and responsibility.

Being explicit about the agency of the Triune God through the Spirit in relation to God's mission in the world and clarifying the church's participation in that mission are important concepts. These perspectives were central to the conception of "missional" when it was first introduced in the 1998 publication of the now seminal book *Missional Church: A Vision for the Sending of the Church in North America*. Continued developments in trinitarian studies since that time, which emphasize the social trinity into relation to the sending trinity, increase the importance of maintaining this perspective. This is the biblical and theological approach that The Missional Network is seeking to contribute to the missional conversation—framing the role of human agency within the divine agency of the Triune God.

In pursuing this contribution, TMN has developed a partnership with Baker Publishing Group to publish a series of books, beginning with this present volume, that will build on the already established tradition of contributing to the missional conversation. This work, we believe, is of great importance to the church today as it seeks to participate more fully in God's mission within our dramatically changed context.

Craig Van Gelder
Editor, The Missional Network Series

# Acknowledgments

This book, like so many, is the result of numerous influences that have shaped our lives, including that of a number of people who have contributed to our thinking. Time and space do not allow for a detailed list of such, but there are several to whom we are particularly indebted and whom we would like to acknowledge specifically.

First, we want to express our appreciation to the leaders of the Gospel and Our Culture Network (GOCN), who had the vision and the courage to take on a writing project that brought missiology into direct conversation with ecclesiology. This work resulted in the publication of *Missional Church: A Vision for the Sending of the Church in North America* in 1998. This volume has substantively reshaped the conversation about the church during the past decade in North America as well as in many other places throughout the world. Special thanks go to George Hunsberger, who provided overall leadership for the GOCN movement, and to Darrell Guder, who guided the work of the writing team and served as editor of that now seminal volume.

Second, we want to acknowledge and thank the scores of church leaders and contributing authors who have engaged the missional church conversation during the past twelve years. Many of these contributors to the conversation are identified in this book. Our thinking about "missional" has been served by their work, and we hope that our work, in turn, will prove helpful to them.

We are blessed to serve in a multifaceted learning community comprised of faculty, students, and staff at Luther Seminary. Ongoing collaboration with our fellow faculty in the Center for Missional Leadership and with the many doctoral and master's students with whom we interact has deeply enriched our understanding of the missional church, particularly in an ever-widening array of global contexts. The collaborative contributions of these conversation partners reflect deeply the theology of participation that this book emphasizes in understanding our relationships with one another in light of our relationship with our Triune God.

Our special thanks to Scott Hagley, who served as a research assistant for this project and gathered information on the development of the missional conversation over the past decade. We also want to express our humble thanks to several colleagues who took time to engage a final draft of our manuscript and to offer us their detailed feedback and critique. Many aspects of our argument were strengthened or corrected as a result of their contributions, although we take full responsibility for anything that still stands in error or is in need of further clarification. These colleagues are Daniel Anderson, Scott Boren, Paul Chung, Terri Elton, Alan Roxburgh, Gary Simpson, Kyle Small, and Jannie Swart.

Finally, we acknowledge our wives, Barbara (Craig) and Blair (Dwight). Their support has been invaluable in bringing this project to fruition.

# Introduction

> The word "missional" seems to have traveled the remarkable path of going from
> obscurity to banality in only one decade.
>
> Alan J. Roxburgh[1]

The word "missional" came into vogue just over a decade ago with the publication of *Missional Church* in 1998.[2] It now appears increasingly in book titles, blogs, and denominational and judicatory literature, and on the lips of church leaders. This word, for most everyone using it, represents a changed relationship between the church and its local context, one that calls for a renewed understanding of the church's identity in God. "Missional" evokes a powerful new imagination for reflecting on the church's nature and purpose in a complex twenty-first-century world.

The word "missional," however, is now being used in very divergent ways by its many advocates. This is evident in the above quote from Alan Roxburgh, one of the contributing authors to *Missional Church*, who suggests that this development has led to the word losing its definitional value. To what extent is this the case? The diverse usage of the word by various authors becomes quickly evident if one examines a few recent publications, as illustrated in the following sample of books published in 2008 and 2009.

*Church Unique: How Missional Leaders Cast Vision, Capture Culture, and Create Movement*, Will Mancini (2008)

---

1. This critique was recently made publicly by Alan Roxburgh, as confirmed in his email of January 25, 2010.
2. Darrell L. Guder, ed., *Missional Church: A Vision for the Sending of the Church in North America* (Grand Rapids: Eerdmans, 1998).

*A Field Guide for the Missional Congregation: Embarking on a Journey of Transformation*, Rick Rouse and Craig Van Gelder (2008)

*Introducing the Missional Church: What It Is, Why It Matters, How to Become One*, Alan Roxburgh and M. Scott Boren (2009)

*The Missional Church and Leadership Formation: Helping Congregations Develop Leadership Capacity*, Craig Van Gelder, ed. (2009)

*Missional House Churches: Reaching Our Communities with the Gospel*, J. D. Payne (2008)

*Missional Renaissance: Changing the Scorecard for the Church*, Reggie McNeal (2009)

*Missions Moments 2: 52 Easy-to-Use Missional Messages and Activities for Today's Family*, Mitzi Eaker (2008)

*The Nehemiah Factor: 16 Characteristics of a Missional Leader*, Frank Page (2008)

*ReJesus: A Wild Messiah for a Missional Church*, Michael Frost and Alan Hirsch (2009)

*Sent and Gathered: A Worship Manual for the Missional Church*, Clayton Schmit (2009)

What an interesting array of themes is represented in this sampling of recent publications, all of which share in common the use of the word "missional." The question naturally arises: how are we to make sense of the diverse ways in which the word "missional" is presently being used throughout the conversation? To answer this question, it is helpful to review in more detail when and how this word became popularized.

"Missional" appears to have been introduced into the English vocabulary in the late nineteenth century and was used only sparingly up until the latter part of the twentieth century (a detailed archaeology of this word is provided in chapter 2). It did not catch on in popular parlance until it was used in 1998 to redefine an understanding of church in *Missional Church*.

That book resulted from a collaborative writing project in the mid-1990s by six participants in the Gospel and Our Culture Network and has now sold over 38,000 copies. This is a remarkable number of sales for such a book, one that has regularly been critiqued for being both quite thick and overly academic in style (charges that are, in fact, true). The concept of missional church apparently struck responsive chords with many of its readers. This responsiveness soon led to the word "missional" being used in diverse ways by a wide range of church leaders.

## Making an Argument for a Missional Understanding

Some argue today, as noted above, that the word "missional" has become vacuous and has thus lost its definitional value. We are proposing a different argument in this book, namely, that "missional" displays an inherent elasticity that allows it to be understood in a variety of ways. This elasticity is actually evident in its use in *Missional Church*. There are several competing interpretive strains evident in that book in relation to the various biblical and theological themes that were formulated by the participants (these competing strains are explored in detail in chapter 2). At present, the inherent elasticity of the word "missional" continues to be demonstrated through its use by various faith traditions to express an understanding of mission from within their own biblical and theological perspectives.

Some commonalities, however, exist within much of this usage. These are primarily the result of the adoption by many authors of one of the key insights offered by *Missional Church*: that mission means *sending* and that God is a *sending* God. The quote from the book that is most frequently referenced in the broader missional literature concerns this point and comes from the introduction by Darrell Guder: "The ecclesiocentric understanding of mission has been replaced during this century by a profoundly theocentric reconceptualization of Christian mission. We have come to see that mission is not merely an activity of the church. Rather, mission is the result of God's initiative, rooted in God's purposes to restore and heal creation. 'Mission' means 'sending' and it is the central biblical theme describing the purposes of God's action in human history."[3]

This important insight continues to lead many authors to draw out further the implications regarding a missional understanding. Our study of the present diverse literature that has emerged in North America[4] led us to identify four themes that appear fairly regularly, although there clearly are some exceptions (especially among those who make the meaning of "missional" equivalent to

---

3. Guder, *Missional Church*, 4. It should be noted that David Bosch is also regularly quoted as a primary source on this point. For example: "The classical doctrine of the *missio Dei* as God the Father sending the Son, and God the Father and Son sending the Spirit, [is] expanded to include yet another 'movement': Father, Son, and Holy Spirit sending the church into the world" (David J. Bosch, *Transforming Mission: Paradigm Shifts in Theology of Mission* [Maryknoll, NY: Orbis Books, 1991], 390).

4. Since the missional conversation is now worldwide, we should note that our intent in focusing primarily on the North American context is not to exclude the significant developments taking place in other contexts around the world but rather to acknowledge the reality that we live and work in, and are primarily shaped by, this particular context. We would invite and encourage those working in different contexts to take up the issues associated with the missional conversation that are unique to their locations.

obedience to the Great Commission). These themes in the North American literature are:

1. *God is a missionary God who sends the church into the world.* This understanding shifts the agency of mission from the church to God. It is God's mission that has a church rather than a church that has a mission.
2. *God's mission in the world is related to the reign (kingdom) of God.* This understanding makes the work of God in the world larger than the mission of the church, although the church is directly involved in the reign (kingdom) of God.
3. *The missional church is an incarnational (versus an attractional) ministry sent to engage a postmodern, post-Christendom, globalized context.* This understanding requires every congregation to take on a missionary posture for engaging its local context, with this missionary engagement shaping everything a congregation does.
4. *The internal life of the missional church focuses on every believer living as a disciple engaging in mission.* This understanding makes every member a minister, with the spiritual growth of every disciple becoming the primary focus as the body is built up to participate more fully in God's mission in the world.

It is important to note that these themes represent powerful insights that significantly redefine how we think about the church. In the present book, we are arguing, first, that these themes represent key insights that are largely derived from the initial argument made in *Missional Church*. We are arguing, second, that the actual use of these themes raises critical questions that many of the authors and movements employing them unfortunately leave unanswered.

It is also important to note that concepts and language do not just drop from nowhere into public conversation. What might be referred to as *new* concepts and ideas always draw to some extent on previous sources. Just as the construction of the original *Missional Church* argument helped to frame the insights now being popularized in the emerging literature, so also that original argument was itself influenced by biblical and theological concepts developed earlier in the twentieth century. Those seeking to utilize missional language today would be served by paying close attention to this earlier cluster of biblical and theological concepts. Some clear areas of convergence among various concepts were drawn together in the argument developed in *Missional Church*. But there were also concepts that were inadequately developed, as well as concepts that were incongruent, if not actually somewhat in conflict with one another. Chapter 2 provides a discussion of these points in an examination of the initial argument presented in *Missional Church*.

We believe that at least some of the confusion generated around the use of missional language today is related to this lack of precision and integration in the initial argument. Those seeking to draw on this language should be aware of how this lack of precision and integration may impact their use of the language as well as their choices and actions. We develop this part of our argument in some detail in chapters 1 through 3.

We believe that those seeking to draw on this language should also be aware of how more recent biblical and theological developments continue to refine and shape the concept of missional. We explore this part of our argument in chapters 4 through 6. We believe that attending to both aspects of what can be described only as a *dynamic* missional conversation can help all of us to enrich and deepen our understanding of God's mission and our participation in it.

## Key Concepts That Influenced the Missional Church Conversation

Ideas matter. They shape our understanding of reality, frame our interpretation of life, and help to inform our choices. But what we really believe, that to which we are truly committed, is what becomes *embodied* in those choices that we actually make and the practices in which we engage. Maintaining this connection is at the heart of understanding "missional" from a biblical and theological perspective. To take one example (which we will explore further in chapter 4), the Bible asserts that we are created in the image of God. This idea has profound ramifications in shaping our choices and behaviors. For example, when embodied, it locates us within a community related to the community of the Triune God, giving us a sense of place; when embodied, it provides us with a story, giving us an identity; and when embodied, it invites us to broaden our community within reciprocal relationships, enabling us to openly welcome and learn from others.

This focus on the embodiment of biblical and theological ideas, in which ideas and behaviors are understood as intricately interrelated, is critical to the missional conversation. We behave our way into new thinking, even as we think our way into new behaving. Throughout our book, we discuss this understanding as representing a "theological imagination" or, more specifically, a "theologically informed social imagination."[5] This approach leads us

5. For a discussion of social imagination, see Alasdair C. MacIntyre, *After Virtue: A Study in Moral Theory* (Notre Dame, IN: University of Notre Dame Press, 1981); and Charles Taylor, *A Secular Age* (Cambridge, MA: Belknap Press of Harvard University Press, 2007).

to consider carefully the biblical and theological ideas, the theological imagination, that informed the conception of missional and its defined practices
in *Missional Church*.

These concepts are identified in the introduction to that book, although
their historical development (embodiment) unfortunately was not pursued
in detail in the book. Specific quotes from the introduction to *Missional
Church* are provided below to help the reader gain perspective on this cluster
of biblical and theological concepts, all of which were developed earlier in
the twentieth century. Guder, as the book's editor, refers to this constella-
tion of themes as a "missiological consensus" that was made available to
the authors primarily through the work of Lesslie Newbigin.[6] This so-called
missiological consensus served as the foundation for the development of the
concept of missional church. It is important when using the word "missional"
to be aware of this cluster of ideas, which conveys important biblical and
theological commitments.

> *Church and missions/mission*: We must overcome the historical dichotomy of
>     church and missions/mission by connecting ecclesiology and missiology.
>
> In the ecclesiocentric approach of Christendom, mission became only one of
> the many programs of the church. . . . What would an understanding of the
> church (an ecclesiology) look like if it were truly missional in design and defi-
> nition? . . . Out of [a discussion of this] emerged the present research project
> to explore the possible shape and themes of a missiological ecclesiology for
> North America.[7]
>
> *Trinitarian missiology*: We must start with the Trinity in order to under-
>     stand mission, for Trinity introduces us to a sending God who is a mis-
>     sionary God.
>
> We have learned to speak of God as a "missionary God." . . . God's character
> and purpose as a sending or missionary God redefines our understanding of
> the Trinity. . . . This Trinitarian point of entry into our theology of the church
> necessarily shifts all the accents in our ecclesiology.[8]
>
> *Missio Dei*: The emergence of this conception of the mission of God re-
>     frames our understanding of mission from being church-centric to be-
>     coming theocentric, a view articulated especially by Newbigin.

6. Guder, *Missional Church*, 3–4.
7. Ibid., 6–8.
8. Ibid., 4–5.

Newbigin brought into public discussion a theological consensus that had long been forming among missiologists and theologians. . . . The missiological consensus that Newbigin focused on our situation may be summarized with the term *missio Dei*, "the mission of God." . . . Mission is the result of God's initiative, rooted in God's purposes to restore and heal creation.[9]

*Reign (kingdom) of God*: The message of Jesus is centered on the reign of God, which must be understood as both *already* and *not yet*.

The centrality of the Gospel as God's good news for all the world pervades our discussion from beginning to end. . . . It has become particularly important to us to focus our discussion on Jesus' message and practice of the reign of God. A vast contemporary biblical discussion of this theme guides us in our thinking.[10]

*Church's missionary nature*: God is a missionary God, and God's mission involves a church sent into the world to represent the reign (kingdom) of God. Thus the church is missionary by nature.

We have begun to see that the church of Jesus Christ is not the purpose or goal of the gospel, but rather its instrument and witness. . . . God's mission is calling and sending us, the church of Jesus Christ, to be a missionary church in . . . the cultures in which we find ourselves.[11]

*Missional hermeneutic*: It is necessary to use a missional hermeneutic to read Scripture in order to understand the full intent of God's mission.

We have been guided by a shared conviction that the Scriptures are the normative and authoritative witness to God's mission and its unfolding in human history. . . . We now agree that one must read Scripture from a missional hermeneutic.[12]

## Missional Church Is Not Just Another Strategy

A key insight of the initial missional church conversation is that it was not *primarily* about the church developing yet another strategic approach for reaching a new generation. Such strategic approaches have usually focused on the purpose/mission of the church. Some dimensions of missional think-

9. Ibid., 3–4.
10. Ibid., 10.
11. Ibid., 5.
12. Ibid., 10–11.

ing clearly lead to such outcomes, but strategy was not the driving force that
initially undergirded the energy and agency associated with this concept. The
authors of *Missional Church* clearly understood that, in fact, a *fundamental
change in perspective* occurs with a missional understanding. Their work
shifted the focus from understanding mission primarily in terms of the "mission of the church" to understanding that the church's mission instead derives
from the "mission of God." With this shift in perspective, the primary agency
for mission moves to divine initiative through the ministry of the Spirit as the
larger framework within which our human responses take place.

This shift in perspective represents a dramatic reframing of the conversation about church in relation to developing strategic approaches to ministry.
Interestingly, a continuous unfolding of movements focusing on strategy can
be observed within U.S. churches during the past half century. These were
generated largely by the church's efforts to respond to continuously changing
contexts. These movements, in focusing primarily on strategy, largely reflect
a deep pragmatism within much of U.S. culture that tends to concentrate
heavily on technique. This focus has led generation after generation of church
leaders to search for fresh approaches to help the church remain successful
within a changing context. These various strategies have typically focused on
redefining the purpose/mission of the church as a way to get the church back
on track in its mission and ministry. Such movements include the following:

- Church renewal movement (1960s and 1970s)
- Church growth movement (1970s and 1980s)
- Church effectiveness movement (1980s and 1990s)
- Church health movement (1990s and 2000s)
- *Emerging church movement (1990s and 2000s)*[13]

Some suggest that a "missional church movement" is yet one more strategic
initiative that should be added to this list. If one takes this approach, then the
missional church becomes yet another effort to help congregations become
relevant in a changing context. Fortunately, many church leaders today who
employ a missional understanding realize that a missional approach actually
draws on a different biblical and theological understanding of God and God's
mission. This different way of thinking helps many of these leaders to move

13. The emerging church is listed here, but in a qualified way (indicated by italics), since
some represent this movement as one that now succeeds previous movements. However, see
the further explanation below regarding some in this movement who are also focusing on the
identity/nature of the church.

beyond the primacy of human agency, which is so deeply embedded in the DNA of these earlier movements, and to shift their focus to the primacy of God's agency.

The initial missional church conversation critiqued these earlier movements as inadequate for understanding the church and its ministry. These movements were viewed as focusing too readily on the purpose/mission of the church without first attending to the reality of God's being and agency. God's being and agency require us to attend first to the identity/nature of the church before seeking to address its purpose/mission—what the church *is* prior to what the church *does*. Thus the missional church conversation presents an alternative way to think about the church, one that focuses on God's mission as determinative for understanding the mission of the church. It should be noted that in the diagram below, as in the list above, the emerging church is included in a qualified way in this shift. Even though the emerging church and missional church movements are somewhat distinct, some emerging church leaders also attend to identity/nature as the formative clue for understanding the church and its ministry.

| Focus on the Church's Purpose/Mission | Focus on the Church's Identity/Nature |
|---|---|
| • Church renewal movement (1960s and 1970s) | • Missional church conversation (1990s and 2000s) |
| • Church growth movement (1970s and 1980s) | • *Emerging church movement (1990s and 2000s)* |
| • Church effectiveness movement (1980s and 1990s) | |
| • Church health movement (1990s and 2000s) | |
| • *Emerging church movement (1990s and 2000s)* | |

## An Initial Mapping of the Missional Literature

The missional conversation is now a little more than a decade old, and, as noted above, the use of this concept has become somewhat diverse. This diversity reflects to some extent the broad range of Christian traditions that employ the concept of missional, including independent evangelicals, evangelical denominations, emerging and emergent churches, mainline denominations, Pentecostal churches, and even some Roman Catholics. However, the diverse usage of the word "missional" today cannot be adequately explained by employing this type of framework. Branches of the missional conversation cut across all these diverse groups. For this reason, we utilize a thematic approach that relates theological imagination to the issue of agency to identify the various branches of this conversation.

A diagram of a tree is used in figure 1 to map the missional conversation in terms of both its original sources and its current expressions. First, the root structure of the tree identifies the key theological concepts in the twentieth century that helped to shape the initial conversation. These concepts were noted above, along with illustrative quotes from *Missional Church*, and are discussed in greater detail in chapter 1. Second, the trunk of the tree represents the contributions made by the *Missional Church* volume. A substantive critique of the strengths and weaknesses of the argument made in that book is presented in chapter 2. Third, the four branches emerging out of the trunk represent the diverse understandings of the word "missional" that have emerged during the past decade. These four branches, along with their various subbranches, are discussed in detail in chapter 3.

### The Four Branches of Conversation Partners

*Discovering missional.* This branch of the missional conversation involves publications and web sources that actually reach back to the previous framework of "church" and "mission," where these concepts are understood as separate though related realities. These authors tend to utilize the popularity of missional language to promote a more traditional understanding of mission, one focusing primarily on human agency.

*Utilizing missional.* This branch of the missional conversation includes those publications and web sources actively trying to utilize the biblical and theological ideas that shaped the initial missional conversation as presented in *Missional Church*. They are working to deepen an understanding of what a missional church looks like, especially in relation to God's agency.

*Engaging missional.* This branch of the missional conversation is found in publications and web sources attempting to engage and live out a missional perspective in relation to some aspect of church life. These authors tend to assume an understanding of missional as they develop the choices and behaviors of a missional approach for some dimension of church life or for the transformation of church systems.

*Extending missional.* This branch of the missional conversation involves publications and web sources seeking to develop further the biblical and theological frameworks that can undergird a missional understanding. Those working in this area usually acknowledge in some detail the concepts that informed the initial missional conversation as they proceed to extend an understanding of it.

Figure 1: **Missional Tree with Primary Branches**

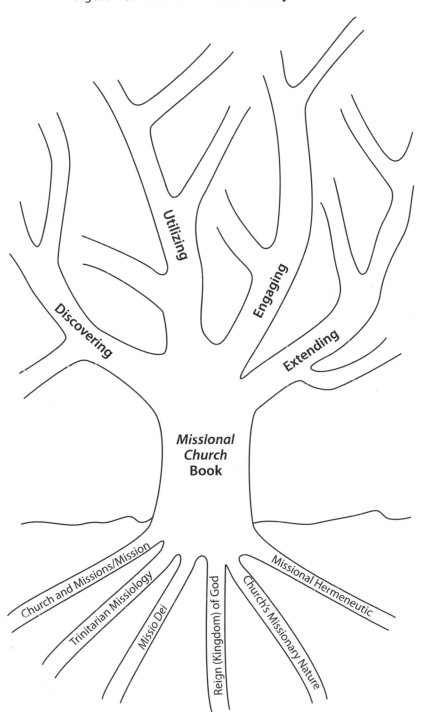

## Why We Are Writing This Book

As coauthors of this book, we believe the time is right to bring greater clarity to the missional church conversation. There are indications that others are also pursuing this task, and we have been helpfully informed by their work.[14] We also believe that we are uniquely situated to contribute to this effort. However, we want to offer the following comments in regard to our own social locations since they influence the way we have framed and pursued this project.

Craig holds doctorates in both missiology and administration of urban affairs. He actively serves as both a theological educator and a church consultant, ministries in which he has engaged for the past thirty years in focusing on the North American context. His church home and ordination are within the Reformed tradition. He was an early leader in the Gospel and Our Culture Network and also served as a member of the writing team of *Missional Church*. After stepping away from the GOCN in 2000, Craig utilized his position at Luther Seminary as professor of congregational mission to continue to pursue the missional church conversation. He helped to develop PhD and DMin degree programs in congregational mission and leadership at Luther and also pioneered an annual missional church consultation that brings together established scholars, graduate students, and local church leaders to consider a designated missional church theme. Each consultation has resulted in a volume in the new Missional Church series published by Eerdmans. To date, Craig has written, edited, or coedited nine volumes related to the missional church conversation.

Dwight is an adult convert to the Christian faith who grew up in a secular home in California as a member of Generation X. His intuitive understanding of the postmodern and post-Christendom world grows out of his life experience. He eventually found a church home in the Anglican tradition, in which he is now ordained. After leadership experiences in several congregations, including serving a church in one of America's least-churched areas, Dwight pursued a PhD at Luther Seminary in congregational mission and leadership. This academic program helped him to explore more deeply the missiological backdrop of the missional church conversation as well as to pursue current developments in thinking biblically and theologically about the missional church. After completing his doctorate, Dwight joined the Luther Seminary faculty, where he now helps to prepare students for leading congregations in ministry from a missional perspective. He remains rooted

14. See especially the recent work by Alan J. Roxburgh and M. Scott Boren, *Introducing the Missional Church: What It Is, Why It Matters, How to Become One* (Grand Rapids: Baker Books, 2009).

within local church leadership as a part-time staff member of a congregation in St. Paul.

We represent different generations but share a common commitment to engaging in the development of a biblical and theological understanding of the missional church. The combination of our training and life experiences provides us with a unique ability to look back as well as to see forward. Although both of us engaged in shaping all the chapters in this book, Craig took the lead in drafting chapters 1 through 3, which deal with the historical development of the missional church conversation, and Dwight took the lead in drafting chapters 4 through 6, which deal with extending the missional church conversation in light of recent biblical and theological developments.

## The Purpose of This Book

Our purpose in writing this book is to place the missional church conversation in perspective in terms of how it was initially understood, how it has become popularized in a wider conversation, how it is being enriched by biblical and theological developments that continue to take place, and how these perspectives can inform the wider conversation that has emerged. This is a timely task to pursue, given the current popularity of the concept of missional, as well as the growing confusion resulting from its diverse usage. Our approach is twofold, as reflected in the two parts of this book.

Part one provides an introduction to the missional church conversation. Chapter 1 explores the historical development of the biblical and theological sources underlying this conception of the church. Chapter 2 examines in some detail the strengths and weaknesses of the argument made in the seminal volume *Missional Church*. Then chapter 3 maps the diverse ways in which the conversation has developed during the past decade, along with identifying how these various perspectives might more fruitfully engage the biblical and theological concepts embedded in the conception of missional church.

Part two extends the missional church conversation. Chapter 4 notes how recent biblical and theological developments continue to contribute to some of the core themes embedded in the original conversation. Chapter 5 draws out further the implications of missional church in relation to the world, which requires careful attention to the concept of culture. Then chapter 6 deepens this conversation in relation to spiritual formation/discipleship and leadership/organization in the life and ministry of the church.

It is our desire to be *invitational* in developing this argument. We are not seeking primarily to critique others' usage of the concept of missional. Rather, our intent is to explore how further examination of the various biblical and theological concepts that helped to shape the initial missional church conversation, as well as concepts introduced through recent biblical and theological developments, might be used by all of us to enrich our understanding of missional within our different Christian faith traditions.

# Part 1

·····················································

# The History and Development of the Missional Conversation

Gaining perspective on the missional conversation requires us to examine in some detail when, how, and why this concept gained currency and became popularized in the last decade of the twentieth century. Chapter 1 provides a detailed account of the development of the important theological concepts underlying the missional church concept in the 1998 book *Missional Church*. The historical background of the formation of these ideas, unfortunately, was not adequately addressed in that volume, so in chapter 1 we discuss the origins of these ideas and offer an assessment of their strengths and weaknesses.

Chapter 2 provides two perspectives regarding the concept of missional. First, it offers a thorough archaeology of the introduction and early use of this word in the English language, with some discussion of the meanings associated with its various uses. Second, we revisit and critique the argument presented in *Missional Church*, paying particular attention to areas that did not sufficiently integrate or thoroughly develop key theological concepts. Additionally, several important themes missing from that book's argument are identified.

Chapter 3 moves the discussion forward by mapping current literature, both conventionally published and available online, that employs the concept of missional. We identify four primary branches of the present usage of this term in relation to how the various authors and publications understand agency. Ten subbranches within these four primary branches are then examined in relation to specific examples from sources that illustrate each subbranch.

# 1

## Concepts Influencing the Missional Church Conversation

Even a cursory review of the literature now being published reveals that the word "missional" is being used in diverse ways. Some of these authors, to their credit, attempt to explain the various influences that helped to give birth to this concept.[1] Many others, however, seem to employ it with little apparent awareness of the complex historical developments underlying its popularized usage during the past decade.

This same problem, in some ways, should be noted regarding the writing team that produced *Missional Church*. They did briefly acknowledge some historical developments associated with the biblical and theological concepts they used to construct an understanding of missional. Unfortunately, however, they devoted little attention to mining this history for insights or examining the historically diverse theological imaginations that gave birth to these concepts. Thus they did not critique sufficiently some of the assumptions—both explicit and implicit—embedded in the use of these concepts. They also neglected to sort out adequately how these various concepts were shaped or reshaped by the diverse theological traditions represented on the writing team—the explicit and implicit assumptions embedded in their own theological imaginations.

1. A good example is Ed Stetzer, who has given extensive treatment to this in his blog (http://blogs.lifeway.com/blog/edstetzer/missional/) as well as in some of his numerous publications.

When concepts are developed and introduced into any conversation, they will always eventually be adapted and modified within different interpretive frameworks. Usually people are not consciously trying to change the meaning of these concepts so much as they are trying to make them understandable within their own faith traditions. They nonetheless often end up either importing untested assumptions into their use or reframing aspects of the initial meaning of a particular concept.

Language is fluid and dynamic, so we are not arguing that such an approach is necessarily wrong when it comes to the use of the concept of missional church. We are asserting, however, that those seeking to utilize missional language would serve their own faith traditions best by paying close attention to the biblical and theological concepts informing the initial use of this term in *Missional Church*, as well as the biblical and theological developments that continue to take place around it. In doing so, those employing the word "missional" might enrich and deepen their understanding of God's mission and their participation in it within their own faith traditions.

This chapter pursues this task in three ways. First, we consider the larger historical backdrop to the emergence of the missional church conversation. This backdrop is discussed in terms of the dichotomized categories of "church" and "mission" that developed in the nineteenth and twentieth centuries, and how this framework influenced the development of the disciplines of ecclesiology and missiology. Second, we examine the development of the biblical and theological concepts that initially shaped the missional church conversation. In the third section we look at the formative work of Lesslie Newbigin, with special attention to how he incorporated these ideas into his own theological and missiological work. We also explore Newbigin's influence on the development of several important gospel and culture networks that emerged in the 1980s, especially the one in England with which Newbigin was directly affiliated and the one in the United States that eventually contributed to the publication of *Missional Church*.

## Background to the Missional Church Conversation: Dichotomy of Church and Missions/Mission

The Protestant Reformation in the sixteenth century represented a significant shift in the development of Christianity in that it gave birth to a variety of institutional expressions of the church. This included primarily the establishment of state churches across northern Europe resulting from magisterial reform movements—for example, Lutheran churches in Germany and the

Scandinavian countries, Reformed churches in the Netherlands and Scotland, and the Anglican Church in England. But this shift also included the emergence of a variety of groups that the state churches tended to persecute, groups usually referred to as sects—for example, Mennonites, Quakers, Amish, and independent Baptists.

All these newly forming churches, whether established or persecuted, were concerned with clarifying what they believed and justifying the legitimacy of their historical existence. Defining what they believed produced a variety of confessions, all of which included major articles explicating their understanding of church, that is, their explicit ecclesiologies—for example, the Augsburg Confession (Lutheran, 1530), the Belgic Confession (Continental Reformed, 1561) and the Heidelberg Catechism (Continental Reformed, 1563), the Dordrecht Confession (Anabaptist, 1632), and the Westminster Confession (English Reformed, 1646).

The understanding of what we refer to today as "God's mission" was developed in these confessional documents within a worldview of Christendom in which the church was established by the state. It was thus assumed that the church was responsible for the world, with the church's direct involvement defined primarily in terms of the magistrate's obligation to carry out Christian duties on behalf of the church in the world. Within a Christendom worldview, the church and the world occupied the same location: the social reality of the church represented the same social reality of the world within that particular context. The Christian groups referred to as sects by default had to function within the same worldview of Christendom, although on the underside of it. Their emphasis on free-church ecclesiology, however, planted seeds that later came to fruition in the development of a more explicit mission theology.

### The Modern Missions Movement

The story of the rise of modern missions out of these Protestant beginnings has been told many times, so we provide here only a cursory overview of its details.[2] It is important to note, however, that what became known as the modern missions movement emerged largely from *outside*, and to some extent *alongside*, the established churches. An organizational structure, able to function beyond the Christian duties assigned to the magistrate, was required for missions to come into their own. Such a structure emerged with the formation of the *mission society* as a specialized organization to engage in missions.

2. See, e.g., Bosch, *Transforming Mission*, 262–345.

Early examples of mission societies were those formed within the Anglican Church, including the Society for the Promotion of Christian Knowledge in 1698 and the Society for the Propagation of the Gospel in Foreign Parts in 1701. These proved to be quite strategic for the spread of Anglicanism within the numerous British colonies then coming into existence around the world (including the North American colonies). More explicit independent societies followed by century's end, patterned after the work of William Carey and the mission society that he proposed in 1792 in *An Enquiry into the Obligation of Christians to Use Means for the Conversion of the Heathen*. Scores of such independent societies soon existed in Europe alongside the state churches—for example, the London Mission Society (1795), the Scottish Missionary Society (1796), the Church Mission Society (1799), and the Berlin Mission Society (1824).

The first immigrants to the American colonies from Europe brought with them their existing churches as well as their ecclesiastical definitions of the church. These immigrant churches included variations of both the established state churches and persecuted Christian sects. This diversity of Christian faith traditions in the colonies eventually led, in the aftermath of the Revolutionary War, to a decision to formally separate the church and the state. This decision had the historical consequence of introducing the *denomination* as the primary organizational form of the church, which represented a remarkable change in the organizational life of the institutional church, the first in over 1,400 years.[3] The denominational church readily became the norm for church life in the newly formed United States, a norm that soon spread around the world through the modern missions movement. This development also signaled that aspects of the free-church ecclesiology of the previously persecuted sects were being incorporated into the polities of all the churches in the United States.

Numerous *interdenominational* mission societies, following the lead of the European state churches, were also organized in the early nineteenth century in the newly formed United States, including the American Board of Commissioners for Foreign Missions (1810), the American Bible Society (1816), the American Education Society (1816), the American Colonization Society (1816), and the American Sunday School Union (1824). Such mission societies during the early 1800s served as vehicles for cooperative mission activities among the more than thirty national denominations that had emerged. Internal church politics, however, soon led increasing numbers of denominations to withdraw from these cooperative agreements in order to form their own internal

3. Martin E. Marty, *Righteous Empire: The Protestant Experience in America* (New York: Dial Press, 1970), 67–68.

denominational boards and agencies, including the American Baptist Foreign Mission Society (1814), the Methodist Missionary Society (1819), and the Presbyterian Board of Foreign Mission (1837). Now mission societies existed in two forms, one version independent of the denominational churches (later taking on names such as "faith missions" and "parachurch organizations") and the other an organizational structure within these denominations (later known as "denominational agencies" with internal governing boards).

### Church and Missions/Mission

It is critical to note that the *foreign* mission societies (societies were formed for many specific purposes) focused primarily on one goal: taking the gospel to other parts of the world. The tasks of evangelizing and church planting, along with numerous benevolent causes such as schools, hospitals, and orphanages, became the order of the day for thousands of missionaries sent out by scores of these independent mission societies and related denominational mission agencies. The peak of this movement, now clear in retrospect, came at the world mission conference convened in Edinburgh in 1910. Over 1,200 delegates from Western churches and mission societies gathered at that time to plan the final advance to complete the challenge of the Student Volunteer Movement's watchword: "the evangelization of the world in our generation." World War I dramatically disrupted the optimistic plans proposed there.

At least two significant developments took place within the modern missions movement following World War I. First, what became known as "younger churches" began to emerge within the Western colonial system. This emergence brought to the surface a critical question: what should be the relationship between the older churches and the younger churches? Embedded in this question were the unresolved issues associated with ecclesiology, both the multiple confessional ecclesiologies of the numerous denominational mission agencies and the lack of less explicit ecclesiologies among many of the independent mission societies.

Second, there was a move in the West toward defining more clearly the relationship of the church to mission. This conversation began to take place within three new organizations, all of which grew out of the work of the Edinburgh conference: the International Missionary Council (IMC), formed in 1921; the Life and Work Movement, formed in 1925; and the Faith and Order Movement, formed in 1927. The same question soon surfaced in all three organizations: how should church and mission be related? Embedded in this question was the growing recognition that the theologies of mission then operative in the modern missions movement were insufficient for answering it.

These two questions—about the relationship of younger and older churches and the relationship of church and mission—especially dominated the discussion within the IMC during the next several decades. It emerged initially at the Jerusalem conference in 1928, became more prominent at the Madras, India, conference (also referred to as Tambaram) in 1938, and was front and center at the Whitby, Canada, meeting in 1947. Attempts to answer these questions also became part of the agendas of the Life and Work Movement and the Faith and Order Movement. It was these two movements that led to the formation of the World Council of Churches (WCC) in Amsterdam in 1948. These questions remained at the forefront of the WCC conversation during the next several decades and in 1961 prompted the merger of the IMC into the WCC, so that the IMC became the Commission on World Mission and Evangelism (CWME). Unfortunately, this structural resolution to the question led at that time to the withdrawal of many evangelicals from the IMC/CWME, a shift that was to have far-reaching implications for the church within another decade. This resolution also confused the interrelationship of mission and the church by assigning the IMC to commission status within the WCC—in effect making mission a subset of church.

### The Challenge of Connecting Ecclesiology and Missiology

The developments that gave birth to the modern missions movement unfortunately led to the conception of church and mission as two distinct entities. This dichotomy was fully established within the institutional and organizational life of Protestant Christianity at the beginning of the twentieth century. By midcentury, it was becoming increasingly clear that the earlier biblical and theological categories used to give expression to the church (ecclesiology) and to mission (missiology) were insufficient to resolve the question of how the two were related.

#### Church—Ecclesiology

Ecclesiology is a theological discipline that seeks to understand and define the church (technically the term refers to the "study of the church": *ecclesiae*, "of the church," and *ology*, "study"). Conceptions of the church traditionally have come primarily from the historical creeds and confessions that were formulated during the past twenty centuries. Few of these conceptions, however, incorporate much explicit awareness of the church's responsibility for engaging in ministry in the larger world, apart from responsibilities assigned to the magistrate.

Two patterns emerged for church life on the foreign mission fields during the modern missions movement. On the one hand, the established churches of Europe and the denominations of the United States for the most part simply transposed their ecclesiastical systems to the mission fields where they worked. This transferal included their confessional understanding of church as well as most of their Western-shaped church practices, including such things as programs, music, organization, and architecture. Over time, the newly formed churches in the mission contexts of the majority world came to challenge many of the underlying assumptions embedded in this transposition of Western church traditions, a challenge that gave impetus to the formation of the WCC in 1948. The newly formed WCC initially focused on finding a biblical and theological basis for cultivating ecclesiastical unity in the midst of ecclesiological diversity. This focus continues to the present and is one that has required a thorough reexamination of confessional definitions of the church. Attention was given to this work over time and eventually produced such documents as *Baptism, Eucharist, and Ministry* (1982)[4] and *The Nature and Purpose of the Church* (1998).[5]

On the other hand, most mission societies and parachurch organizations had little commitment to any particular confessional understanding of the church. Ecclesiology for them was largely a matter of attending to the pragmatic development of the church in diverse foreign mission contexts. Efforts at church planting by these organizations typically followed what is often referred to as the "restoration tradition," which used the New Testament to find the patterns of church life that can serve as the basis for organizing new churches. The diversity of organizational practices in the New Testament, however, plagued these efforts in terms of finding common ground for developing church life. Interestingly, this approach to missions and church planting still serves as the primary vehicle for many evangelicals.

These developments on the church/ecclesiology side of the dichotomy confronted Western churches with the dilemma of having to sort out their ecclesiological understandings. It also required the emerging younger churches to sort through the diverse confessional approaches of Western churches as well as the pragmatic practices of many mission societies in reaching some understanding of what it meant to be the church in their own context.

### MISSION—MISSIOLOGY

Missiology is a theological discipline that seeks to understand and define both the creating and the redeeming works of God in the world (technically the

4. Faith and Order, *Baptism, Eucharist, and Ministry* (Geneva: World Council of Churches, 1982).

5. Faith and Order, *The Nature and Purpose of the Church* (Geneva: World Council of Churches, 1998).

term refers to the "study of mission": *missio*, "mission," and *ology*, "study"). Traditionally, conceptions of mission have primarily come from organizational entities—such as monastic orders, mission societies, parachurch organizations, and denominational boards and agencies—that developed inside or alongside the church. Few of these conceptions incorporated any meaningful interaction with the historic creeds and confessions of the church.

A systemic challenge embedded within these developments impacted the emerging discipline of missiology. The modern missions movement was already nearly a century old before there was significant development of the formal discipline of missiology. Friedrich Schleiermacher offered an early conception of missiology as a discipline in his 1811 proposal for a theological curriculum, in which he designated missions a subdiscipline of practical theology. This understanding of mission as a practical discipline, one that dealt primarily with matters of mission practice rather than with theology proper, was reinforced through early appointments of mission professors at several seminaries, including Charles Breckenridge at Princeton in 1836, as the professor of practical theology and missionary instruction, and Alexander Duff in 1867, as the chair of evangelistic theology at Edinburgh.

As noted above, the Protestant version of the modern missions movement emerged largely outside the established, institutional church. It was conducted in Europe primarily by mission societies that operated alongside the state churches, and in the United States through a combination of mission societies, parachurch organizations, and denominational agencies. The most prevalent theology of mission undergirding these structures followed Carey's argument regarding the necessity to obey Christ in seeking to fulfill the Great Commission (Matt. 28:18–20). This represented what later came to be called a "church-centric" view of mission for denominational churches, which views the church as the primary acting subject responsible for doing something on God's behalf in the world.

The devastation experienced by the West as a result of World War I eventually led to sweeping changes for both the churches and missions, including the gradual dismantling of the colonial system. Ironically, at the same time these changes were occurring, the theological academy was just beginning to expand courses as well as the number of teaching positions for the newly emerging discipline of missiology. In 1910 about half the theological schools in the United States offered courses in missions, although most of these were elective offerings. By 1934 the majority of theological schools offered at least some courses in missions, with about half of them requiring such courses.

Just as the discipline of missiology was gaining viability in the academy, the climate related to foreign missions began to shift. By the 1950s the validity of the foreign missions enterprise was increasingly being called into question, and the discipline of missiology within theological education was becoming *marginalized* at the very time it was becoming *institutionalized*. The discipline of missiology had gained a foothold in the conversation, but it was a tenuous hold at best, one that would require significant biblical and theological development to move the discipline to more stable foundations. During this time several biblical and theological developments introduced a different mission theology that led many in the field of missiology both to reshape the conversation about church and missions/mission and to reframe the relationship between ecclesiology and missiology.

The approach of developing an alternative mission theology and theological understanding of missiology was pursued primarily in ecumenical, Roman Catholic, and Orthodox circles. But it is important to note that during this same period, in the 1960s, a substantial renewal occurred regarding the classical evangelical approach to missions. This resurgence was stimulated by two strains of evangelicalism. One was the focus on church growth pioneered by Donald McGavran and his colleagues at the School of World Missions at Fuller Theological Seminary. This approach sought to reclaim the priority of the Great Commission. The other strain came from a focus on world evangelization and was championed by the Billy Graham Association, a stream that soon morphed into the Lausanne Committee for World Evangelization (LCWE).

These alternative ecumenical and evangelical missiologies are still very much at work within the church today, where each movement continues to express high levels of suspicion toward the other. The ecumenical approach seeks to attend primarily to a larger theological understanding of mission, especially the mission of the Triune God, leaving many evangelicals concerned that evangelism is being diluted or lost. The evangelical approach seeks to attend primarily to obeying the Great Commission and thereby focuses especially on Christology and human obedience, leaving many ecumenicals concerned that a holistic gospel is being compromised. The introduction of the missional church conversation, along with earlier initiatives, helped to provide for some bridging, with ecumenicals becoming more aware of evangelism's role in the discussion and evangelicals beginning to reconceive mission in light of the mission of the Triune God.

## Biblical and Theological Themes of the Missional Church Conversation

Several significant biblical and theological concepts were developed during the twentieth century that substantially reoriented an understanding of church and mission. As noted in this book's introduction, these concepts provided a framework that helped to give birth to the conception of missional church. This section explores the specific historical circumstances associated with the formulation of each of these important concepts. It is unfortunate that the writing team for *Missional Church* did not give more attention to this history. As will be explored in chapter 2, doing so might have enabled them to develop a more integrated argument in utilizing these biblical and theological themes.

### Trinitarian Missiology—God Is a Missionary God

One of the key theological developments in the first half of the twentieth century that began to shift the conversation from a *theology of mission* to *mission theology* was the renewal of interest in trinitarian studies. Trinitarian theology had fallen on hard times during the Enlightenment. Even though confessional churches held firm to their beliefs, little theological work was done to bring classical trinitarian formulations into conversation with contemporary worldviews. These classical formulations became increasingly irrelevant to theological discussions within the church and were largely dismissed by those outside the church. Representative of this view was Immanuel Kant, who noted that "the doctrine of the Trinity, taken literally, has *no practical relevance at all.*"[6]

A profound shift in trinitarian thinking took place, however, in the early twentieth century through the influence of Karl Barth. Barth reclaimed a theological understanding of God's trinitarian self-revealing in the midst of the demise of classical liberalism. The logic of liberalism had collapsed in the face of the devastation wreaked upon Europe and the so-called Christian West during World War I. Barth clearly saw that the theological architecture that had supported the dominance of Christendom as a viable social reality was faulty and was also collapsing.

Barth, in developing his doctrine of the Word of God, utilized a Western trinitarian understanding to reframe discussion of God theologically. This tradition focused on the essential unity within the divine community and then proceeded to elucidate the distinct roles of the three persons of God. In returning to this Western trinitarian tradition, Barth reclaimed the classical meaning of "mission" within the interrelations of God as that of *sending*—the Father sent the Son, and the Father and the Son sent the Spirit.

This conception changed the playing field for thinking about mission by shifting the rationale and agency for mission away from the church and placing them instead within the life of the Trinity. Barth stressed that "the term *missio* was in the ancient Church an expression of the doctrine of the trinity—namely

---

6. Immanuel Kant, *Religion and Rational Theology*, trans. Allen W. Wood and George Di Giovanni (New York: Cambridge University Press, 1996), 264. Italics in the original.

the expression of the divine sending forth of self, the sending of the Son and Holy Spirit to the world."[7] He then proceeded to connect these movements within the Trinity to the gathering, forming, and sending of the church into the world. Although the notion of *missio Dei* (the mission of God) was not conceptualized until later, Barth's point was that there is mission because God is a sending God.

The church could no longer serve as the starting point in thinking about mission. Instead, the church was now understood as being the result of God's mission. This meant that God needed to be understood as being a missionary God. It also meant that a theology of mission could no longer be adequately informed by drawing primarily on either ecclesiology (emphasizing the mission of the church) or Christology (stressing human obedience to the Great Commission) as the starting point. A theology of mission required one to understand mission in relation to the Trinity. This important conceptual move had significant implications for the theological work done in the following decades. Drawing out these implications continues to the present time in the missional church conversation, which focuses on God as a *sending Triune God*. This view, which was mediated into the missional church conversation primarily through the writings of Lesslie Newbigin, stands at the center of the formative cluster of biblical and theological concepts that helped give birth to the *Missional Church* book.

### The Reign (Kingdom) of God[8]

The intellectual viability of the classical liberalism that developed during the latter part of the nineteenth century, as noted above, became obsolete for most Western church leaders in the aftermath of World War I. Also, as noted above, a renewed appreciation of God's revelation emerged in this context under the influence of Barth and the moniker of neoorthodoxy. His work, in turn, had been significantly influenced by the formative contributions of both Johannes Weiss and Albert Schweitzer, who had set in motion in the late nineteenth and early twentieth centuries a fresh examination of eschatology and the kingdom of God in the Gospels in a search for the historical Jesus.[9]

7. This quote by Barth from his 1932 address to the Brandenburg Mission Conference appears in English in *Classic Texts in Mission and World Christianity*, ed. Norman E. Thomas (Maryknoll, NY: Orbis Books, 1995), 106; the original source in German appears in Karl Barth, *Theologische Fragen und Antworten* (Zollikon: Evangelischer Verlag, 1957), 104–5, 114–15.

8. Because of problems in using the word "kingdom" today in light of historical meanings, we have chosen to use the word "reign" to represent this biblical concept.

9. See Johannes Weiss, *Jesus' Proclamation of the Kingdom of God*, trans. Richard Hyde Hiers and David Larrimore Holland (1892; repr., Philadelphia: Fortress, 1971); and Albert

The neoorthodoxy movement, once again, took Scripture seriously and gave impetus to further development of a field of study known as biblical theology. The heyday of the biblical theology movement occurred in the 1940s and 1950s as various theoretical proposals were made for how the biblical materials came into existence as biblical authors interacted within the realities of their diverse contexts. It should be noted that a more theologically conservative version of the biblical theology movement developed alongside this broader movement. It built on the work of Princeton scholar Geerhardus Vos and included such figures as George Eldon Ladd and Herman Ridderbos, who contributed substantially to New Testament studies and especially to a focus on the "already" and "not yet" of the reign of God.[10]

Various aspects of this approach to biblical materials became problematized over time, especially in relation to Old Testament studies. But one of the significant fruits of this return to Scripture from the perspective of a self-revealing God was the development of the concept of the reign of God. This biblical theme in the Gospels became a major focus during the 1940s and 1950s and came to be seen as the primary organizing concept of the message articulated by Jesus. The distinction was made between those aspects of the reign of God that were already present, the *already* of the reign, and those aspects of the reign of God that were yet to come, the *not yet* of the reign. Various conceptions of this polarity emerged in such phrases as "the church between the times" and "the presence of the future."

This focus on the reign of God with its already/not yet dimensions was foundational for broadening the focus of mission theology in contrast to what had functioned so long as "Great Commission theology." That church-centric view focused on the mission of the church and emphasized human agency being responsible to work on behalf of God in the world by obeying Jesus in carrying out his commission. This theological understanding shaped and drove much of the modern missions movement for over one hundred years (note that its influence today remains strong in some parts of the church, especially among evangelicals).

Many church leaders in the 1950s and 1960s, however, began to broaden their understanding of mission to include a more holistic understanding of God's work in the world in sending God's Son. Their approach reframed the

Schweitzer, *The Quest of the Historical Jesus: A Critical Study of Its Progress from Reimarus to Wrede*, trans. W. Montgomery (London: A & C Black, 1910).

10. Geerhardus Vos, *Biblical Theology: Old and New Testaments* (1948; repr., Carlisle, PA: Banner of Truth, 1975); George Eldon Ladd, *Gospel of the Kingdom: Scriptural Studies in the Kingdom of God* (Grand Rapids: Eerdmans, 1959); Herman Ridderbos, *The Coming of the Kingdom* (Phillipsburg, NJ: Presbyterian & Reformed, 1962).

necessity of obeying the Great Commission within the larger message of the reign of God. Many evangelicals, however, were slow to embrace this new understanding of Jesus's life and ministry and were critical of the emphasis by many on the social dimensions of the gospel. This was especially the case for those influenced by a premillennial dispensationalist understanding of Scripture, an approach that sees the kingdom of God as related to a future thousand-year reign of Christ[11] and views the world as evil and largely outside the work of Christ's redemption.

Two important implications for thinking about mission and the church resulted from focusing on the reign of God. First, it was now necessary to keep the entire gospel message in perspective when considering the redemptive work of God in the world. Narrower concepts of the gospel, such as viewing it in terms of individualized salvation focusing primarily on securing eternal life, were regarded as inadequate to convey the fullness of the good news as announced by Jesus. Second, it was now necessary to frame God's mission in relation to the reign of God as announced by Jesus and, thereby, to understand the church as deriving from this larger redemptive work of God in the world—the *missio Dei*.

A convergence was now clearly beginning to emerge in understanding that the missionary Triune God through Jesus was announcing God's redemptive work in the world in terms of the already/not yet of the reign. Thus it was God through the Spirit who was gathering, forming, and sending the church into the world to bear witness to this good news. This convergence of thought that emerged in the 1950s and 1960s is clearly evident in the theological thinking that undergirds the missional church conversation as introduced in *Missional Church*.

### Missio Dei—*The Mission of God*

The renewal of trinitarian studies laid the necessary theological groundwork for formulating an understanding of mission as *missio Dei*—the mission of God. This phrase came into vogue following the Willingen conference of the International Missionary Council in 1952. Karl Hartenstein used it in his follow-up report on the Willingen meeting to speak of mission as "participation in the sending of the Son, in the *missio Dei*, with an inclusive aim of establishing the lordship of Christ over the whole redeemed creation."[12] Wil-

---

11. This understanding was recently popularized in the *Left Behind* series by Tim LaHaye and Jerry B. Jenkins, published by Tyndale House in the 1990s.

12. Rodger C. Bassham, *Mission Theology, 1948–1975: Years of Worldwide Creative Tension, Ecumenical, Evangelical, and Roman Catholic* (Pasadena, CA: William Carey Library, 1979), 332.

lingen provided a trinitarian basis for mission by stressing that the missionary movement has its source in the Triune God. This represented a dramatic shift away from what had been primarily a church-centric view of mission based on a high Christology, one that became operational through the church's obedience to the Great Commission. It shifted the rationale for mission to God's initiative and the agency for mission to God's activity through the Spirit in the church in relation to the world.

The conception of *missio Dei* was further popularized in Georg F. Vicedom's book *Missio Dei* (translated into English in 1965), which reported his reflections on the Willingen conference. Vicedom's understanding of *missio Dei* emphasized that mission needs to be understood as God's mission "from beginning to end."[13] He included the church in this understanding but made it clear that God is the acting subject. "The mission, and with it the church, is God's very own work. . . . [Both the church's mission and the church] are only tools of God, instruments through which God carries out His mission."[14]

### Two Strains of the *Missio Dei*—Creation Focus and Redemption Focus

The utilization of this concept, however, was fraught with some complexity.[15] This was evident even in the several versions of the reports coming out of Willingen. The basic issue was left unresolved: Should the *missio Dei* be understood primarily in relationship to God's work of redemption and thereby see the church as the primary way in which God works in the world—a *specialized* way of understanding God's work in the world? Or should the *missio Dei* be understood as the broader agency of God in relation to all creation and God's continuing care of that creation—a *generalized* way of understanding God's work in the world? The majority at Willingen clearly leaned toward the former understanding, but it was not long before others began to act on the latter understanding.

A key figure for this approach was J. C. Hoekendijk, a Dutch missiologist who published several volumes during the 1960s and who was influential in helping to shape the conversation within the WCC at that time. His primary approach was to shift the focus of God's work in the world to that of establishing *shalom*, a concept that reframed previous understandings of Christology. "This

13. Bosch, *Transforming Mission*, 482.
14. Georg F. Vicedom, *The Mission of God: An Introduction to the Theology of Mission* (St. Louis: Concordia, 1965), 5–6.
15. For further discussion of the development of *missio Dei*, see John Flett, *The Witness of God: The Trinity, Missio Dei, Karl Barth, and the Nature of Christian Community* (Grand Rapids: Eerdmans, 2010).

concept in all its comprehensive richness should be our leitmotif in Christian work. God intends the redemption of the whole of creation."[16] Broadening the understanding of God's mission in this way had the effect of making the world the primary locus of God's mission. The church, in the midst of this shift in perspective, was largely displaced in terms of its necessary participation in that agency of God. This shift is best summarized in the popular reframing of the equation from God-Church-World to God-World-Church. With this shift came an understanding that the world sets the agenda for the church.

This understanding corresponded well to the increased secularization of the day and led to a generalized understanding that in reality became a secular version of the *missio Dei*. In this approach, God is understood to already be present and active in the world, with the church being responsible for discovering what God is doing and then seeking to participate in that. This understanding of *missio Dei* came to clear expression in the 1967 WCC publication that reported on the work of two study teams, *The Church for Others*.[17] The *missio Dei* had come to be identified with a process of historical transformation whereby humankind would gradually achieve the goals of the messianic kingdom through the processes of secular history. Clearly, these different perspectives associated with the use of *missio Dei* must be understood if we are to assess the biblical and theological assertions offered by the authors of *Missional Church*.

## MERGING MISSIONS/MISSION INTO THE CHURCH (1961)

To more fully appreciate the theological developments that were taking place during this time, we should note again the events that were unfolding within the WCC. It was becoming increasingly clear by the mid- to late 1950s that the so-called younger churches, many of which were now becoming organized as national churches within newly formed independent nations, were no longer satisfied with relating to the larger world church movement through the various mission society structures that had helped to birth them. Increasing pressure was being placed on the IMC to address this situation, and by the Ghana meeting in 1958 it was clear that a merger of the IMC and the WCC needed to take place. This was effected at the New Delhi assembly of the WCC in 1961, when the IMC ceased to exist and was reorganized as the Commission on World Mission and Evangelism (CWME) of the WCC.

Interestingly, Lesslie Newbigin was serving as the general secretary of the IMC at the time of this merger, and he became the first director of the newly

---

16. J. C. Hoekendijk, *The Church Inside Out* (Philadelphia: Westminster, 1966), 19–20.
17. World Council of Churches, *The Church for Others: Two Reports on the Missionary Structure of the Church* (Geneva: World Council of Churches, 1967).

formed CWME. Unfortunately, this integration left many evangelicals in the former IMC feeling that they had lost their theological and organizational home. By the 1960s, the seedbed for a new movement of evangelicals had already been planted through conferences sponsored by the Interdenominational Foreign Mission Association (IFMA) and the Evangelical Foreign Mission Association (EFMA) in Wheaton in 1966, as well as the Graham Evangelistic Association in Berlin in the same year. The major conference at Lausanne in 1974 led to the formation of the Lausanne Committee on World Evangelization (LCWE), an organization that continues to serve as the major clearinghouse for evangelical mission activities around the world.

This merger of the organizational structure of the various national councils of mission (IMC) into the structure of the World Council of Churches had both generative and limiting consequences. On the one hand, new energy was channeled toward understanding the church in relationship to God's mission. Various study projects were initiated that led to volumes like Paul Minear's *Images of the Church in the New Testament* in 1960[18] and Johannas Blauw's *The Missionary Nature of the Church* in 1962.[19] Also, future conferences of the CWME, such as the Mexico City conference in 1963 and the Bangkok conference in 1972–73, were devoted to this task. On the other hand, many evangelical voices were lost to the conversation, especially with the formation of the LCWE in the 1970s. Also lost was a sustained focus on what is understood as frontier missions as many former mission societies and denominational agencies shifted their focus to supporting national church bodies.

### The Church's Missionary Nature

Barth's theological influence continued to shape both the ecclesiological and the missiological conversations during the 1950s and 1960s. His return to a trinitarian view of God's mission and an understanding of the church being sent into the world contributed to the conception of the church as missionary by nature. This view of the church meant that ecclesiology should be understood as derived from missiology. Mission precedes the church, and mission must be understood as God's mission, where "missionary activity is not so much the work of the church as simply the Church at work."[20] The understanding of church as missionary by nature stems from realizing that God is missionary

18. Paul Minear, *Images of the Church in the New Testament* (Philadelphia: Westminster, 1960).

19. Johannas Blauw, *The Missionary Nature of the Church: A Survey of the Biblical Theology of Mission* (New York: McGraw-Hill, 1962).

20. John C. Power, *Mission Theology Today* (Dublin: Gill & Macmillan, 1970), 41–42.

in God's very being. If the church is missionary by nature, then participating in God's mission is the responsibility of the whole church, involving all of God's people. This approach collapses the dichotomy of church and mission.

This particular conception of the church was under construction at the same time that Vatican II was convened in the early 1960s. Numerous Roman Catholic theologians contributed to the work of that council, but of special note were Karl Rahner and Hans Küng. Both theologians helped to mediate the influence of Barth into the Roman Catholic conversation in their service as theological advisers to the council.

Rahner's trinitarian perspective was somewhat unique in its proposal that "the economic Trinity is the immanent Trinity, and the immanent Trinity is the economic Trinity" (known as Rahner's Rule). That is to say, God communicates Godself to humanity as God really is in the divine life.[21] This connection between God's divine life and the work of God in the world clarified that the church was, in fact, missionary by nature. Küng's influence on the discussions taking place at Vatican II are well documented and were made clear in his 1967 work, *The Church*.[22] In this volume, Küng argues that the kingdom of God is a larger framework for understanding the church, one in which the missionary church is sent into the world by a missionary God.

The work at Vatican II brought these influences regarding a different understanding of God's mission and the kingdom of God into a clear expression for understanding the church. We find it most clearly expressed in *Ad Gentes: Decree on the Church's Missionary Activity* in the following assertion: "The Church on earth is by its very nature missionary, since, according to the plan of the Father, it has its origin in the mission of the Son and the Holy Spirit."[23] This represented a foundational shift in ecclesiology for the Roman Catholic Church, but it would take several more decades for the fuller implications to be explored.

### Mission Theology and a Missional Hermeneutic: Convergence and Divergence

#### CONVERGENCE

The biblical and theological developments noted above had led by the 1970s to a transition from a "theology of mission" to "mission theology," where the larger framework of Scripture was beginning to be viewed from the perspective of the mission of God. Substantive documents produced within different expressions of the church during this period drew on many of the

21. Karl Rahner, *The Trinity*, trans. Joseph Donceel (New York: Herder, 1970), 22.
22. Hans Küng, *The Church* (New York: Sheed & Ward, 1967).
23. Austin P. Flannery, ed., *Documents of Vatican II* (Grand Rapids: Eerdmans, 1975), 814.

same biblical and theological concepts that were later to contribute to the missional church conversation. A key focus of these documents was an effort to bring together evangelism and social concerns as part and parcel of the same holistic gospel.

The Roman Catholic Church further developed its mission theology through the *Consejo Episcopal Latinoamericano* (CELAM) conferences of bishops in Latin America in the 1960s and 1970s, where liberation theology and an understanding of God's preferential option for the poor shaped the discussion. In 1975 Pope Paul VI interacted with this understanding in his apostolic exhortation *Evangelii Nuntiandi*, in which he expressed the growing theological consensus linking evangelization with concerns for peace, justice, and development. Through the work of the CWME, the ecumenical movement brought together in 1982 its version of the growing consensus in mission theology in the document *Mission and Evangelism: An Ecumenical Affirmation*. This document sought to frame some of the classic evangelical themes of the legacy of missions within the larger framework of the mission of God and the announcement of the reign of God by Jesus. At the Grand Rapids consultation of the Lausanne Committee on World Evangelization in 1982, progress was made toward affirming this growing consensus in mission theology in the follow-up work on the affirmations of the Lausanne Covenant adopted in 1974. The representatives employed a reign of God theology in an effort to build a bridge between evangelism and social involvements.

These developments, in addition to numerous other initiatives within the larger world church community, demonstrated an amazing *convergence* of thinking that was emerging about mission and mission theology in relation to the concepts of the *missio Dei* and the reign of God.[24] In the midst of this increasing convergence of thinking, a growing number of people from the two-thirds world viewed themselves as evangelical ecumenicals. They found value in associating with both streams of the multiple conferences and congresses sponsored by the CWME of the WCC and the LCWE.[25]

### DIVERGENCE

Many evangelicals, however, remained deeply concerned about the WCC. The gains made within the CWME through a growing consensus regarding mission theology were not sufficient to overcome long-standing suspicions

---

24. See Bosch, *Transforming Mission*; and James A. Scherer, *Gospel, Church, and Kingdom: Comparative Studies in World Mission Theology* (Minneapolis: Augsburg, 1987).

25. Examples include Emilio Castro, a Methodist from Uruguay who was director of the CWME during this time, as well as Orlando Costas from Puerto Rico, David Gitari from Kenya, and Samuel Escobar from Peru.

of the WCC. A significant alternative to the emerging consensus in mission theology developed around the work of Donald McGavran in the 1970s in what became known as "church growth." The debate regarding the shift toward a more secular understanding of the *missio Dei* in the 1960s came to a head at the Uppsala assembly of the WCC in 1968, when McGavran laid down a critical challenge by asking, "Will Uppsala betray the two billion?"[26] This question was shorthand for his concern that bringing the gospel to those who had not heard it was being left behind in the ecumenical movement.

Organizationally, the evangelical movement had already gained momentum, as noted above, in conferences sponsored in 1966, first by the EFMA and the IFMA at Wheaton, and second by the Graham Evangelistic Association in Berlin. The Lausanne Congress in 1974 solidified this emerging movement, and the formation of the LCWE carried forward classical evangelical concerns inherited from the modern missions movement. Unfortunately, the growing consensus in mission theology during the 1980s failed to bridge sufficiently the differences between ecumenicals and evangelicals at that time—this in spite of the CWME's work with the *Ecumenical Affirmation* document and the work of the LCWE in Grand Rapids in 1982.

In the midst of a significant convergence in understanding mission, there was at the same time a growing *divergence* organizationally between these movements. Illustrative of this growing divergence in the United States was the gradual withdrawal in the early 1990s of numerous evangelical missiologists from the American Society of Missiology,[27] a group that had been formed in 1973 to give expression to the growing convergence among evangelicals, ecumenicals, and Roman Catholics. They left to join the Evangelical Missiological Society that had been reorganized in 1990 out of the former Association of Evangelical Professors of Missions.

### Renewal of Missiology

The developments taking place during the 1970s and 1980s, however, did lead to a renewal of the discipline of missiology. There was a clear transition in missiology from focusing on the Western modern missions movement to focusing on a global church sharing a common mission. David Bosch is one of the key representatives of this renewal in missiology. His seminal work

26. Donald McGavran, "Will Uppsala Betray the Two Billion?" *Church Growth Bulletin: Institute of Church Growth* 7, no. 6 (July 1971): 149–53.

27. For example, Craig recalls professors from various Southern Baptist seminaries withdrawing from active participation in the early 1980s as that denomination took a more conservative turn theologically.

published in 1991, *Transforming Mission*, brought together the primary themes of mission theology emerging from the theological consensus discussed above.

A critical contribution of Bosch's work was his use of what came to be called a "missional hermeneutic" to read both Scripture and church history. Unfortunately, Bosch did not use his missional hermeneutic to reframe fully the discussion of the concepts of "church" and "mission," although his own work offered the tools for doing so. He continued to work to a large extent within this dichotomized way of understanding the organizational expressions of the church and was unable to move the discussion forward to the development of a missiological ecclesiology, or missional church. However, the biblical and theological proposal of a missional hermeneutic demonstrated by Bosch in his book was adopted by the writing team of *Missional Church*. There it was employed to develop their proposal for a missional ecclesiology, even though the book did little to extend the specifics of the argument.

Another important figure in the renewal of missiology was Lesslie Newbigin, whose influence is discussed below in greater detail. Newbigin's life and work have both parallels with and distinctions from the life and work of his contemporary Donald McGavran, which are interesting to note. For example, both served as missionaries in India. Newbigin was at the center of many of the developments in thinking regarding mission theology and contributed greatly to the missiological consensus discussed above. In contrast, McGavran's work sought to reclaim and extend the more classical evangelical themes of the modern missions movement, and he opposed the growing ecumenical movement. His work contributed substantially to the increasing divergence between evangelicals and ecumenicals in the late twentieth century. Curiously, many evangelicals today who share in the legacy of McGavran and church growth have begun to come to terms with the influence of Newbigin by adopting missional language to speak about God's mission.

## The Seminal Influence of Lesslie Newbigin

Lesslie Newbigin was born in 1909 into an English Presbyterian family. As a university student he initially pursued studies in the field of economics, but gradually his interest turned to theology. He prepared for ministerial ordination at Cambridge, where he worked for a period with the Student Christian Movement. Following graduation and ordination in the Church of Scotland, he and his wife, Helen, were appointed missionaries to India by that church. Newbigin worked in the Madras area as a village evangelist for several years until he was injured in a bus accident. After recovering in England, he returned to India and became a leading figure in the formation in 1947 of the Church of South India, a church union that brought together Presbyterians, Congregationalists, Methodists, and Anglicans. Newbigin was appointed one of the new church's bishops (a Reformed bishop!) and soon established himself through his substantial writings as a theologian and missiologist of note.

Newbigin was present at the Willingen conference in 1952, which greatly influenced his understanding of mission theology, and by 1959 he was persuaded to become the general secretary of the International Missionary Council. In this role, he oversaw the merger of the IMC with the WCC as the CWME in 1961, serving in many ways as a bridge person between evangelicals and ecumenicals. He held the position of general secretary until 1965, when he returned to India to serve as bishop of Madras in the Church of South India, a position he occupied until his retirement in 1974.

Newbigin returned to England and taught missionary theology in the Selly Oak Colleges for a number of years; he also worked within the United Reformed Church. After years on the foreign mission field, Newbigin's return to England forced him to encounter head-on the late-modern culture of the West. This encounter deeply engaged Newbigin's missiological instincts. He took up the challenge to envision what a fresh encounter of the gospel with late-modern Western culture might look like. During this time he was invited by the British Council of Churches to join a planning team working toward a major conference on the relationship of Christianity and society.

His writing of a publication for this planning team, *The Other Side of 1984*,[28] represented a major breakthrough in framing the issues that would eventually result in the formation of a gospel and culture movement. His way of framing the issue is probably best focused in his 1986 book, *Foolishness to the Greeks*, in the form of a question: "What would be involved in a missionary encounter between the gospel and this whole way of perceiving, thinking, and living that we call 'modern Western culture'?"[29] In seeking to address this question, Newbigin drew on his years of involvement in missions to generate a consensus around mission theology by focusing specifically on his own context—the late-modern Western culture of England.

Newbigin's work with the British Council of Churches led in the 1980s to the formation of a movement in England that gave organizational support to

---

28. Lesslie Newbigin, *The Other Side of 1984: Questions to the Churches* (Geneva: Consul Oecumenique, 1983).

29. Lesslie Newbigin, *Foolishness to the Greeks* (Grand Rapids: Eerdmans, 1986), 1.

his important theological work, which came to be known as the Gospel and
Our Culture (GOC) Programme. Although the GOC discussion first surfaced
in England, it soon spread to the United States, where it was engaged by a
new generation of missiologists who focused on addressing the U.S. context as
its own unique mission location. This development is discussed in chapter 2.

Newbigin's missiology had been largely shaped by the mission theology that
emerged within the IMC and CWME conferences during the 1950s and 1960s.
This theology comes best to expression in his 1978 publication, *The Open
Secret*.[30] His approach integrated a high Christology into a larger framework
of the *missio Dei* in relation to the reign of God. Newbigin understood the
work of the Triune God as *calling* and *sending* the church through the Spirit
into the world to participate fully in God's mission within all creation.

This participation, for Newbigin as well as for Barth, is tied to the doctrine
of election and is pivotal for both of them in understanding the identity of the
church in relation to God's mission. God's pattern through the biblical narrative is to choose the one for the sake of the many, the particular for the sake
of the universal. This plays out in the calling of Abraham and Sarah, in the
vocation of Israel as a light to the nations, and also in the church. The church
is chosen and called, not as a privilege, but as a responsibility to witness to
God's purposes for all humanity. In God's words to Abraham in Genesis 12,
it is *blessed to be a blessing*. In this theological understanding, the church is
understood to be the "hermeneutic of the gospel." It exists in the world as a
"sign" that the redemptive reign of God is already fully present. It serves as a
"foretaste" that the eschatological future of the redemptive reign has already
begun. It also serves as an "instrument" under the leadership of the Spirit to
bring that redemptive reign to bear on every dimension of life.[31]

### The British GOC Programme

The British version of the GOC conversation, as noted above, was a movement developed during the 1980s and came to be referred to as a "program."
It was shaped largely by the writings of Newbigin during that period, which
included *The Other Side of 1984* (1983), *Foolishness to the Greeks* (1986),
and *The Gospel in a Pluralist Society* (1989).[32] Newbigin's intellectual leadership of the program was augmented by the administrative and organizational
contributions of Dan Beeby and Bishop Montefiore. An occasional newsletter

30. Lesslie Newbigin, *The Open Secret: An Introduction to the Theology of Mission* (Grand
Rapids: Eerdmans, 1978).
31. Ibid., 124.
32. Lesslie Newbigin, *The Gospel in a Pluralist Society* (Grand Rapids: Eerdmans, 1989).

began publication in 1989, but the initial program culminated in many ways in 1992 with the National Consultation at Swanwick. A volume of essays edited by Hugh Montefiore, titled *The Gospel and Contemporary Culture*, served as the agenda for discussion at that consultation.[33]

The British GOC Programme floundered during the early 1990s for a number of reasons. One reason was primarily organizational, as reflected in its failure to secure sufficient funding and to find an institutional home within the church. A move was made to merge the GOC Programme with the C. S. Lewis Center in 1994, but this effort proved to be short-lived, and the program suspended activity for several years.[34] Another reason for the program's faltering in the early 1990s, which in many ways was more substantive in terms of the overall failure of the initiative, was primarily strategic, as probably best illustrated in the 1992 national consultation. The British program—following the organizational design used by J. H. Oldham in preparation for the 1937 conference of the Life and Work movement, "Church, Community, and State," held at Oxford—conceived of its work largely as being a battleground of ideas. In this approach, Christian scholars attempted to make a cogent argument for the validity of the gospel by convincing the educated elites to effect change from the top down. By approaching its work in this way, the British program failed to connect with the church at the grass roots and also failed to clarify how congregations and their leaders might engage in missional practices in light of the gospel.

The death of Newbigin in 1998 brought a sense of further closure to this initial phase of the GOC Programme. However, the Bible Society in England picked up the dormant GOC Programme later that year and provided it with an institutional home. This renewed initiative continues to function today under this sponsorship with the leadership of David Kettle. It maintains fraternal relations with other GOC networks around the world, especially the DeepSight Trust in New Zealand, originally led by the late Harold Turner, and the GOCN in North America, led by George Hunsberger.

## Conclusion

Numerous concepts helped to influence the emergence of what became the missional church conversation in the late 1990s, and many sources contrib-

33. Hugh Montefiore, ed., *The Gospel and Contemporary Culture* (London: Cassell Academic, 1992).

34. A brief history of the British GOC Programme is available at www.deepinsight.org /articles/engchis.htm.

uted to the shaping of these concepts. While these concepts and sources were not without certain ambiguities, they did coalesce as a type of missiological consensus that led to the publication of *Missional Church* in 1998. As part of our examination in chapter 2 of both the content of *Missional Church* and the impulses that helped shape it, we will look more closely at the GOCN in the United States.

# 2

## Revisiting the Seminal Work
### *Missional Church*

The widespread use of the word "missional" in many publications and numerous websites today indicates how influential *Missional Church* has been. That book's influence in popularizing the word "missional" along with its strong sales justifies the claim that it represents a seminal contribution to the reshaping of the conversation about church in the United States at the beginning of the twenty-first century.[1]

The biblical and theological concepts that helped to stimulate the missional church conversation were identified in the introduction and discussed in some detail in chapter 1. This chapter moves the discussion forward by examining the actual content of *Missional Church*. First, a bit of archaeological work explores the use of the word "missional" prior to its appearance there. Although the word was used in certain contexts prior to the publication of *Missional Church*, clearly the book popularized it and led to its widespread use in the church.

---

1. The popularizing of the word "missional" is evident in the abundance of literature reviewed in chapter 3; the sales of *Missional Church* now stand at over 38,000 copies. Strong sales for a book of this type might normally range anywhere from a low of 3,000 to a high of 10,000.

Second, some attention is given to the formation of the Gospel and Our Culture Network (GOCN) in the United States. The emergence of this network along with the focus of its work in the 1980s and 1990s is examined, with particular attention given to the writing of *Missional Church*.

Finally, the book's content is critically examined in some detail in three ways: (1) a review of the basic argument of the book; (2) an examination of the themes that were underdeveloped as well as concepts that appear to be somewhat in conflict with one another; and (3) an exploration of several key themes that were not addressed in the book.

## Linguistic Archaeology of the Word "Missional"

It is interesting to engage in language archaeology to explore how a new word or phrase becomes a part of our public vocabulary. The formation of ideas, as noted in chapter 1, is always dynamic and fluid, for the meaning of words often morphs over time. This was certainly the case regarding the introduction of the theological concept of the *missio Dei* in the last half of the twentieth century (see the discussion of *missio Dei* in chapter 1). The initial use of this concept was somewhat poorly defined and carried with it some unexamined assumptions. It was a concept, however, that offered great potential for reframing a prior understanding of church and missions/mission. *Missio Dei* quickly attracted widespread interest and use, and within a decade different strains of meaning were being proposed. The definitive meaning of this concept, as well as its conceptual value, continue to be debated in missiological circles. The word "missional" appears to be following a similar trajectory.

### Some Early Uses of "Missional"

According to the *Oxford English Dictionary*, the word "missional" was first used in the early twentieth century, but an earlier usage should be noted. In his 1883 book, *The Heroes of African Discovery and Adventure, from the Death of Livingstone to the Year 1882*, C. E. Bourne states, "Bishop Tozar is called the 'Missional Bishop of Central Africa' and by some the 'fighting parson.'"[2] The usage here clearly relates to the missionary character of the activities of the bishop. The word next occurred in W. G. Holmes's 1907 work, *The Age of Justinian and Theodora*, where he employs it in the following way: "Several prelates, whose missional activities brought over whole districts and even na-

---

2. C. E. Bourne, *The Heroes of African Discovery and Adventure, from the Death of Livingstone to the Year 1882* (London: W. S. Sonnenschein, 1883), 191.

tionalities to their creed . . ."[3] This usage is tied to a historical understanding of the missionary work carried out by church leaders in extending the sphere of influence of the institutional church in the East.

Another use of the word appears to have been in 1975, when it surfaces in the title of a DMin thesis by Edsel Albert Ammons, "Congregational Linkage for Missional Ministry: Examination of the Endeavor of Two Urban Churches to Create a New Form of Faithful Witness."[4] This usage reflects an understanding of a type of shared ministry practiced by two urban congregations. The word appears again in 1976 in P. J. McCord's *Pope for All Christians?* where it is used in an article by J. R. Nelson as follows: "In fairness to John Wesley, it can be presumed that in his self-awareness as a virtually monarchical leader of the movement he was guided by this missional principle."[5] "Missional" is used here as an adjective to accentuate a key conviction of Wesley, one that implies some historical association with the mission of the church, but there is little indication of content beyond that.

### A More Explicit Organizational Use of "Missional"

A more explicit organizational use of the word "missional" occurs in the 1977 book by Lindgren and Shawchuck, *Management for Your Church*. The authors focus on applying an organizational open-systems perspective to the life and ministry of the church and use the word "missional" several times in referring to the purpose of the church and calling for every church to have a clear mission statement: "A systems view of any organization is concerned with its mission. . . . Every church must answer the missional question of what it purposes to do, and every organization within the church must be clear as to why it exists and what it expects to accomplish."[6] A clear missional awareness of what the church seeks to achieve is crucial to the entire transformation process of the church system.

A similar use is found in the 1983 publication by Kennon L. Callahan, *Twelve Keys to an Effective Church*, where the word appears as an adjective in the following ways: "missional objectives" and "missional outreach." Callahan's focus

3. William Gordon Holmes, *The Age of Justinian and Theodora: A History of the Sixth Century AD* (London: G. Bell & Sons, 1907), 687.

4. Edsel Albert Ammons, "Congregational Linkage for Missional Ministry: Examination of the Endeavor of Two Urban Churches to Create a New Form of Faithful Witness" (DMin thesis, Chicago Theological Seminary, 1975).

5. Peter J. McCord, *Pope for All Christians? An Inquiry into the Role of Peter in the Modern Church* (New York: Paulist Press, 1976), 165.

6. Alvin J. Lindgren and Norman Shawchuck, *Management for Your Church* (Nashville: Abingdon, 1977), 49.

is clearly on trying to help the church more strategically engage in ministry, both within its context and among its members. He provides the following definition of the term: "'Missional' refers to the fact that in doing effective mission, the local congregation focuses on both individual as well as institutional hurts and hopes. . . . 'Objectives' refers to missional direction stated in a sufficiently clear fashion that it is possible to know when they have been achieved."[7] His 1990 book, *Effective Church Leadership*, continues to use the word "missional" in the same organizational way—for example, "missional structures."[8]

None of these authors provides any explicit biblical or theological framing for the introduction of the word "missional." Their use of the word connects it primarily to the church's mission and to the agency of the church in carrying out that mission. They largely employ organizational language—words like "systems," "transformation," "effectiveness," and "objectives"—to make the point that a congregation is responsible for engaging its larger context. Those who do are missional. Interestingly, this understanding of missional as the church strategically engaging its context is one of the primary ways in which the missional church conversation has been redirected by some during the past decade, a pattern that is explored in detail in chapter 3.

### More Substantive Theological Uses of "Missional"

A more substantive, theologically informed use of the word "missional" can be attributed to Francis DuBose in his 1983 work, *God Who Sends*.[9] He first uses the word in the introduction of the second phase of his five-phase argument about a "God who sends": "The Sending: Biblical Theology as Missional Theology." Thus DuBose ties the use of "missional" to the mission of a *sending* God, which is the focus of his argument throughout the book. He reinforces this with his second use of the term in chapter 24, in a subsection titled "Toward a Missional Theology," where he argues that "what is needed is not so much a theology of mission but a missional theology. In other words, mission does not so much need to be justified theologically as theology needs to be understood missiologically."[10]

DuBose employs the same theological understanding as those working within the Western trinitarian tradition in the mid to latter part of the twen-

7. Kennon L. Callahan, *Twelve Keys to an Effective Church* (San Francisco: Harper & Row, 1983), 2.

8. Kennon L. Callahan, *Effective Church Leadership: Building on the Twelve Keys* (San Francisco: Harper & Row, 1990), 222.

9. Francis DuBose, *God Who Sends: A Fresh Quest for Biblical Mission* (Nashville: Broadman, 1983).

10. Ibid., 148–49.

tieth century. Barth had reclaimed from this tradition an understanding of the classical meaning of mission as the *sending* of God, which originates in the relations of the Trinity within the divine community. DuBose explicitly acknowledges his debt to Barth as he proceeds to develop a fuller scriptural argument that the Triune God is a sending God and that mission needs to be understood as originating from within God. The substance of his meaning is clear: biblical theology is a *missional (sending) theology*, and taking a missiological approach to understanding theology requires the development of a *missional theology*. In many ways, DuBose was anticipating the development called for within *Missional Church*: Scripture must be read through the lens of a "missional hermeneutic."

Missiologist Charles Van Engen likewise made explicit use of "missional" in 1991 with the publication of his book *God's Missionary People*. Here the word "missional" appears several times as an adjective describing relationships.

> We might highlight the following types of missional relationships: covenanters, illustrations, family, pilgrims, foreigners, witnesses, enfolder-gatherers, providers, lovers, and ambassadors. . . .
>
>     It is through all the various subsystems of the congregation that the people of God preserve their saltiness so they may contribute missionally to the transformation of the world. . . . Goal-setting gives concrete shape to the missional relationship of church and context.[11]

Additionally, Van Engen uses the phrase "the church's missional actions in the world" as a descriptive title in a diagram depicting the multiple ways that a church intersects with its local context.[12]

Van Engen's multiple uses of the word "missional" reflect the basic biblical and theological argument that he is making, that the church is missionary by nature. This argument encompasses some of the key developments in thinking about church and mission that emerged in the 1950s and 1960s. He focuses on a congregation's relationships and actions when he uses the word "missional." Some of the deeper biblical and theological concepts underlying Van Engen's use of the word are similar to those found among the authors of *Missional Church*. These include especially the concept of the "mission of God" (*missio Dei*) and the notion that "the church is missionary by nature." Although Van Engen does not explicitly connect "missional" to "church" in *God's Mission-*

---

11. Charles Van Engen, *God's Missionary People: Rethinking the Purpose of the Local Church* (Grand Rapids: Baker Academic, 1991), 127, 141.
    12. Ibid., 185.

*ary People*, his biblical and theological understanding of the church as God's missionary people comes very close to making this connection.

## The Development of *Missional Church*

The previous uses of the concept of missional are instructive. We find historical and organizational meanings applied to early uses of the term, but we also find clear theological meanings by the late 1980s and early 1990s. "Missional" was beginning to be understood as tied to the mission of God and God's *sending*. But as yet a definitive connection had not been made in the adjectival use of the word to define church. This was a natural next-step linkage in the use of the word "missional" in the late 1990s with the publication of *Missional Church*. The authors of that volume proceeded to take this step since they were intentionally working to make an explicit connection between missiology and ecclesiology as a missiological ecclesiology—a missional church.

### *The Gospel and Our Culture Network in North America*

The important influences of Lesslie Newbigin and the Gospel and Our Culture (GOC) Programme in England were reviewed in chapter 1. As the British program began to gain public recognition in the mid-1980s, a North American version of the GOC conversation also began to emerge. Several consultations were sponsored during that time by the Overseas Ministries Study Center because of interest in the question Newbigin had posed in the Warfield Lectures at Princeton in 1984 (later published as *Foolishness to the Greeks*): "What would be involved in a missionary encounter between the gospel and this whole way of perceiving, thinking, and living that we call 'modern Western culture'?"[13] The shorthand version of this question soon became, can the West be converted?

Growing out of these early events, the GOCN took shape by the late 1980s under the leadership of George Hunsberger, who began circulating an occasional newsletter in the mid-1980s. Hunsberger finished his doctoral studies in ecumenics at Princeton in the late 1980s and then in 1990 accepted a position as professor of mission at Western Theological Seminary in Holland, Michigan. This institution eventually became the organizational home of the GOCN. Some of the early participants contributing to the formation of this emerging network in the late 1980s were Wilbert Shenk, Charles West, and Craig Van Gelder. Soon joining them were Darrell Guder, Jim Brownson, Alan Roxburgh, and Lois Barrett.

13. Newbigin, *Foolishness to the Greeks*, 1.

A formative development for the GOCN's visibility occurred with the October 1991 publication of the American Society of Missiology journal, *Missiology*.[14] This issue was dedicated to the gospel and culture conversation being generated at that time. By the early 1990s the GOCN was publishing a regular quarterly newsletter and convening a yearly consultation. The primary focus of the conversation in those initial years centered on the gospel and culture question that Newbigin had originally posed. Considerable attention was devoted to understanding the North American version of what Newbigin referred to as "modern Western culture." This discussion soon became nuanced with descriptors like "late-modern" and the "emerging postmodern" in discussing the North American context.

The continuing conversation within the network was organized around three loci: culture, gospel, and church. Work groups were formed around these loci with an open invitation for any and all interested persons to participate. The work groups met twice a year and typically attracted about thirty to forty participants. In 1996 essays developed in relation to the activities of these work groups as well as those resulting from the annual consultations were collected into a volume edited by George Hunsberger and Craig Van Gelder, *The Church between Gospel and Culture*.[15] The initial strong sales of this volume soon led Eerdmans Publishing to agree to the publication of the Gospel and Our Culture series, with Craig Van Gelder serving as general editor for the series.

The GOCN received during this same period a three-year grant from the Pew Charitable Trust that provided helpful funding for study and writing projects. Securing sufficient funding for travel and meeting expenses had always presented a challenge. This grant finally placed the network on surer footing to pursue larger projects. One of the projects built into the Pew grant design was hosting a major national conference in 1996. Approximately 250 people attended this conference, which was organized around the theme "Confident Witness—Changing World: Rediscovering the Gospel in North America." An edited volume containing the plenary and workshop presentations from that conference was published in 1999 under the same title as a part of the Gospel and Our Culture series.[16]

Another project built into the Pew grant design called for the collaborative writing of a major work that proposed the development of what was then referred

14. "The Gospel and Our Culture," *Missiology: An International Review* 19, no. 4 (October 1991): 391–473.

15. George R. Hunsberger and Craig Van Gelder, eds., *The Church between Gospel and Culture: The Emerging Mission in North America* (Grand Rapids: Eerdmans, 1996).

16. Craig Van Gelder, ed., *Confident Witness—Changing World: Rediscovering the Gospel in North America* (Grand Rapids: Eerdmans, 1999).

to as a "missiological ecclesiology." Only three of the six people serving on the writing team had formal training in the discipline of missiology, but all six shared strong missiological instincts. The missiological approach they pursued reflected a reality that had become an evident strength within the GOCN in the early to mid-1990s. It was clear that a broad range of diverse participants were attracted to the conversation about the engagement of the gospel and our culture. This participation included a cross section of academics, denominational leaders, and local pastors from a variety of faith traditions—ecumenical, evangelical, and Roman Catholic. Early on, the GOCN leadership recognized that the strong commitment to a missiological focus provided the bridge for keeping such diversity within a common conversation. This missiological framing of the GOCN conversation became formative in shaping the work of the writing team as it began working in 1994 to formulate a missiological ecclesiology.

This team approached its work, which stretched over three years, by engaging in daylong consultations with four well-known theologians—Justo González, Douglas John Hall, Stanley Hauerwas, and John Howard Yoder—who were deemed able to offer insights into the shaping of a missiological ecclesiology.

Interestingly, the team soon discovered, to its surprise, that the formulation of a missiological ecclesiology mystified all these theologians. Probably the greatest value of this phase of the project was the empowerment that the members of the writing team felt in turning to their own training, experiences, and perspectives for shaping an argument for what was to become known as "missional church."

### *The Writing Team of* Missional Church

The writing team that collaborated to produce *Missional Church* consisted of six people: the coordinator Darrell Guder, Lois Barrett, Inagrace Dietterich, George Hunsberger, Alan Roxburgh, and Craig Van Gelder. This team, although comprised entirely of white Protestants, was nonetheless quite diverse in terms of its makeup, consisting of

- two women and four men
- three academic missiologists, a denominational agency executive, a church consultant, and a pastor
- three from Presbyterian/Reformed backgrounds, a United Methodist, a Mennonite, and a Canadian Baptist
- five with academic PhDs and one with a DMin
- at least three who had extensive backgrounds in evangelical parachurch organizations

The three-year process of collaborating on writing the book required numerous meetings. The first year and a half was spent trying to frame an argument regarding what the team thought a missiological ecclesiology might look like. The last year and a half was spent with team members drafting assigned chapters and then having these reviewed again and again by the full team, since the conversations regularly led to substantial editing in each chapter. Interesting discussions, and at times challenging debates, were a part of the dynamic of the team's work. Encouragingly, the end result of this intensive collaboration was a multiauthored volume that reads, for the most part, as a coherent argument. But interestingly, this final product also contained underexamined concepts, unresolved theological tensions, and unexplored theological issues.

## The Argument of *Missional Church*

*Missional Church* has regularly been critiqued, as noted in the introduction, as being both quite long and overly academic. Some of this was due to the authors' purposeful attempt to construct an argument that would hold up under academic scrutiny. The resulting book was not intended to be a popular read as much as a thoroughly documented, cogent argument for a missiological ecclesiology—a missional church. It is, therefore, somewhat surprising how widely the book has circulated among church leaders. We believe that this widespread circulation reflects primarily the substance of the argument being made, one that appears to have resonated deeply with many church leaders. So, what is this argument? There are essentially six movements.

*Movement 1: The church in North America is now located within a dramatically changed context.* An often noted strength of *Missional Church* is that it makes a serious attempt to review the context of North America in terms of both Canada and the United States. Chapter 2, "Missional Context: Understanding North American Culture," and chapter 3, "Missional Challenge: Understanding the Church in North America," argue that each country's history followed a different but parallel path in the formation of a favored-status arrangement for the church (a functional Christendom) within a cultural context shaped by modernity. However, this favored-status arrangement began to significantly change with the shift in the twentieth century to late modernity and had all but collapsed by the late twentieth century in the midst of an emerging postmodern culture. The collapse of this functional Christendom increasingly pushed the church to the margins in privatizing the faith. Recent strategies to retool the church were critiqued as well intentioned but largely ineffective in addressing the underlying systemic crisis of a changed cultural context. The church needed to return to a deep examination of its very identity/nature and discover what it means to be a missional church.

*Movement 2: The good news of the gospel announced by Jesus as the reign of God needs to shape the identity of the missional church.* Chapter 4, "Missional Vocation: Called and Sent to Represent the Reign of God," focuses on the life and message of Jesus Christ centered in his announcement of the reign of God as being both already and not yet. This gospel calls on the church to reorient itself away from an overreliance on its own agency for carrying out its mission in the world. Relying on its own agency has resulted in the church functioning primarily as a vendor of religious goods and services within a consumer society. The grammar of the kingdom invites the missional church to understand how the agency of the Triune God is at work in shaping its true identity. This Triune God is a missionary God who sends the church as a community into the world to represent the reign of God to a watching world. The identity of the missional church in this understanding stands in sharp contrast to the increasingly marginalized church of late modernity and of the emerging postmodern culture, a church that has lost its favored-status arrangement.

*Movement 3: The missional church with its identity rooted in the reign of God must live as an alternative community in the world.* Chapter 5, "Missional Witness: The Church as Apostle to the World," extends the argument regarding how the reign of God shapes the life and ministry of the missional church. The principalities and powers that pervade the world are fallen and stand in opposition to God, although they can be redeemed. God's intent is to bring such redemption to bear on the world through the life and ministry of an alternative community: the missional church. This community is to base its life and ministry on the redemptive realities of the reign of God so that it can bring to full expression the image of the church provided in 1 Peter, where the church is called to be a holy nation among the nations. The missional church as an alternative community is called to demonstrate an alternative culture in a fallen world, to engage in practicing alternative economics, and to provide the world with an example of living out an alternative approach to the exercise of power. This takes place as the missional church embodies Jesus's mission and patterns as its own actions in the world.

*Movement 4: The missional church needs to understand that the Holy Spirit cultivates communities that represent the reign of God.* Chapter 6, "Missional Community: Cultivating Communities of the Holy Spirit," picks up the agency of the Holy Spirit and makes clear the importance of understanding that the Spirit of God is the creator of Christian community—the missional church.

But it is also important to understand that the Spirit of God is the source of all life in creation. Both works of the Spirit continue to be active in the world today in relation to the eschatological fulfillment of the reign of God, where there is an already and a not yet that focuses on the reconciliation of all humanity as well as the healing of all creation. It is the work of the Spirit to cultivate missional communities that represent both dimensions. The Spirit gifts and empowers these communities to accomplish this task, helping them to focus on specific ecclesial practices that demonstrate God's intent for all creation. These practices include socially embodying the reign of God, being baptized, breaking bread together, engaging in reconciliation and mutual accountability, practicing corporate discernment, demonstrating hospitality, and engaging in common witness.

*Movement 5: The missional church is to be led by missional leadership that focuses on equipping all of God's people for mission.* Chapter 7, "Missional Leadership: Equipping God's People for Mission," makes the point that the historical church always had leadership, but that its approach to leadership has changed over time. The primary changes taking place are typified by the priest of the medieval church, the pedagogue of the Reformation church, and the professional of the church of modernity. The missional church calls for the necessity of missional leadership that can focus on God's work in both creation and redemption by helping Christian communities to announce and demonstrate the new creation in Jesus Christ—the full realities of the already present reign of God. Creation itself is a missional act of a Triune God that establishes the interrelationship of all life. Missional communities bear witness to this interrelatedness as they work to bring healing and wholeness to the particular location in which they exist. They are to live as a people of God where all God's people are equipped for ministry in the world, and they are to be led by a covenantal community of missional leadership.

*Movement 6: The missional church needs to develop missional structures for shaping its life and ministry as well as practice missional connectedness within the larger church.* Chapter 8, "Missional Structures: The Particular Community," and chapter 9, "Missional Connectedness: The Community of Communities in Mission," address the structural realities to which any and every church must attend. The missional church approaches the development of structure by beginning with the *missio Dei*—the mission of the Triune God. The Triune God implements the mission of God within the world by calling and forming a particular people. Since the time of the New Testament, this particular people has been known as the church. To understand God's intent for the church, including its structures, one must engage in a missiological reading of the New Testament. Here we find the reign of God reframing how power is to be exercised, and we find the eschatological perspective always calling the church to be flexible and dynamic as it seeks to live into the future that is already present. The most basic expression of the missional church is the congregation. Structuring congregations requires us to attend carefully both to the diversity of contexts and to continual reform as congregations seek to participate in God's mission. This participation calls on all expressions of the church to recognize the inherent necessity of connectedness, a connectedness that is well summarized in the Nicene attributes of the church as being apostolic, catholic, holy, and one (the order of these attributes has been intentionally reversed).

## Underdeveloped Concepts and Unresolved Theological Issues in *Missional Church*

The basic argument developed in *Missional Church* as outlined above is fairly well integrated, considering that it is the product of six somewhat diverse authors. The level of integration that was achieved clearly reflects the common missiological lens employed by the writing team, but it is also likely due in part to their intensive efforts at collaboration. However, this argument does include some concepts that were underdeveloped and some theological issues that were unresolved, four of which are examined below.

### Trinitarian Missiology

At the heart of the argument of *Missional Church* is an understanding that the Triune God is a missionary (sending) God who sends the church into the world to participate in God's mission—the *missio Dei*. As discussed above in chapter 1, this trinitarian missiology was mediated into the argument of this book primarily through the work of Newbigin. The introduction of this understanding of the Trinity at the IMC Willingen conference represented a Copernican revolution in many ways in the field of missiology. It provided a way forward in overcoming the dichotomy of the categories of "church" and "mission" that plagued the missiological conversation by the middle of the twentieth century.

This view of the Trinity, as discussed in chapter 1, is rooted in the classic Western emphasis on the single divine substance of God and the separate actions of the three persons in relation to the world. This view focused on the mission/sending of God, with the Father sending the Son into the world, and the Father and the Son sending the Spirit into the world. Barth extended this classical understanding of *mission as sending* by including the Father and the Son through the Spirit sending the church into the world. Relying primarily on this Western conception of the Trinity, however, carries with it at least two problems, both of which are clearly present in the argument proposed in *Missional Church*.

The first problem with this understanding of the Trinity concerns the tendency to view God in modalistic terms.[17] Thus the works of the Father, the Son, and the Spirit are subject to being separated and individualized, with God conceived of as one subject who acts in three different modes. This tendency emerges in the book in several ways. Chapter 4, for example, focuses primarily on Jesus and his announcement of the reign of God and on how the church is now responsible for *representing* this reign within the world. Mention of the work of the Spirit is present in the earlier sections of this chapter, mostly as scriptural references. But as the argument proceeds in the latter sections to the church representing the reign in the world, the author moves back and forth between the example of Jesus and the responsibility of the church in relation to the reign without ever explaining how the ministry of the Spirit mediates this *representing* work in the life of the church. This approach to using the example of Jesus to inform the responsibility of the church in relation to the reign, with the agency of the Spirit functioning primarily as subtext, is played out even further in chapter 5, where the church is presented as apostle to the world.

A quite different approach to understanding the work of God through the Spirit is presented in chapter 6, which focuses on ecclesial practices. In this chapter, the work of the Spirit is front and center in terms of initially infusing life into all creation, continuing to bring about the healing of all creation, and also bringing about reconciliation in the world. Similar strains are developed in chapter 7, which deals with leadership. Both of these authors present a foundational understanding of the work of Christ—a Christology in relation to the Spirit—but the relationship between Jesus and the Spirit is not adequately integrated regarding the reign of God as presented especially in chapter 4 and to some extent in chapter 5.

One is left with a missional church that has two underintegrated views of the work of God in the world in relation to the *missio Dei* and the reign of God. One view posits a missional church shaped primarily by the message of Jesus and responsible for embodying and emulating the life that Jesus lived. The other view proposes a missional church shaped primarily by the power

17. See especially Jürgen Moltmann, *The Trinity and the Kingdom* (Minneapolis: Fortress, 1993).

and presence of the Spirit, who creates, gifts, empowers, and leads the church into engaging in a series of ecclesial practices. Clearly all these authors understood these views to be complementary. But the argument in the book did not adequately integrate the *sending* work of God in relation to the work of the Son and the work of the Spirit.

The critique offered here does not argue that the authors did not have an understanding of the person and work of Christ or the person and work of the Spirit; evidence is clear that they did. Rather, the point being made is that utilizing primarily a Western view of the Trinity can lead to a *functional modalism* where the works of the three persons of God become separated from one another. It should be noted that this tendency is not limited to *Missional Church*. It emerges regularly in theological discussions within the Western tradition of the church. It also surfaces regularly among many authors who have acquired missional language, whose theological starting point is Christology, and who also stress the example of Jesus as the model to be emulated. These patterns are discussed in detail in chapter 3 below.

The second problem associated with the trinitarian approach utilized in *Missional Church* is related to the issue discussed above, but it goes deeper in exploring trinitarian theology. At the time of the book's writing in the mid-1990s, another understanding of trinitarian theology was emerging within missiological conversations. This approach drew primarily from the Eastern tradition of the church and especially from the Cappadocian fathers of the fourth century. Their conception stressed the relational personhood of the Triune community. This view has come to be referred to as the "social Trinity."

The social Trinity is conceived as a relational community of equality and mutuality within which the distinctive identity of each person of the Trinity is fully maintained as Father, Son, and Spirit. There is an irreducible otherness within God in relation to each person of the Trinity. This deep interrelated communion of the three persons of the Trinity is often expressed by the word *perichoresis*, which refers to the mutual indwelling within the threefold nature of the Trinity. All three persons of the divine community mutually indwell one another in a relational unity while maintaining their distinct identities.

At the time *Missional Church* was being written, only one person on the writing team proposed drawing both Western and Eastern understandings of the Trinity into the argument. This person was the primary author of chapter 6, a chapter that clearly reflects a relational-communal understanding of God, creation, and the church. The other members of the writing team, for the most part, were new to this understanding and continued to rely on the Western view of *sending* as the primary way to conceive of God's work in relationship to the church and the world. This is clearly evident in chapter 4, where the primary author introduces the concept of *perichoresis*, noting that it reveals that "the nature of God is communion." Although observing that this concept has missiological value, he proceeds to note, "What is not yet fully developed in these fresh approaches to trinitarian doctrines is the missional implication for ecclesiology."[18] Disappointingly, the writing team of *Missional Church* in general was not able in that book to develop such missional implications, and this lack of development continues today in the vast majority of publications that employ a missional understanding, conceiving of the Triune God exclusively as a *sending* God.

It is unfortunate that the writing team could not at that time explore more fully these two distinct but complementary approaches to understanding the Trinity. Doing so would have helped them to overcome the pitfall of the functional modalism that tends to emerge in the book. It would also have deeply enriched their understanding of the church as a relational community, which has extensive implications for understanding both the world and the church's relationship with the world. A fuller integration of these two approaches to trinitarian theology is a significant part of what *Missional Church in Perspective* attempts to do, particularly in chapter 4.

### Missio Dei *and the Reign of God*

Another major concept undergirding the argument proposed in *Missional Church* concerns the mission of God—the *missio Dei*. A critical issue, however, concerns how this concept is understood and used. It is essentially the same issue that surfaced in the debate about *missio Dei* in the 1960s. As noted in chapter 1, at that time two versions of the *missio Dei* emerged: a *specialized* view that understood God as working in the world through a redeemed people who were called and sent, and a *generalized* view that understood God as working in the world beyond the church through secular history. Which version of the *missio Dei* did the authors of *Missional Church* propose?

Two preliminary factors should be noted regarding the use of *missio Dei* in *Missional Church*. First, the only person on the writing team to regularly employ the actual phrase *missio Dei* was Darrell Guder, the primary author of the introduction and chapters 8 and 9. His use of this concept, however, leaves unexplored the earlier debate that surfaced around the concept as well as any discussion of the interrelationship of the specialized and generalized understandings embedded in it. Second, this earlier debate regarding the di-

18. George R. Hunsberger, "Missional Vocation: Called and Sent to Represent the Reign of God," in Guder, *Missional Church*, 82.

vergent views of the *missio Dei* is only briefly acknowledged and discussed in chapter 4, where the actual interrelationship between these views is left largely unresolved. The author opts for a reign of God approach to the issue, expressed as follows: "We are led to capture the biblical sense of the church's calling and vocation this way: *the church represents the reign of God.*"[19] It is likely that a fuller examination of the earlier debate within missiology could have led to a more robust discussion of how the specialized and generalized views might be interrelated. The fact that this was not pursued likely contributed to the inconsistent ways in which *missio Dei* was ultimately used in the book's argument.

It is important to nuance the two alternative ways of understanding the *missio Dei* when critiquing its use in *Missional Church*. Two variations of the specialized view should be considered, as well as two variations of the generalized view. There is also an approach that attempts to integrate several of these views.

1. **Specialized views of *missio Dei* and the reign of God**
   - *The church embodies the reign of God.* The church represents the reign of God before a watching world; God's redemptive work in the world is limited primarily to what takes place within the church. This view tends to collapse an understanding of the reign of God back into the church—ecclesiology.
   - *The church witnesses to the reign of God.* The church witnesses to the reign of God within the world; God's redemptive work extends beyond the church, but the church is directly involved in bearing witness to this work. This view engages the world redemptively but leaves unanswered the place of God's generalized work in the world beyond the redemptive work related to the reign of God.
2. **Generalized secular views of *missio Dei* and the reign of God**
   - *God's mission unfolds through secular history.* God's mission in the world is a result of the historical transformation taking place as humankind gradually achieves the goals of the messianic kingdom through the processes of secular history. This view, for all practical purposes, removes the church from the equation of how God works in the world.
   - *God's mission unfolds in the midst of secular history.* God's mission in the world takes place in the midst of secular history through the agency of the Spirit, who continues to bring about God's creation

19. Ibid., 100. Italics in original.

purpose that all life might flourish and who leads God's people into participating as creaturely cocreators with God in pursuing this mission.

## 3. Integrated view of *missio Dei* and the reign of God

- *The church participates in God's continuing creation and redemptive mission.* People in the church pursue God's mission in the world both as cocreative creatures engaging with God in the Spirit's continuing work in all creation and by bearing witness to the reign of God. This view attempts to integrate the other two views, but exactly how the specialized and generalized works of God are interrelated is typically left unexplained. (Our approach to integrating these perspectives is provided in chapter 4.)

The different perspectives associated with the use of *missio Dei* in relation to the reign of God are important for understanding the biblical and theological assertions offered by the authors of *Missional Church*. Variations of these five approaches are used in the argument, sometimes in conflicting ways. This leads to confusion regarding how God works in the world in relation to the church and to the reign of God. This confusion seems to continue today within the expanding missional conversation, where variations of these approaches surface among different authors seeking to utilize a missional understanding (see chapter 3).

As we turn to the question of which understanding of *missio Dei* was actually used in *Missional Church*, it is interesting to note the first use of the concept in the introduction. "The missiological consensus that Newbigin focused on our situation may be summarized with the term *missio Dei*, 'mission of God.'" Guder then proceeds to use this understanding to critique the church-centric view of Christendom and to emphasize the importance of understanding the "profoundly theocentric reconceptualization of Christian mission."[20] This approach, however, largely sidesteps the question of how to understand this theocentric reconception relative to the work of God in creation and in redemption. The ambiguity regarding what is understood by this concept is demonstrated by various authors utilizing a mixture of the first three approaches listed above.

Chapter 5 of *Missional Church* takes primarily a "church embodies the reign of God" approach to understanding the mission of God in the world. It focuses on the redeemed community's responsibility to live as an alternative community before a watching world. "The more accurately the church

20. Guder, *Missional Church*, 3–4.

locates the key points of difference between its surrounding culture and that culture called for by the reign of God, the more faithfully the church lives a distinctively holy life in its place. And the more the church lives such distinctive faithfulness, the more visible the reign of God will be for all to see."[21]

Chapter 4 of the book takes primarily a "church witnesses to the reign of God" approach to understanding the mission of God in the world. It focuses on the redeemed community's responsibility to engage the world by representing the reign of God in its life and ministry. "Therefore the church's own mission must take its cues from the way God's mission unfolded in the sending of Jesus into the world for its salvation. In Jesus' way of carrying out God's mission, we discover that the church is to represent God's reign as its community, its servant, and its messenger."[22]

In contrast to these approaches, chapters 6 and 7 take primarily an "integrated view" approach to understanding the mission of God in the world. Two dimensions of this participation are offered. First, it includes an understanding of God as present in the world beyond the church, where God is at work through both the initial life-giving work of the Spirit and the continuing work of the Spirit to bring healing to all creation, with the church participating in that healing. Second, it includes an understanding of God through the Spirit working to bring reconciliation to the world through God's redeemed community. Unfortunately, how these two works of God are interrelated is not made adequately explicit.

An excerpt from chapter 6, for example, reads, "The community-forming activity of the Holy Spirit challenges us to move beyond the contemporary assumption that the Spirit's actions center exclusively, or even primarily, on the individual soul. Not only does the Creator Spirit renew particular lives, but the Spirit is the source of all life in creation. . . . The Holy Spirit's participation in the primal and ongoing action of creation [is] the foundation for the saving presence of the Spirit in the life of Christian communities."[23] And from chapter 7: "The creation is the missional act of the triune God. . . . As an expression of God's own nature, creation itself is to reflect the dynamic interrelationship of God [which] means that creation is fundamentally and inherently relational in nature and intention. . . . We are offered the opportunity to unfold the relational mystery of the created order. . . . We have the

21. Lois Barrett, "Missional Witness: The Church as Apostle to the World," in Guder, *Missional Church*, 129.

22. Hunsberger, "Missional Vocation," 102.

23. Inagrace T. Dietterich, "Missional Community: Cultivating Communities of the Holy Spirit," in Guder, *Missional Church*, 143.

missional responsibility to show forth both the sovereignty and healing power of the Creator in relation to the creation."[24]

On the one hand, *Missional Church* ultimately offers multiple views of how the specialized mission of God is to be understood in relation to the church. Not surprisingly, these multiple views continue to surface today in the expanding missional literature. On the other hand, *Missional Church* leaves unresolved the conundrum of exactly how the generalized understanding of *missio Dei* is related to a specialized understanding of this concept. This unresolved conundrum has led many in the larger missiological conversation during the past several decades to abandon the use of the term *missio Dei* as overly problematic. It is our purpose in chapters 4 through 6 of this book to offer a synthesis of the multiple views of the specialized mission of God and to suggest a resolution to the conundrum of how the specialized and generalized works of God are interrelated.

### Church and Culture/World

A related issue to the one discussed above is how *Missional Church* develops an understanding of the relationship between the church and the culture/world. Several conceptions are offered, and it becomes readily clear that they are not of the same cloth. These diverse conceptions also raise important issues that need further exploration.

Chapter 7 makes it clear that the church is deeply embedded within culture. Culture is not something *out there* that the church enters to engage in ministry. Rather, the church is fully enmeshed in its host culture even as it seeks to live out a redemptive lifestyle within its local context. "The church's eschatological vision of the future-present reign of God is universal. But it is always and everywhere lived out in the particular locales of created existence. The created order locates people in specific cultures, and God invites the missional community to cooperate with the ongoing work of God's creating in their particular location."[25]

Quite differently, chapter 5 portrays the church as a contrast society within a fallen world. It is the responsibility of the church to develop an alternative culture to that of the world. This approach reflects a classical Anabaptist understanding of ecclesiology and, interestingly, is a view that much of the present missional literature promotes. "The church exists as community, servant, and messenger of the reign of God in the midst of other kingdoms, communities,

24. Alan J. Roxburgh, "Missional Leadership: Equipping God's People for Mission," in Guder, *Missional Church*, 188–89.
25. Ibid., 188.

and powers that attempt to shape our understanding of reality. The world of those kingdoms, communities, and powers often opposes, ignores, or has other priorities than the reign of God. . . . The missional church differs from the world because it looks for its cues from the One who has sent it out, rather than from the powers that appear to run the world."[26]

The question of how missional church is to be understood is involved in this discussion. At stake is how culture and the world are to be viewed: are they to be viewed primarily in positive terms or in negative terms? Chapters 6 and 7 each propose a more positive view of the world as the location of God's continuing creation, where the Spirit is still very active in carrying out the intent of God. This approach suggests a more engaged role for the church in the world in trying to discern how God is already at work, and then seeking to participate more fully in what God is already doing. Chapter 5, in contrast, views the work of God as taking place primarily in and through the church, which is responsible for living as an alternative community. This view presents a more negative view of culture/world, one that sees it as fallen and alien to the redemptive purposes of God.

Interestingly, missiologist Stephen Bevans republished his *Models of Contextual Theology* in 2002[27] after reading all the Gospel and Our Culture series books that had been published at that time. As a result, he was prompted to add a sixth model to the five he had proposed in the original 1992 edition of his book. Bevans called this additional approach a "countercultural model" of the church, which represented his reading of the Gospel and Our Culture series. Hunsberger challenged Bevans on this point, but Bevans responded that the series proposed such an understanding of the church as an alternative community within the world.[28] It is important to note that this was not the only understanding of the relationship of the church to culture/world presented in the series, but it was the one that came to the fore for Bevans and apparently for many other readers as well.

Also at stake in this discussion is how the church engages the culture/world. Is this engagement to be shaped primarily by the relationship of "gospel and *culture*" or by the relationship of "gospel and *church*"? The latter becomes the focus when one emphasizes the alternative church as a contrast society. Such a shift in focus to "gospel and church" is represented in at least one primary

26. Barrett, "Missional Witness," 110.

27. Stephen Bevans, *Models of Contextual Theology*, rev. ed. (Maryknoll, NY: Orbis Books, 2002).

28. As reported to Craig Van Gelder by George Hunsberger in a conversation at an annual American Society of Missiology meeting in the early 1990s following the publication of Bevans's book.

strain of the argument of the book and was critiqued by missiologist Michael Goheen as having redirected the missionary ecclesiology that Newbigin had originally proposed.[29] Newbigin had focused on the church's role in the engagement of "gospel and culture," a focus that was also the initial conversation for the first decade of the GOCN. An important implication of this perspective shift in *Missional Church* is that much of the missional literature today fails to adequately engage the complex interaction between the gospel and *our* culture(s). It tends to follow the logic of the approach of a sending God. This logic conceives of the world as something "out there" into which the church is being sent. The church's embeddedness in culture is left unexplored, and the reciprocal interactions between church and culture are left unexamined.

### Worship, Sacraments, and Ordination

A larger ecumenical conversation took place in the last half of the twentieth century that engaged the concepts of worship, sacraments, and ordination as crucial for building bridges between different faith traditions. This conversation focused largely on the theme of church unity, an important concept. Starting with the church as the crux of the conversation, however, has the effect of keeping the architecture of the house in place while engaging in redecorating the rooms. The missional church conversation, with its focus on the mission of God as the key to understanding the church in relationship to the world, offered the possibility of constructing a different architecture for discussing ecclesiology. Given the importance of worship, sacraments, and ordination to all faith traditions, a critical opportunity was available to engage this set of issues.

The authors of *Missional Church* did introduce some discussion about worship and sacraments into the construction of their argument. Chapter 5 offers some understanding of worship as a public political act, while chapter 6 explores the exercise of sacraments as key ecclesial practices. In addition, chapter 8 relates worship and sacraments to the topic of developing organization within the life of the church. While none of the authors addresses the issue of ordination in relation to what it means to be missional, chapter 8 does provide a largely functional approach to understanding the development of church officers in the New Testament.

The book's efforts to relate worship and the sacraments to an understanding of missional church are helpful. But because of the limits of these modest efforts, as well as the failure to address ordination, the book falls short of substantively engaging the historical realities of how various understandings of

29. Michael W. Goheen, "The Missional Church: Ecclesiological Discussion in the Gospel and Our Culture Network in North America," *Missiology* 30, no. 4 (October 2002): 479–90.

the critical issues of worship, sacraments, and ordination have shaped church life and how these understandings are in need of reshaping from a missional perspective. It is worth noting that these historical realities are made explicit in the important ecumenical publication *Baptism, Eucharist, and Ministry*, which appeared in 1982 and laid the groundwork for a meaningful engagement with the issues, with the potential for the authors to offer a missiological conversation about these matters. But unfortunately this was not pursued in *Missional Church*, and little work on this issue has been done subsequently. An exception is one of the volumes in Eerdmans' new Missional Church series, *The Missional Church and Denominations*.[30]

## Unexamined Issues in *Missional Church*

Several important themes did not receive explicit treatment in the development of the argument of *Missional Church*. Although no single book can address every issue, the omission of these themes is, on the one hand, curious and, on the other hand, unfortunate, especially in light of the subsequent developments of missional language adopted by so many in diverse faith traditions. Here we address two of the more important of these issues.

### Examining the Historical Development of Ecclesiology

The primary argument of *Missional Church* is that we must bring into an integrated conversation the disciplines of missiology and ecclesiology to construct a missiological ecclesiology. The authors claim to introduce a new ecclesiological understanding of how to conceive of the church in relation to the mission of God. It is therefore curious that the writing team pursued the construction of their argument without engaging in a serious review of the historical development of ecclesiology. The issue of whether to include some examination of historical ecclesiologies was raised at one point by several team members, but the majority felt that this would introduce more problems than they wanted to address and so chose not to pursue this task.

An understanding of missional church did not just drop out of the sky from nowhere. Extensive historical and theological developments in ecclesiology deeply inform the construction of this conception of church—both positively and negatively. Not examining these historical developments in ecclesiology is problematic for at least two reasons. First, the authors did not explore how the

---

30. Craig Van Gelder, ed., *The Missional Church and Denominations: Helping Congregations Develop a Missional Identity* (Grand Rapids: Eerdmans, 2008).

mission of God, as understood in other times and places, might have informed the understanding of missional church that they were proposing. For example, how does a Word and sacrament ecclesiology (usually referred to as two marks of the church) relate to missional church? Or how might a fuller exploration of free-church ecclesiology have informed the conversation? In not pursuing these connections, the authors were unable to help church leaders translate an understanding of their proposal for a missional church into different faith traditions with different ecclesiologies. This work remains largely undone, even after a decade of missional church conversation.

Second, by leaving these issues unexplored, the authors left missional church "hanging out there" as if it were a dramatically new ecclesiological understanding of the church without historical dependency. This appears to have made *Missional Church* appeal especially to many in the evangelical movement, where attention to historical ecclesiologies is lacking, and to many in the emerging movement, with its desire to create a new understanding of the church. We should note that those in mainline and conservative denominations with distinct ecclesiological traditions have for the most part been less receptive to engaging the missional church conversation. Where there are pockets of such engagement, the hard theological work of integrating a missional church understanding with a particular historical ecclesiology still largely remains to be done. An exception is the Presbyterian Church (USA), which is presently pursuing the development of a missional polity in light of a missional ecclesiology (see chapter 3).

### Examining the Historical Development of Missiology

The construction of the argument within *Missional Church* relies heavily on the discipline of missiology, especially as it was reframed and renewed in the last half of the twentieth century. The authors do provide some introduction to aspects of the renewal of this discipline, but not in any systematic way. This is unfortunate since the publication of this book provided a strategic opportunity to introduce the critical perspective of the discipline of missiology to a larger audience of church leaders. The default code in Western Christianity in general and U.S. Christianity in particular is always to frame the conversation in terms of the church. The primary argument of *Missional Church* is that the conversation needs to be framed first and foremost in terms of the mission of God—a missiological understanding. This represents a substantially different orientation of thinking about Christianity.

The book does make some significant progress toward arguing that the mission of God (missiology) needs to frame our understanding of the church (ecclesiology). But all too quickly the current conversation about missional church has tended to again focus on the mission of the church, as evidenced by the vast majority of missional literature during the past decade. The issue has everything to do with agency: who is the acting subject in one's understanding of missional church? Many who have adopted this conceptual language have applied it all too readily to a renewed understanding of the mission of the church, as we will see in chapter 3. This understanding shifts the focus from God as the acting subject to human agency as the acting subject doing something on behalf of God in the world. At the crux of this lies the question of whether one starts with the identity/nature of the church or with the purpose/mission of the church.

Identity/nature concerns what the church *is*. Purpose/mission concerns what the church *does*. The key premise of missional church, as proposed in *Missional Church*, is that what the church *is* must deeply inform what the church *does*. Human agency is fully implicated in the doing, but such doing is always deeply informed and empowered by the agency of God working through the Spirit. Getting the sequence right is crucial for allowing God's person and power to become fully operative within the life and ministry of the church. That sequence flows as follows: The church *is*. The church *does* what it is. The church *organizes* what it does.[31]

It is through understanding and engaging the discipline of missiology that the church can remain focused on the agency of God in the conversation. The failure of the authors to provide a more explicit introduction to this discipline also accounts for some of the ways in which the concept of missional church has been used by many during the past decade to try to pour new wine (starting with the agency of God) into old wineskins (focusing on the mission of the church). One interesting development in recent missional literature, however, is the importance that many authors place on the discipline of missiology.

## Conclusion

*Missional Church* offers a substantive and generative argument for reconceiving both the identity/nature and the purpose/mission of the church in relation to the mission of the Triune God. Understandably, no single book can do everything; therefore, inadequately developed concepts, unresolved theological issues, and unexplored themes leave the argument of the book vulnerable to diverse interpretations. Confusion tends to reign where lack of definition resides.

---

31. An explicit argument for this approach is offered by Craig Van Gelder, *The Essence of the Church: A Community Created by the Spirit* (Grand Rapids: Baker Academic, 2000).

Perhaps this factor is one reason for its popularity; readers from a variety of different faith traditions can *find themselves* in the argument. Whatever the reason, a conversation utilizing missional language has exploded during the past decade. It is now time to turn to a more detailed mapping of the various branches that have grown out of the initial conversation.

# Mapping the Missional Conversation

"Missional" is clearly a word of choice today for many Christian authors, as well as for a large number of church leaders around the world. The introduction to this book summarizes the emergence of this term in popular usage and also provides an initial framework for mapping the diverse ways in which it is presently being used. This chapter picks up the mapping discussion and explores in detail the primary branches and various subbranches of the missional conversation.

This mapping framework identifies the distinguishing characteristics of each major branch in terms of key biblical and theological ideas that various authors use to construct their missional argument. As noted in the introduction, one might think of each cluster of ideas as constituting a particular *theological imagination*, or, more specifically, a *theologically informed social imagination*, which helps to shape each approach to missional. Not only do ideas matter profoundly in influencing our choices and actions, but the socially embedded character of our choices and actions also shapes our ideas—our social imagination.

Such a particular theologically informed social imagination was constructed in *Missional Church*. In light of this imagination, the authors made an effort to identify certain actions and practices for shaping the life and ministry of congregations. This was especially the case in terms of the church's stance toward the world (chapter 5), the particular practices that are to be cultivated by congregations (chapter 6), and approaches to be utilized in leadership and organization (chapters 7 and 8). It is thus interesting that many readers of this book have raised the question: what does a missional church actually look like?

One suspects that those who ask this question are probably seeking a more discrete how-to list. It should be noted that the authors actually made an explicit effort to avoid taking such a functional approach, lest the argument they were making default all too quickly once again to strategy as the primary focus. This probably helps to explain to some extent the numerous volumes appearing in the past decade that provide concrete lists of characteristics or behaviors defining what the authors believe "being missional" represents. Closer examination of these lists, however, reveals that many of them are, in reality, simply repackaged practices from church growth and church effectiveness literature, but are referred to now as missional. One good example is the list available at the website of the Evangelical Covenant Church;[1] another obvious example is the twenty-eight characteristics ascribed to missional congregations by the LCWE.[2]

### Developing a Hermeneutic for Mapping the Missional Conversation

Surprisingly few efforts have been made to map the diverse uses of the concept of missional in the midst of the explosion of missional literature during the past decade. One suggestive map is available on the website of Ed Stetzer, where it is referred to as a "Missional Family Tree."[3] Stetzer, to his credit, is one of the few authors publishing on the missional theme who has examined more carefully, both historically and theologically, the cluster of ideas associated with the use of the word "missional."

The trunk of Stetzer's tree starts with *Missional Church* and then spreads out to show books that are part of three distinct branches, with several books displayed for each of the following: (1) missional leaders, (2) missional communities, and (3) missional disciples. His approach suggests a starting point for distinguishing between various publications using a missional understanding. However, a more fruitful approach is to utilize the issue of *agency* for mapping the extensive diversity within the missional literature that has now emerged.

---

1. The denominational website provides a link to "Healthy Missional Markers," where one finds a list of ten characteristics all supported by specific biblical texts, such as intentional evangelism (Matt. 28:18–20), compelling Christian community (Acts 2:42–47), and heartfelt worship (John 4:23). Little attention is paid to framing these markers within a larger theological understanding. See http://covchurch.org/resource/healthy-missional-markers.

2. Lausanne Committee for World Evangelization, "The Local Church in Mission: Becoming a Missional Congregation in the Twenty-First Century Global Context and the Opportunities Offered through Tentmaking Ministry," Lausanne Occasional Paper no. 39, 2005.

3. http://blogs.lifeway.com/blog/edstetzer/2009/02/missional-family-tree.html.

### Theological Imagination in Relation to Agency

We propose that a fruitful hermeneutic for constructing a map of the present missional conversation involves exploring how the theological imagination used by various authors shapes their understanding of agency in relation to church life. The key issue, comprised of two closely related questions, is: to what extent are we simply dealing with human agency, and to what extent is God's agency operative and discernible within human choices? This issue represents a significant distinction that allows us to discern several branches of the missional conversation. The dividing line between branches revolves around the extent to which one starts with the *mission of the church* and the extent to which one starts with the *mission of God*; when starting with the mission of God, it also has to do with how robust the trinitarian theology is. This dividing line around the issue of agency is related to the issue of theological imagination. The key question is: how do we understand God's presence in the world, in general, and in the midst of the church, in particular?

### Using This Hermeneutic for Mapping the Missional Literature

As noted in the introduction, applying this hermeneutic of theological imagination in relation to agency to the current missional literature led us to identify four primary branches that have emerged within the missional conversation during the past decade. We also identify in this chapter the several distinguishable subbranches that are evident within each of the four branches (see figure 2). Our method for employing this approach proceeds in four steps.

First, each major branch with its subbranches is identified in relation to the biblical and theological ideas that inform it. Second, specific examples of relevant literature are provided as representative of each subbranch. These examples include books as well as online sources such as websites, electronic publications, and blogs. Third, a critique of the limits of each branch and its subbranches is provided that attempts to illustrate how a theologically informed social imagination impacts various practices within churches and how such practices work to shape and reinforce a particular social imagination. Finally, those working within the biblical and theological imagination of each branch and subbranch are invited to consider how they might deepen their understanding of missional. This invitation draws on both the initial cluster of ideas that gave birth to the missional conversation and recent biblical and theological developments that are working to extend this conversation.

Figure 2: **Missional Tree with Branches and Subbranches**

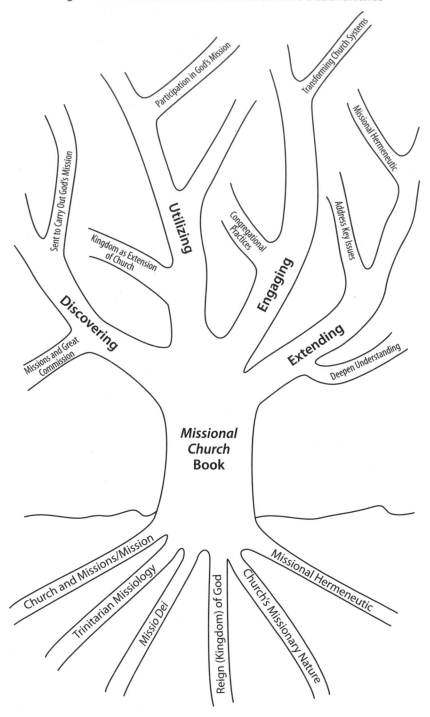

## Conversation Partners "Discovering" Missional

One branch of the missional church conversation today actually reaches back to the previous framework of "church" and "mission," where these were understood as being separate though related realities. The authors representative of this position tend to utilize missional language to promote a more traditional understanding of mission. They are categorized here as still "discovering" the meaning of missional in the sense that they leave much of the biblical and theological imagination associated with the meaning of missional in *Missional Church* largely unexplored. These conversation partners tend to emphasize, as an alternative, some combination of the following ideas, which constitute what might be called their "theological imagination": (1) obedience to the Great Commission and Great Commandment; (2) Christology as the starting point of mission; (3) incarnational versus attractional ministry in a local context; and (4) the church as the location of God's work in the world.

### Examples of Subbranches within the Discovering Branch

At least two subbranches are discernible within the missional literature that is part of the Discovering branch. One is represented by those publications that understand missional to be the equivalent of the historical understanding of mission/missions, that is, as obedience to the Great Commission. A second is represented by those publications that continue to emphasize the Great Commission but frame it theologically in terms of God being a *sending* God.

#### Subbranch 1: Missional as Missions and Great Commission Obedience

A typical example of the word "missional" used as a substitute for what has traditionally been understood as "mission/missions" is found in Mitzi Eaker's 2008 publication, *Missions Moments 2: 52 Easy-to-Use Missional Messages and Activities for Today's Family.*

> Missional Message: God wants Christians to do missions. . . . We do them because God tells us to do missions and because we want to do missions. In the Bible, one of the last things Jesus did before going to heaven was to tell His disciples to go and make disciples of all nations (Matt. 28:19–20). . . . Jesus's disciples obeyed what Jesus told them to do. . . . We should do missions because God tells us to and because we feel compelled by the love that God has shown us.[4]

4. Mitzi Eaker, *Missions Moments 2: 52 Easy-to-Use Missional Messages and Activities for Today's Family* (Birmingham, AL: New Hope, 2008), 118–19.

This basic understanding is expanded by Frank Page in his 2008 publication, *The Nehemiah Factor*. His usage reflects the classical understanding of mission as obedience to the Great Commission, though he nuances this a bit with involvement in social concerns. Page writes, "Missional is a buzzword in evangelical circles today. . . . The word has replaced other terms, such as *missionary, purpose driven, evangelistic,* or *socially intentional*. It involves a way of looking at Christianity that integrates concern for both evangelism and social ministries. It is a kind of acting out of the faith in daily life. . . . [This] is called *missional leadership*, and it offers a type of leadership providing vision and strategy for living a lifestyle that is an example to others."[5]

A very interesting expression of this understanding of missional as mission/missions is offered in the critique of the missional movement in 2007 by the *Leadership Journal*. A variety of articles in that year's winter edition discussed the missional conversation. A few offered at least some background to the more substantive biblical and theological developments that gave birth to the recent movement. But the overall thrust of the critique consistently viewed missional as primarily concerning the church's task of obeying the Great Commission through engaging changed local contexts. This is clearly illustrated in the cover article by the journal's managing editor, Eric Reed, in which he writes, "The word *missional* . . . [is about] focusing on the church's role in the culture. It refers to a philosophy of ministry: that followers of Christ are countercultural, on a mission to change culture. Missional refers to the specific activity of churches: to build the kingdom of God in all settings where church members are at work, rather than building up the local congregation, its programs, numbers, and facilities."[6]

Similar approaches to using the word "missional" in the sense of representing the more traditional understanding of mission/missions can be found in the following publications and websites:

Abilene Christian University, http://www.acu.edu/aboutacu/vision.html

Dennis Bickers, *Intentional Ministry in a Not-So-Mega Church* (2009)

Bob Hopkins and Freddy Hedley, *Coaching for Missional Leadership* (2008)

Georgia Baptists with the Christian Index, http://www.christianindex.org

Alan C. Klaas and Cheryl D. Klaas, *Flexible, Missional Constitution/By-Laws* (2000)

Kara E. Powell and Brad M. Griffin, *Deep Justice Journeys* (2008)

5. Frank Page, *The Nehemiah Factor: 16 Characteristics of a Missional Leader* (Birmingham, AL: New Hope, 2008), 19.
6. Eric Reed, "New Ownership: Missional Is More Than a Trend as Today's Christians Recover an Old Calling," *Leadership Journal* (Winter 2007): 20.

Gary Rohrmayer, *First Steps for Planting a Missional Church* (2006)

Rick Rusaw and Eric Swanson, *The Externally Focused Church* (2004)

### SUBBRANCH 2: MISSIONAL AS BEING SENT TO CARRY OUT GOD'S MISSION

This subbranch slightly nuances the conversation about obeying the Great Commission by stressing that it is God's mission in and to the world, a mission that involves a sending activity on behalf of God. The operational framework of obedience to the Great Commission is still at work here, but it is presented in terms of God sending Christians into the world to carry out God's mission. An interesting use of this understanding of missional is demonstrated by the LCWE in the paper that developed from its 2004 consultation, "The Local Church in Mission." It offers, consistent with the diversity of the consultative work group, a comprehensive list of twenty-eight characteristics of missional congregations. The paper's introduction states:

> Missional congregations are those communities of Christ followers who see the church as the people of God who are sent on a mission. . . . These Christ followers seek to embody the way of Christ within their particular surrounding cultures. . . .
>
> Every local congregation is only a true representative of the body of Christ when they serve the world in mission. If a local church fails to "go" and instead waits for others to "come," they are disobedient. The local church must regain the reputation as mission-driven.[7]

Another typical example of this approach is found in the 2001 publication *Next Door and Down the Freeway*, edited by Nazarene author Neil Wiseman.

> The Great Commandment and the Great Commission move us to engage the world in evangelism, compassion, and justice. . . . The church is sent into the world to participate with God in this ministry of love and reconciliation. . . .
>
> In the 20th century, we were a *sending* church . . . sending missionaries around the world. But in the 21st century, we must be a *sent* church, because the mission field is all around us—right here in North America.[8]

A similar understanding is employed by the North American Mission Board of the Southern Baptist Convention in the edited work of John Bailey, *Pursuing the Mission of God in Church Planting*.

7. Lausanne Committee for World Evangelization, "The Local Church in Mission."
8. Neil B. Wiseman, ed., *Next Door and Down the Freeway: Developing a Missional Strategy for USA/Canada* (Kansas City, MO: Beacon Hill, 2001), 7, 11. Italics in the original.

Today, across North America there is a renewed emphasis upon the *sending* of believers into the world to live as missionaries who seek to fulfill the Great Commission. . . .

Therefore, in the *missional church* there must be a shift from just a programmatic and attractional approach to doing church. . . . In essence, the followers of Christ become an extension of God's mission in the world as missionaries. . . . *They become partners with God.*[9]

Similar approaches to using the word "missional" in the sense of being sent by God into mission can be found in the following publications and websites:

Assemblies of God, *Enrichment Journal*, http://enrichmentjournal.ag .org/200802/200802_050_DevMissMind.cfm

Timothy Cowin's blog, http://timothycowin.com

Dave Dunbar (president of Biblical Seminary), "Missional Journal," http:// www.biblical.edu/index.php/missional-journal

Evangelical Lutheran Church in America, http://www.elca.org/Growing -In-Faith/Discipleship/Missional-Leaders.aspx

Todd Harrington, Resonating the Gospel within a Post Christian Culture (2008)

Rick Meigs's blog, http://www.friendofmissional.org

J. D. Payne, *Missional House Churches* (2008)

Bo Prosser, *Approaching a Missional Mindset* (2008)

Vineyard USA, http://www.vineyardusa.org/site/content/how-be-missional -your-church

Joe Waresak, *The Missional Life* (2008)

Barry E. Winders, *Finding the Missional Path* (2007)

### A Critique

Most of the publications that are representative of the Discovering branch have clearly grasped several things about the concept of missional that were intended in its initial use, especially (1) the engagement of believers/the church with the church's own immediate context, and (2) that all believers must be understood as being missionaries. The missional concept allows many of the contributors within this branch to begin to bridge the classic dichotomy that

9. John M. Bailey, ed., *Pursuing the Mission of God in Church Planting: The Missional Church in North America* (Alpharetta, GA: North American Mission Board of the Southern Baptist Convention, 2007), i, 41. Italics in the original.

has plagued much of the evangelical world: the separation of evangelism and social involvement. The incarnational theology associated with the use of the term "missional" allows for fresh engagement in a context that is more holistic in character.

However, for many who are within this branch, important aspects of their biblical and theological understanding of missional continue to limit its usefulness for reframing their approach to church and mission/missions from a missional perspective. First, they continue to frame agency primarily in human terms as either obedience to the Great Commission or the responsibility of the church to carry out its mission, thereby diminishing an understanding of God's agency. Second, the central role that Christology plays for most of them tends to (1) downplay the role of the Spirit, (2) reinforce hierarchical patterns of authority and decision making, and (3) focus attention on our responsibility to emulate the example of Jesus—a perspective not wrong in and of itself, but insufficient for disclosing the fullness of God's intent in sending God's Son. Third, their focus on mission/missions tends to promote a functional understanding of ecclesiology, which diminishes an appreciation for the nature of the church as the creation of the Spirit. Finally, any discussion of the reign of God is either very limited or absent in defining God's redemptive work in relation to the church and world, which makes the church the primary locus of God's redemptive activity.

### An Invitation

We return in chapters 4 through 6 to a further discussion of the issues identified above by bringing them into conversation with insights from recent biblical and theological developments. There we invite those pursuing this missional approach to explore more fully a trinitarian understanding of mission, which recognizes that the *social* and *sending* Triune God has a mission in the world. This would help to cultivate the understanding of a more active engagement of the Spirit in relation to redemption in the life of the church and in regard to the reign of God within the larger world. It would also invite a fundamentally different approach to understanding agency by opening up the horizon of God's leading in the life of the church in relation to God's continued presence in the world.

### Conversation Partners "Utilizing" Missional

A second branch of the current missional conversation includes publications that utilize the framework of God's agency as a sending God as the key to understanding the role of human agency. In doing so, they actively draw on the larger cluster of biblical and theological ideas that initially stimulated the missional conversation in *Missional Church*. These publications are categorized here as "utilizing" the meaning of missional because their authors are actively attempting to identify implications that this understanding of missional has for the ministry of the church.

These conversation partners tend to emphasize some combination of the following ideas, which constitute what might be called their "theological imagination": (1) the mission of the *sending* Triune God and the church being called to participate in this mission; (2) the importance of the reign of God in understanding God's mission in the world; and (3) the responsibility of the church to engage the world, though there are different versions of what this engagement should be.

### Examples of Subbranches within the Utilizing Branch

At least three subbranches are discernible within the missional literature that pursues the Utilizing approach. One is represented by publications that clearly frame the sending character of a missionary God but then proceed to frame the redemptive work of God's reign as basically an extension of the church's ministry in the world. A second is represented by publications that frame their understanding of missional in terms of both the sending character of God and the redemptive nature of God's reign, but then make the church a contrast community within the world as the primary place where that redemptive work takes place. A third is represented by publications that draw fairly consistently on the whole cluster of biblical and theological ideas informing the initial conversation, which focused on illuminating further the implications of this understanding.

#### Subbranch 1: Missional as the Kingdom of God Being an Extension of the Church's Ministry

The publications representative of this subbranch clearly begin with an assertion of the central importance of the Triune God's mission—the *missio Dei*. This is stressed as foundational for framing the life and ministry of the church in the world. They also emphasize the importance of understanding the church's life and ministry in relation to the reign of God. However, publications in this subbranch tend to revert to stressing human responsibility in defining the relationship of the church to the reign of God. They do so by making it, in effect, an extension of the church's ministry in the world. A good example of this is found in Milfred Minatrea's 2004 publication, *Shaped by God's Heart*.

No significant Kingdom accomplishment will occur until churches value Kingdom more than their own sectarian accomplishments. Missional churches seek
to raise the standard of the cross in territories currently occupied by forces of
the enemy. . . . The church serves as the contemporary representative of . . . the
Kingdom of God. . . .

Jesus taught "the Kingdom of God is within you" (Luke 17:21). . . .

Although the church and Kingdom are not synonymous, the church is a current expression of the Kingdom of God. The church is the corporate domain
of the Kingdom. . . .

The Kingdom within will manifest itself in the external activities of disciples. . . . Individual servants are the building blocks of the Kingdom. . . . Each
disciple comes into the Kingdom individually.[10]

This understanding ultimately folds the reign of God back into the life
and ministry of the church rather than viewing it as extending beyond the
church, calling the church into a fuller participation in what God is doing
in the world.

A similar understanding is presented by Will Mancini in his 2008 publication, *Church Unique*.

The first step in ascertaining a unique vision is to discover your Kingdom Concept. The Kingdom Concept is the simple, clear, "big idea" that defines how
your church will glorify God and make disciples. . . . Your Kingdom Concept is
what differentiates you from every other church in *how* you develop followers
of Christ for God's ultimate honor. The Kingdom Concept answers important
questions such as "What is our greatest opportunity to have an impact for the
kingdom?" . . . Think of it as your organizational sweet spot. It is the place
where your church's unique experiences flow as a body of Christ. With a clear
understanding of a Kingdom Concept, your leadership can capture and release
amazing energy toward a better future.[11]

This understanding captures an important dimension of the biblical teaching
that the reign of God works to reframe a church's self-understanding. However,
this approach also tends to default back to the church developing, yet again, a
more strategic focus for its future without considering the deeper realities of
God's work in the world. This approach can also be found in Reggie McNeal's
2009 publication, *Missional Renaissance*. After clearly articulating a missional

10. Milfred Minatrea, *Shaped by God's Heart: The Passion and Practices of Missional
Churches* (San Francisco: Jossey-Bass, 2004), 127–32.

11. Will Mancini, *Church Unique: How Missional Leaders Cast Vision, Capture Culture,
and Create Movement* (San Francisco: Jossey-Bass, 2008), 84.

sending theology, he proceeds to connect this theological understanding to the relationship of the church and the reign of God.

> Today's spiritual realities call for the third shift of the missional renaissance, from church-based to kingdom-based leadership. . . . [This] requires spiritual leaders who understand the culture's search for God and who are willing to engage this discussion.
>       . . . Much of the kingdom movement will be focused outside the "organized" church, exercising its influence in the world beyond the church by bringing church into every domain of the culture.
>       Missional leaders . . . find themselves thinking of kingdom impact more than church growth. . . . [They] are imaging the church as a catalyst to mobilize all the community, synergizing the altruistic impetus, to work on the big things that God cares about.[12]

Similar approaches to using the word "missional" in the sense of God's reign functioning essentially as an extension of the church's ministry can be found in the following publications and websites:

Brother Maynard, http://subversiveinfluence.com

Evangelical Presbyterian Church, http://www.epc.org/about-the-epc/missional-church-and-denomination

Mark Liederbach and Alvin L. Reid, *The Convergent Church* (2009)

Reggie McNeal, *The Present Future* (2003)

Milfred Minatrea of the Missional Church Center, http://www.missional.org/who_we_are/our_identity

Hugh and Matt Smay of Missio, http://missio.us/about

Ed Stetzer and Philip Nation, *Compelled by Love* (2008)

Ed Stetzer and David Putman, *Breaking the Missional Code* (2006)

Daniel Vestal of the Cooperative Baptist Fellowship, http://www.thefellowship.info/News/Words-from-the-Coordinator/lilg

### Subbranch 2: Missional as the Church Being a Contrast Community

Authors writing from this perspective clearly understand and draw on the biblical and theological ideas initially presented in *Missional Church*. They stress the mission of the Triune God and God's sending of the church

---

12. Reggie McNeal, *Missional Renaissance: Changing the Scorecard for the Church* (San Francisco: Jossey-Bass, 2009), 14–15.

into the world to participate in God's mission. They also clearly distinguish between the church and the reign of God with the latter serving as the key for framing the intersection of the church with the world. But they especially emphasize one strain within that cluster of ideas that deals with the church being understood primarily as a contrast community.[13] This focus appears to be tied, at least for some authors, to their use of Christology rather than Trinity as a starting point in defining missional. This approach, in turn, leads them to view missiology primarily as an applied, rather than a theological, discipline.

An example of this approach is found in Michael Frost and Alan Hirsch's 2009 book, ReJesus. They begin by clearly stating a robust understanding of missional.

> God's mission in this world is his and his alone. The glory of God, not the church, is the ultimate goal of mission. Our role as the church, however, is a humble participation in his grand scheme—the kingdom of God.
> . . . It is one of our greatest mistakes to equate the church with the kingdom of God. The kingdom is much broader than the church—it is cosmic in scope.[14]

They then proceed, however, to formulate their understanding of God's mission in relation to Christology and the biblical Jesus.

> We believe it is not possible to be following the biblical Jesus and not end up being molded by the missio Dei, participati Christi, and imago Dei.
> . . . His passions and concerns must become ours. . . . Christology must determine missiology (our purpose and function in this world), which in turn must determine ecclesiology (the cultural forms and expressions of the church). . . . We believe that Christology is the singularly most important factor in shaping our mission in the world and the forms of ecclesia and ministry that result from that engagement. . . .
> . . . There ought to be a thoroughgoing attempt to reconnect the church with Jesus; that is, to reJesus the church as the first order of business.[15]

13. The use here of "contrast community" to describe the church refers primarily to the strain of ecclesiology that promotes a more sectarian understanding of the church in relation to the world, typically referenced as an Anabaptist approach. There is also a use of the term "contrast society" that draws on the work of Gerhard Lohfink, Jesus and Community: The Social Dimension of Christian Faith, trans. John P. Galvin (Philadelphia: Fortress, 1984), 122. His usage focuses on the distinctiveness of the people of God in the midst of their full engagement with the world. Interestingly, both uses are evident in Missional Church, with the former being prominent in chapter 5 and the latter coming to the fore in chapter 6.

14. Michael Frost and Alan Hirsch, ReJesus: A Wild Messiah for a Missional Church (Peabody, MA/Grand Rapids: Hendrickson/Baker Books, 2009), 29–30.

15. Ibid., 41–43.

Frost and Hirsch fail to realize that the trinitarian understanding of God's mission they use to frame their Christology is in fact a theological missiology—a missiological framework that defines the interrelationship of God, church, and world. They choose instead to make Christology their starting point and as a result tend to (1) diminish the role of the Spirit in the life of the church as well as in the world; (2) foster an understanding of the church as a contrast community within the world that seeks to emulate the example of Jesus; and (3) reduce missiology to an applied discipline, thus eclipsing its richer biblical and theological assertions.

Another example of someone who takes this approach is Mark Driscoll in his 2006 publication, *Confessions of a Reformission Rev*.

> Reformission . . . begins with a simple return to Jesus, who . . . saves us and sends us into reformission. . . .
>
> . . . A third incarnation of the church is arising [in contrast to the *traditional and institutional* and the *contemporary and evangelical*], the *emerging and missional church*, which is marked by . . . every Christian being a missionary to their local culture . . . [and where the] church is a counterculture with a new kingdom way of life through Jesus. . . .

Driscoll goes on to list the four priorities of the "missional ministry matrix" as Christology, ecclesiology, missiology, and ministry.[16]

A critique similar to the one offered above regarding the proposal of Frost and Hirsch can be offered in relation to Driscoll's argument. He utilizes a substantive trinitarian theology to frame God's mission, but his christological approach culminates in the church becoming a countercultural society attempting to emulate the example of Jesus by living out kingdom values.

Although not proposing as strong of a christological starting point, Gary Nelson's 2008 publication, *Borderland Churches*, offers an additional example of this approach.

> The *missio Dei* emerges from the very nature of who God is. It takes place long before the church is formed and it implicates everything we do. As we reimagine the church in our crossover to the borderlands, we do so in the profound belief that we are not taking God there; God is already there. . . .
>
> The church as it existed in the New Testament times is only a means to an end whereby the reign of God is made possible even in the smallest, most imperfect way. . . . The church [is] the only part of God's kingdom with a consciousness

16. Mark Driscoll, *Confessions of a Reformission Rev.: Hard Lessons from an Emerging Missional Church* (Grand Rapids: Zondervan, 2006), 15, 19, 41–51.

of the kingdom[,] and therefore [it has] a responsibility for its preservation, celebration, and extension.[17]

Similar approaches to using the word "missional" in the sense of the church being a contrast community of God's reign can be found in the following publications and websites:

Allelon: A Movement of Missional Leaders, http://allelon.org

Cooperative Baptist Fellowship, *It's Time* (2005)

Eddie Gibbs, *ChurchMorph* (2009)

Eddie Gibbs and Ryan K. Bolger, *Emerging Churches* (2005)

Alan Hirsch, *The Forgotten Ways* (2006)

Andrew Jones's blog, http://tallskinnykiwi.typepad.com/tallskinnykiwi

Brian D. McLaren, *A Generous Orthodoxy* (2004)

Mennonite Mission Network of the Mennonite Church USA, http://www
   .mennonitemission.net/aboutus/FAQs/MissionalChurch.asp

Cam Roxburgh of Forge Canada, http://www.forgecanada.ca

Howard Snyder, *Decoding the Church* (2002)

Mark Van Steenwyk of Missio Dei church in Minneapolis, http://www
   .jesusmanifesto.com

Jason Zahariades of The Off Ramp, http://www.theofframp.org/missional_
   comm.html

### SUBBRANCH 3: MISSIONAL AS PARTICIPATING IN GOD'S MISSION IN THE WORLD

Several publications have followed the other strain regarding the relationship between the church and the world as proposed in the initial argument of *Missional Church*. This approach views the mission of God as involving God's work not only in and through the church but also within the larger world through the Spirit, which makes the church more responsive in discerning how to participate more fully in both aspects of God's mission. Although the trinitarian theology undergirding God's mission is still framed primarily in sending terms, it is nuanced to some extent by these authors. The conundrum of how the works of God—the reign of God and the Spirit of God's broader work in the world—are to be interrelated, however, is left largely unresolved in this approach.

17. Gary V. Nelson, *Borderland Churches: A Congregation's Introduction to Missional Living* (St. Louis: Chalice, 2008), 39, 45, 122.

One example of this more substantive approach to understanding missional is found in Ed Stetzer's 2008 publication, *Sent*. In this volume, Stetzer moves beyond some of his previous publications that tended toward a more functional understanding of how the church and the reign of God are related.

> Missional is an important word because it doesn't describe what we *do* as Christ-followers; it describes who we *are* as Christ-followers . . . [sent] into the world for the sake of the kingdom. . . . Our mission is not our mission at all. It's God's. So if we don't understand His purpose, we can do all the right *things* and still miss the point. . . .
> . . . According to God's will, Jesus sent the Holy Spirit to empower those He would be sending into the world. . . . Our sending God sends the church—the body of Christ—as His missionary in the world. . . .
> God doesn't limit Himself to working only through the church. Though the church is God's plan for reaching the world, He isn't limited to us to build His kingdom on the earth. . . . So what we're doing isn't "taking God to others" by any stretch. We're really simply pointing out to people the presence of God who is already among them.[18]

This broader view of God's work within the world is also expressed by Linda Bergquist and Allan Karr in their 2010 publication, *Church Turned Inside Out*.

> God is the life-giving Creator/Designer of everything that exists. He creates in His image, sustains what He creates, and as Creator of the universe His perspective as cosmic God has placed His creative Holy Spirit in us; therefore we are creative by nature. . . .
> God is the Creator-community of Father, Son, and Spirit, the three in One. He is the image of unity in diversity, and the model for true community. . . . We are called to be a relationally based spiritual community created in the image of the Trinity, drawn together by spirit and the person of Christ, led by the abiding Spirit. . . .
> Today's church has posed itself a serious challenge: to live according to its missional nature rather than simply organize around mission activities. This challenge is something of an antidote to the church's practice of piecing together a theology out of the . . . Great Commission . . . rather than from the entire biblical story.[19]

The authors engage several aspects of the initial missional church argument that most have not attended to very well, if at all. These include

18. Ed Stetzer, *Sent: Living the Missional Nature of the Church* (Nashville: LifeWay, 2008), 10, 14, 19–20, 24.
19. Linda Bergquist and Allan Karr, *Church Turned Inside Out: A Guide for Designers, Refiners, and Re-Aligners* (San Francisco: Jossey-Bass, 2010), 65–66, 75.

understanding God as Creator who is continuing to create, emphasizing the role of the Spirit in shaping the life and ministry of the church, and acknowledging the importance of the social Trinity for understanding the church as community.

Two additional books fit fairly well within this subbranch. Both were written by members of the writing team that produced *Missional Church*. One is the book authored by Darrell Guder in 2000, *The Continuing Conversion of the Church*, in which he employs the cluster of biblical and theological ideas used in the initial missional church argument and focuses on the tendency of the church throughout the ages to reduce the meaning of the gospel in relation to an understanding of church and culture—what he refers to as "the challenge of reductionism."[20] The other book, published in 2000 and authored by Craig Van Gelder, is *The Essence of the Church*. This volume restates the basic argument developed in *Missional Church* but does so by addressing some of the gaps and lack of integration in that original argument. In particular, attention is given to providing a framework for understanding the history of ecclesiology and incorporating a more explicit emphasis on the role of the Spirit in the life of the church as well as in the world.

Similar approaches to using the word "missional" in this sense can be found in the following publications and websites:

Ray S. Anderson, *An Emergent Theology for Emerging Churches* (2006)

Todd Billings, "What Makes a Church Missional?" (2008)

Brad Brisco of Missional Church Network, http://missionalchurchnetwork
   .com

Paul W. Chilcote and Laceye C. Warner, *The Study of Evangelism* (2008)

Nate C. P. Frambach, *Emerging Ministry* (2007)

Reformed Church in America, "Reformed and Missional Video Discussion,"
   http://www.rca.org/Page.aspx?pid=4758

Ed Stetzer, *Planting Missional Churches* (2006)

### A Critique

Most of the publications listed above as being representative of the Utilizing branch demonstrate a clear commitment to most of the core ideas of the initial missional church understanding, especially (1) how the sending Trinity shapes an understanding of *missio Dei* and (2) the importance of stressing the

---

20. Darrell Guder, *The Continuing Conversion of the Church* (Grand Rapids: Eerdmans, 2000), 97.

reign of God in relation to the church and the world. However, the theological imagination exercised by at least some in this branch, primarily the first two subbranches, tends to produce a number of difficulties.

First, there is a tendency to limit the fuller work of the reign of God to the life and ministry of the church, thus making it either an extension of the church's ministry or restricting its power to bring the church into intersection with the world. Second, the failure to consistently develop a trinitarian understanding of God's mission in relation to Christology tends to do three things: (1) contributes to focusing on individual Christians as the focal point of God's redemptive work, rather than the church in relation to the world; (2) emphasizes our responsibility to emulate the example of Jesus rather than our calling to live into the fullness of a new communal identity "in Christ"; and (3) diminishes the role of the Spirit, especially in relation to the broader work of the Spirit in the world. A third difficulty is that the ecclesiology of the church as a contrast community tends to limit the ability of the church to actively discern God's work through the Spirit within the larger world in order to more fully participate in it.

### An Invitation

We return in chapters 4 through 6 to a further discussion of the issues identified above by bringing them into conversation with insights from recent biblical and theological developments. There we invite those pursuing this conception of missional to consider a more robust approach to the Trinity by integrating a view of the social Trinity with their understanding of the sending Trinity. This can strengthen their approach to framing the communal nature of the church as well as the corporate nature of discipleship. It would also invite a fuller understanding of God's work through the Spirit within creation in relation to God's work through the Spirit in redemption. In addition, it would assist these authors in engaging more substantively the question of how the reign of God serves as the point of intersection between the church and the world and how this intersection provides a framework for integrating God's works in creation and redemption.

### Conversation Partners "Engaging" Missional

A third major branch of the missional conversation today finds expression in publications that apply an understanding of missional to some aspect of church life. These publications tend to assume, without much review, the basic cluster of biblical and theological ideas associated with missional as well as the primacy of the agency of God. They primarily focus on exploring some of the implications of what a missional approach would mean for some dimension of church life.

### Examples of Subbranches within the Engaging Branch

At least two subbranches are discernible within the missional literature that pursues the Engaging approach. The first is represented by publications that focus on the life and ministry of congregations in seeking to address the issue of how a missional understanding would shape, or reshape, one or more practices of church life. A second is represented by publications that focus on bringing a missional understanding into engagement with the transformation of church systems. The midlevel judicatory, in particular, has been taken up as a key point for leveraging such change.

#### SUBBRANCH 1: A MISSIONAL UNDERSTANDING OF CONGREGATIONAL PRACTICES

The literature in this subbranch of the missional conversation ranges across a broad array of congregational practices. A generalized approach toward clarifying what constitutes missional practices is found in the follow-up study by the GOCN, a study that was conducted in the early 2000s and published in 2004 as *Treasure in Clay Jars*. This study attempted to address the question often raised by readers of *Missional Church*: what does a missional congregation actually look like? The results of the intensive field study of nine congregations led the team to identify what they describe as "eight patterns—patterns on clay jars—of church life that let the 'light of the knowledge of the glory of God in the face of Jesus Christ' shine through."[21] The eight patterns emerging from the nine congregations were identified as

1. Missional vocation: discovering together our missional vocation
2. Biblical formation and discipleship: all members growing as disciples
3. Taking risks as a contrast community: learning to take risks for the sake of the gospel in light of being different from the world
4. Demonstrating God's intent for the world: embodying a demonstration of what God intends for the world
5. Worship as public witness: celebrating God's presence with joy
6. Dependence on the Holy Spirit: demonstrating dependence on the Spirit, especially through prayer

---

21. Lois Y. Barrett et al., *Treasure in Clay Jars: Patterns in Missional Faithfulness* (Grand Rapids: Eerdmans, 2004), xi.

7. Pointing toward the reign of God: serving as instrument, agent, and
   sign of that reign
8. Missional authority: functional roles that cultivate communal discernment[22]

Another example from this type of missional literature is the 2009 book by
Clayton J. Schmit, *Sent and Gathered*, which focuses on the important role
of worship in the life of a missional congregation. He begins by laying out a
biblical and theological understanding of what it means to be missional—what
he stresses as the sent aspect of church life—and then proceeds to engage
all aspects of the practice of worship from this perspective. His operational
framework is as follows:

> Central to our discussion are two key observations: that there is an increas-
> ing awareness among the denominations and traditions that public Christian
> worship consists of the faithful gathering themselves around the Word and the
> sacraments, and that from those gatherings we are sent out into the fields of
> mission that lie beyond each church door. Along the way several key theological
> ideas have been identified:
>
> 1. Worship is relevant only because God chooses to relate to humanity and
>    to invest God's self in our gatherings.
> 2. Liturgy consists of the egalitarian activities engaged in by people who
>    gather for worship and who go forth in service in the world. . . .
> 3. The role of worship leaders is to serve, drawing the assembly into an
>    encounter with the One who made, redeems, and sustains them.
> 4. The *missio Dei* is the mission of the church today: to be called and
>    gathered . . . and sent forth as the active people of God.[23]

This understanding of worship clearly represents an awareness of the post-
Christendom reality of church life today. Interestingly, however, the author does
not engage in any substantive critique of the Christendom-shaped historical
understanding of the place of Word and sacrament within worship, especially
in the context of the Protestant Reformation.

A similar approach, applied specifically to understanding the role of preaching from within a missional perspective, is available in the 2008 publication by
John Addison Dally, *Choosing the Kingdom*. The author does a good job of
reframing an understanding of preaching in light of the inbreaking of God's
reign, but he does not offer a substantive critique of the historical rise of the
role of preacher and the practice of preaching.

22. Ibid., xii–xiv.
23. Clayton J. Schmit, *Sent and Gathered: A Worship Manual for the Missional Church*
(Grand Rapids: Baker Academic, 2009), 40–41.

If mission is not an activity of the church but an attribute of God, what are the implications for preaching? . . . If I've learned anything about missional preaching in the past six years, it is that it's hard work, mentally and spiritually. It takes its cue from the announcement of Jesus at the inauguration of his public ministry in the gospel of Mark: "The kingdom of God has come near. . . ."

These simple words remind us that the "crisis in preaching" may be due to our long amnesia about the preaching of *krisis*, the judgment of God breaking in to human history.[24]

Similar approaches to using the word "missional" in the sense of reshaping congregational practices can be found in the following publications and websites:

Jim Belcher, *Deep Church* (2009)

Earl Creps, *Off-Road Disciplines* (2006)

Inagrace T. Dietterich, *Cultivating Missional Communities* (2006)

David Fitch of Reclaiming the Mission, http://www.reclaimingthemission .com

Tim Keller, "The Missional Church," http://download.redeemer.com/pdf /learn/resources/Missional_Church-Keller.pdf

Dan Kimball, *The Emerging Church* (2003)

Dan Kimball, "Missional Misgivings" (2008)

Louise Nelstrop and Martyn Percy, eds., *Evaluating Fresh Expressions* (2008)

David Putman, *Breaking the Discipleship Code* (2008)

Rick Rouse and Craig Van Gelder, *A Field Guide for the Missional Congregation* (2008)

Jim Thomas, "The Missional Church," http://www.urbana.org/articles /the-missional-church

### Subbranch 2: Missional Leadership and Transforming Church Systems

The missional church conversation clearly has significant implications for congregations, as illustrated in the discussion above about the first subbranch of the Engaging branch. There is also an emerging awareness for some regarding how to bring this conversation into engagement with larger church systems

24. John Addison Dally, *Choosing the Kingdom: Missional Preaching for the Household of God* (Herndon, VA: Alban Institute, 2008), 11.

in seeking their transformation—especially judicatories and national-level denominational agencies. Several recent publications, all by church consultants, have offered insights into how to pursue such an engagement.

The first book to appear in this area was *Robust Church Development*, written by Mike Regele and published in 2003. Drawing from the extensive database that his Percept organization had produced on congregations, Regele lays out an approach for judicatories to pursue in seeking to help congregations become more missional.

> The last few years have seen a floodgate opened around the recognition that North America has become a primary mission field. . . .
>
> The emergence of a missiologically defined vision of the church has taken firm root. . . . The missional nature of the church is being embraced. . . . We greatly encourage denominational leaders to aggressively engage this conversation at any level you can. . . .
>
> As we try to rethink and reshape church development efforts around this new missionary context, what principles should be the foundation of our thinking, our shaping and ultimately, our provision of support and resources?
>
> First principle: God is a missionary God
> Second principle: God calls us to participate
> Third principle: A cross-cultural missionary enterprise
> Fourth principle: Contextual analysis is critical
> Fifth principle: Translate the story
> Sixth principle: Missionary leadership required[25]

A similar understanding is provided by Patrick Keifert in his 2006 publication, *We Are Here Now*. Drawing on the experiences that his consulting organization, Church Innovations, has had with its Partnership for Missional Church, Keifert lays out an approach for helping judicatories and their congregations to enter into an extensive process of engagement that can lead to missional transformation in the system. He provides an initial summary of a biblical and theological framework that reflects the logic of the initial missional church conversation.

> This is God's mission, not ours. . . . For it is the reign of God that is near, not just the church. The reign of God is far more than the church, though of course the church continuously experiences the breaking in of the reign of God. . . .

25. Mike Regele, *Robust Church Development: A Vision for Mobilizing Regional Bodies in Support of Missional Congregations* (Rancho Santa Margarita, CA: Percept Group, 2003), 29–45.

In this New Missional Era, this time of the missional church, those congregations that are faithful, effective, and efficient will be a part of transforming mission. They will be transformed by the mission—called, gathered, and centered in Word and sacrament, and sent into the mission of God in daily life.[26]

Keifert then develops the phases of transformation and renewal as discovering ("living within the life of the Trinity"), experimenting, visioning for embodiment, learning and growing, and sharing and mentoring.

A third publication that fits into this subbranch is the 2006 volume coauthored by Alan J. Roxburgh and Fred Romanuk, *The Missional Leader*, in which the authors draw on their extensive experience as church consultants to offer a framework for helping church leaders, especially judicatory and denominational leaders, to engage in the process of change—missional transformation. They assume for the most part a biblical and theological understanding of missional in light of the initial missional church conversation and then proceed to stress the importance of cultivating a biblical imagination as the key to engaging the journey.

> The narrative imagination of Scripture challenges our assumptions about what God is up to in the world. . . . An important role of a missional leader is cultivating an environment within which God's people can discern God's directions and activities in them and for the communities in which they find themselves. . . . We, like the people in these biblical stories, are invited to cultivate our imagination to see the possibilities of what the Spirit wants to do in and among the people we are called to lead.[27]

In part two of the book, titled "The Missional Leader," the authors discuss the skills that are necessary for leading missional transformation in terms of "Missional Readiness Factors and the Nature of Leadership," "The Character of a Missional Leader," "Cultivating the People of God for a Missional Future," "Forming a Missional Environment and Culture," and "Engaging Context with a Christian Imagination."[28]

### A Critique

Most of the publications listed above as representative of the Engaging branch appear to have accepted the basic tenets of the initial missional church

26. Patrick Keifert, *We Are Here Now: A Missional Journey of Spiritual Discovery* (Eagle, ID: Allelon, 2006), 37.

27. Alan J. Roxburgh and Fred Romanuk, *The Missional Leader: Equipping Your Church to Reach a Changing World* (San Francisco: Jossey-Bass, 2006), 16–17.

28. Ibid., 109–206.

argument, thus they do not spend much time rehearsing that material. They focus instead on trying to identify what an engagement of this perspective might look like in terms of the choices congregations make and the practices they seek to embody. Although we recognize that most of these books are not written primarily for academic audiences, we believe that readers would nonetheless be better served if the authors made more explicit the fuller connections between their biblical and theological framework and the engagement of practices on which they focus. First, doing so would have led to a more critical awareness of the historical conditioning of all church practices. Second, it would have led to more reciprocal interaction between biblical and theological perspectives and the particular practices that are engaged. Finally, it would have helped the authors to distinguish more substantively between their approaches and those that turn missional into a pragmatic how-to list.

### An Invitation

We will return in chapters 4 through 6 to a further discussion of the issues identified above by bringing them into conversation with insights from recent biblical and theological developments. There we invite those pursuing this approach of missional engagement in relation to church practices to explore more critically the full range of biblical and theological concepts associated with a missional understanding—especially the social and sending aspects of God's mission and the intersection of the reign of God with the church and the world. It is likely that their experience and expertise in engaging congregational practices would make a significant contribution toward enriching these biblical and theological perspectives. It is also likely that their input would lead to a richer understanding of how the church might more fully participate in God's mission in the world. Finally, their work could be fruitful in helping to address the conundrum of relating God's work in redemption to God's continuing work in creation.

## Conversation Partners "Extending" Missional

A fourth branch of the missional conversation today is represented in publications that seek to extend the initial missional argument by further developing the biblical and theological frameworks that undergird this conversation. Those working in this area usually acknowledge in some detail the concepts underlying the initial missional conversation as they proceed toward extending an understanding of it.

### *Examples of Subbranches within the Extending Branch*

At least three subbranches are discernible within the current missional literature that pursues the Extending approach. The first subbranch consists of publications working to further develop the basic argument about missional church by bringing additional biblical and theological insights to bear on the initial "missiological consensus" identified in *Missional Church*.[29] A second subbranch is comprised of publications working to bring a missional church understanding into engagement with key issues by exploring the implications of a missional understanding in relation to a particular theme. A third subbranch is exemplified by those who return to a critical agenda remaining from the initial missional conversation to formulate a missional hermeneutic as the basis for developing a missional theology.

### SUBBRANCH 1: DEEPENING OUR UNDERSTANDING OF MISSIONAL

The literature in this subbranch of the missional conversation is characterized by its explicit attention to the biblical and theological concepts used to frame a missional understanding. Some of this literature seeks to address the gaps or areas that lack integration in the initial construction of the argument; other literature in this subbranch moves the missional conversation in new directions. A good example of the latter is *Mission-Shaped Church*, a 2004 publication that grew out of the Fresh Expressions movement within the Church of England. It begins by framing God's mission in terms of both the social Trinity and the sending Trinity.

> We have entitled this report *Mission-Shaped Church*. This echoes two themes within this report: that the Church is the fruit of God's mission, and that as such it exists to serve and to participate in the ongoing mission of God. . . .
>
> When Christians speak of "God," it is as shorthand for the Holy Trinity. . . . First, God has to be understood relationally and communally: "Father, Son, and Holy Spirit, who mutually indwell one another, exist in one another and for one another, in interdependent giving and receiving." Second, God is a missionary. We would not know God if the Father had not sent the Son in the power of the Spirit. In fact the mission of God (*missio Dei*) itself expresses God's relational nature.[30]

*Mission-Shaped Church* then proceeds to make the connection between this integrated trinitarian approach and God's works of creation and redemption.

29. Guder, *Missional Church*, 3–4.
30. Archbishops' Council 2004, *Mission-Shaped Church: Church Planting and Fresh Expressions of Church in a Changing Context* (London: Church Publishing House, 2004), xii, 84–85.

"The communion of the persons of the Trinity is not to be understood as closed in on itself, but rather open in an outgoing movement of generosity. Creation and redemption are the overflow of God's triune life." . . . The mission of God as creator, through Christ, in the Spirit, is to bring into being, sustain and perfect the whole creation. . . . The mission of God as redeemer, through Christ, in the Spirit, is to restore and reconcile the fallen creation. . . . The "mission of the Church is the gift of participating through the Holy Spirit in the Son's mission from the Father to the world."[31]

There were glimpses of this approach to a missional understanding in one strain of the initial missional church construction (chapters 6 and 7 of *Missional Church*), but this strain was not developed in any detail. *Mission-Shaped Church*, however, does pick up this strain in order to develop it more fully. Key to this approach is the intersection between the social Trinity and the sending Trinity in regard to the works of both creation and redemption as representing the mission of God. Also of note is the careful way in which the works of all three persons of the Trinity are consistently integrated within their understanding. The writing team of this document proceeds to utilize this framework to address the dramatically changed context in which the church now finds itself in England.

A different approach to extending the missional conversation is utilized by coauthors Alan Roxburgh and Scott Boren in their 2009 publication, *Introducing the Missional Church*. As one of the original authors contributing to *Missional Church*, Roxburgh has been engaging the missional conversation now for well over a decade and has written several other volumes utilizing this understanding. However, in this volume he teams up with coauthor Boren to place into perspective the ever-expanding missional conversation. They begin by clarifying what a missional church understanding is *not*—at least is *not* in relation to its initial formulation in *Missional Church*.

> *Missional church* is not a label to describe churches that emphasize cross-cultural missions. . . .
> *Missional church* is not a label used to describe churches that are using outreach programs to be *externally focused*. . . .
> *Missional church* is not another label for church growth and church effectiveness. . . .
> *Missional church* is not a label for churches that are effective at evangelism. . . .

31. Ibid., 84–85. Quotations from House of Bishops of the General Synod, *Eucharist Presiding: A Theological Statement of the House of Bishops of the General Assembly* (London: Church Publishing House, 1997), x; and James Torrance, *Worship, Community and the Triune God* (London: Paternoster, 1996), ix, respectively.

*Missional church* is not a label to describe churches that have developed a clear mission statement with a vision and purpose for their existence. . . .

*Missional church* is not a way of turning around ineffective and outdated church forms so that they can display relevance in the wider culture. . . .

*Missional church* is not a label that points to a primitive or ancient way of being the church. . . .

*Missional* is not a label describing new formats of church that reach people who have no interest in traditional churches.[32]

The authors proceed to frame their approach to an understanding of missional, one that is best conceived of as a journey.

In the biblical imagination, dictionary definitions as we know them are not the norm. . . . The implications for the missional conversation are clear. We have to become willing (like little children) to enter the strange world of the Bible. . . . The thing about definitions is that we use them to provide clarity that, in turn, has the potential of giving us control over our world. . . .

Scripture does not so much define reality as invite us onto a journey in which we discover the world God is creating. . . . If we persist on this journey into the strange world of the Bible, it will form our imaginations in radically new ways; it will change how we see the world. . . .

It's as though missional life is discovered out of a wide, wild river. . . . It has been shaped by the confluence of three powerful currents we call *mystery*, *memory*, and *mission*. Entering the missional waters is not about strategies or models; it is about working with the currents that shape our imagination of what God is doing in the world.[33]

This shifting of the landscape (or riverscape!) of the missional conversation provides an important insight into the whole conception of missional. Roxburgh and Boren propose that missional must be conceived of primarily as a dynamic relationship that God has with God's world; they also suggest how the church comes to experience this relationship and participate in its implications for God's mission in the world.

A similar approach was pursued by Craig Van Gelder in the 2007 publication, *The Ministry of the Missional Church*, in which he sought to redress some of the underdeveloped attention to the ministry of the Spirit that was part of the initial missional conversation. Van Gelder utilizes an awareness of the dynamic ministry of the Spirit as a key hermeneutic for understanding the mission of God and the church's participation in that mission.

32. Roxburgh and Boren, *Introducing the Missional Church*, 31–33. Italics in the original.
33. Ibid., 37–39.

This volume makes the connection between the church's nature and its purpose in relation to changing contexts more explicit by focusing on the ministry of the church as being Spirit-led. . . .

The premise is that it is crucial to understand the Spirit's role in the creation of the church if we are to correctly understand its missionary nature. So also, it is crucial to understand the leading of the Spirit in shaping the church's ministry if we are to correctly understand its purpose.[34]

This book represents a more thoroughgoing integration of the work of the Spirit in relation to the works of the Father and the Son within the missional conversation. It uses a trinitarian approach that avoids some of the problems of the functional modalism that plagued the initial argument as formulated in *Missional Church*.

Taken together, these three efforts to extend the missional conversation indicate that there is much work still to be done in formulating a fully developed biblical and theological understanding of missional.

### Subbranch 2: Addressing Key Issues

This subbranch attempts to extend the missional conversation by utilizing a well-developed understanding of missional to engage critical issues that the church must address. A good example of this approach is found in the work being done by the Presbyterian Church (USA). The 2006 General Assembly of this denomination directed a task force to prepare a revised polity (known as a "Form of Government"). The 2008 General Assembly received the report and then directed a task force to engage all the churches and presbyteries in a study process and to revise the report based on this work.

Polity is a matter of great importance to this historic denomination with its deep roots in Reformation traditions, traditions that are not easily renegotiated. It is important to note that the framework employed to explicitly guide this reexamination and reformulation of polity is a missional understanding of the church—a missional ecclesiology. Making an explicit connection between a missional ecclesiology and a missional polity represents new territory in the missional conversation. The 2009 online report, "What Is Missional Ecclesiology?" by Paul Hooker, offers an update of the work that is being done. It begins by providing an explanation of what it means to be missional.

First, the *foundation for all mission*—all "sending"—*is the act of the Triune God to enter the world in Christ, to suffer and die and be raised again.* At heart, mission is about the *missio Dei*. . . .

34. Craig Van Gelder, *The Ministry of the Missional Church: A Community Led by the Spirit* (Grand Rapids: Baker Academic, 2007), 17, 19.

Second, *it is not the Church who sends; it is God who sends the Church*. . . . Just as Christ was sent into the world, so also is the Church sent into the world. . . .

Third, *the calling of the church is to be a community of witness to the future God is creating*. The church is gathered by God's Spirit and called through its corporate witness to proclaim that, in Christ, God is shaping a new life for the world.[35]

This explanation is followed by a more explicit statement about what a missional polity might look like in light of such a missional ecclesiology.

Polity is the architecture of mission. Polity describes the structure and governance by which a church lives out its calling to be a community of witness. . . .

- *A missional polity starts by understanding that the mission of the Church is grounded in God's self-sending into the world*. . . .
- *A missional polity clarifies that the calling of the Church is to witness to and to participate in the work of Jesus Christ in the world*. . . .
- *A missional polity locates the congregation—not the individual believer— as the basic form of the Church*. Just as the being of the Triune God is relational in nature . . . so also is the basic nature of the Christian life relational. . . .
- *A missional polity defines the ministry of the councils of the Church as shaped around the calling of the Church*. . . .
- *A missional polity provides flexibility for mission*. . . .
- *A missional polity encourages accountability on the part of its covenantal partners to one another.*[36]

It is worth noting that an understanding of the social Trinity is part of the theological framework for understanding missional polity, but unfortunately it appears basically as a subtext. The primary trinitarian understanding that is utilized draws from the Western emphasis on the God who sends (the sending Trinity). This work, however, represents a significant contribution toward beginning to image how a missional understanding intersects with the critical issue of church polity.

In addition to the document discussed above, the Missional Church series, published by Eerdmans as the result of an annual missional church consultation conducted at Luther Seminary, seeks to draw connections between a missional understanding and important issues of church life. To date, three series volumes have appeared, with additional volumes forthcoming. The

35. Paul Hooker, "What Is Missional Ecclesiology?" http://61122.netministry.com/images /06WhatIsMissionalEcclesiology.doc. Italics as in original.

36. Ibid., 7–8. Italics as in orignal.

themes of the consultations and the series volumes that have appeared, or are scheduled to appear, are:

> *The Missional Church in Context: Helping Congregations Develop Contextual Ministry* (2007)
>
> *The Missional Church and Denominations: Helping Congregations Develop a Missional Identity* (2008)
>
> *The Missional Church and Leadership Formation: Helping Congregations Develop Leadership Capacity* (2009)
>
> *Cultivating Sent Communities: Missional Spiritual Formation* (forthcoming, 2011)
>
> *Created and Led by the Spirit: Planting Missional Congregations* (forthcoming, 2012)
>
> *The Missional Church and Global Civil Society: Helping Congregations Engage as Public Church* (forthcoming, 2013)

The essays published in the volumes of this series have made an explicit effort to develop a more substantive understanding of the biblical and theological concepts that shape a missional approach. In particular, they have worked to integrate an understanding of the social Trinity with that of the sending Trinity. They have also sought to cultivate a more robust understanding of the relationship between the Triune God's continuing presence and work within all creation and the Triune God's redemptive work through Christ within the reign of God. As evident from the titles of the consultations and their subsequent published volumes, this series also seeks to apply a missional perspective to the realities that congregations face within their particular contexts.

### Subbranch 3: Developing a Missional Hermeneutic

A third subbranch working to extend a missional understanding involves the development of an explicit missional hermeneutic that can help to shape a missional theology. The importance of developing such a hermeneutic was stressed in the original argument in *Missional Church*, but this task was not pursued in that volume. The GOCN, following the completion of the study projects that led to the publication of *Missional Church* and *Treasure in Clay Jars*, turned its attention in the mid-2000s to this issue. Utilizing the annual gatherings of the American Academy of Religion and the Society of Biblical Literature as a vehicle, the GOCN has hosted a conversation around this theme every year since 2005 by inviting key presenters to offer their perspectives.

George Hunsberger took the opportunity to reflect on the presentations made at the sessions held between 2005 and 2008 by drafting and posting a summary article in early 2009, "Proposals for a Missional Hermeneutic."[37] He identified four key proposals that had emerged for the development of a missional hermeneutic.

1. *The missional direction of the story* [missio Dei]. The *framework* for biblical interpretation is the story that tells of the mission of God and the formation of a community sent to participate in it.

   Chris Wright is perhaps the prime exemplar of this model. . . . His presentation . . . offered a detailed rationale for interpreting the Bible in light of the mission of God as the heart and core of the biblical narrative. . . .

2. *The missional purpose of the writings* [equipping witness]. The *aim* of biblical interpretation is to fulfill the equipping purpose of the biblical writings.

   [This stream] pertains to the character of the biblical literature itself. . . . [It] has to do with the purpose and aim of the biblical writings, and the canonical authority by virtue of their formative effect. Darrell Guder is the one who has most forcefully made this case.

3. *The missional locatedness of the readers* [located questions]. The *approach* required for a faithful reading of the Bible is from the missional location of the Christian community.

   . . . Michael Barram shifts the perspective by looking . . . from the position of the community being thus formed. . . . A missional hermeneutic [is] "an approach to the biblical text rooted in the basic conviction that God has a mission in the world and that we read Scripture as a community called into and caught up by those divine purposes."

4. *The missional engagement with cultures* [gospel matrix]. The gospel functions as the interpretive *matrix* within which the received biblical tradition is brought into critical conversation with a particular human context.

   By proposing "elements of a missional hermeneutic," [James] Brownson . . . focuses on what is taking place in the missional moment, . . . in which biblical writers are addressing the people of their own time and place in terms of the received tradition.[38]

37. George R. Hunsberger, "Proposals for a Missional Hermeneutic: Mapping the Conversation," The Gospel and Our Culture Network, January 28, 2009, http://www.gocn.org/resources/articles/proposals-missional-hermeneutic-mapping-conversation.

38. Ibid., 3–10.

Following the posting of this paper on the GOCN website, a further dimension was offered by James Brownson, one of the key contributors to the conversation during the past decade.

> I want to push a little further on this, particularly in conversation with the more explicitly post-modern hermeneutical literature that begins with the notion of *difference*.
>
> . . . It's not only the great powers of the world that construct . . . metanarratives which seek to suppress difference. *We* construct metanarratives together with people who are like us, and in so doing, we reassure ourselves that difference is not absolute. . . . Our images of God—even a "missional" God—may be just such a metanarrative. . . .
>
> . . . If a missional hermeneutic is going to avoid becoming either a totalizing narrative that suppresses difference, or a pastiche that simply satisfies for the moment, a missional hermeneutic must take the reality of *difference* with utmost seriousness.[39]

### A Critique and an Invitation

These approaches to extending the missional church conversation offer intriguing possibilities for deepening and expanding the biblical and theological frameworks of this concept. Unfortunately, there does not appear to be as yet much collaboration or coordination between these efforts, which would enable contributors to inform and learn from one another. Given the creative work that these authors are pursuing and the importance of the missional conversation to the life of the church today, we might all be served if this were to take place. It would also be helpful to have contributors within this branch interact more directly with those working in the first three branches. We will return to this matter of engaging in mutual conversation in the epilogue.

### Conclusion

The missional church conversation today is clearly a significant force in shaping the theological imagination of the church in our context. But this conversation has also become incredibly diverse. Further work on developing the biblical and theological concepts that undergird a missional imagination would help to deepen this influence and to create a more substantive framework for integrating diverse approaches. It is to this task that we turn in part 2.

39. James A. Brownson, "A Response at SBL to Hunsberger's 'Proposals . . .' Essay," The Gospel and Our Culture Network, January 28, 2009, http://www.gocn.org/resources/articles/response-sbl-hunsbergers-proposals-essay.

# Part 2

.......................................................................................................................

# Perspectives That Extend
# the Missional Conversation

In the first three chapters, we laid a foundation for understanding the present missional conversation—when, how, and why this concept emerged and became popularized. In the following three chapters, we build on this foundation, suggesting key biblical and theological resources for extending the conversation.

Chapter 4 returns to the discussion of the Trinity and extends the missional conversation by developing a more integrated view of the social Trinity and the sending Trinity. This theological framework provides the basis for offering a more robust understanding of God's relationship to the world through creation, Christ, and the Spirit. The theme of participation is introduced as the key for resolving the question of how the works of God in continuing creation and redemption are related.

Chapter 5 takes up the complex matter of how to understand culture, dealing with both the historical development of the concept and its current fluidity within our present globalized, networked world. God's hospitality and the church's working within diverse cultures are explored in terms of reciprocity and mutuality in relationships. A missional theology of culture is proposed for framing the church's public engagement with diverse contexts even as it seeks to participate more fully in God's ongoing mission.

Chapter 6 revisits the impact of missional theology on congregational practices, leadership, and organization. The theological commitments offered in chapters 4 and 5 serve as the basis for deepening the missional conversation about how to reframe church life in a new apostolic era.

# 4

## Expanding and Enriching
## the Theological Frameworks

The missional church conversation, as evidenced in chapter 3, has clearly branched off in multiple directions. One of the most promising developments has been the way in which the conversation has expanded to engage and incorporate a much wider variety of voices and traditions. This indicates how deeply the missional conversation resonates with the wider Christian church. We want to affirm and encourage this expansiveness.

This chapter offers biblical and theological resources for clarifying and deepening the conversation and also for resolving some of the ambiguities, tensions, and underdeveloped threads in the missional church literature. These resources are by no means exhaustive. Rather, we offer them as an invitation to use a missional imagination in engaging the riches of the Christian theological tradition, discovering "treasures new and old" (in the words of Matt. 13:52).

Theology matters more deeply than we often recognize. As we noted in the introduction, theological commitments are embodied in and shaped by practices in community. They reflect particular historical and contextual realities. The theological frameworks for the missional church warrant careful attention. These frameworks and assumptions, as noted in chapter 3, have not always been adequately addressed in the missional literature. In this chapter, we revisit some key theological themes from the perspective of missional theology. We believe these resources have the capacity to enrich the missional conversation in substantive ways. A more robust missional theology offers the promise of rendering more faithful and more fruitful our imagination of who God is, what God is doing in the church and the world, and how we can better participate in these works of God.

## The Trinity

In chapter 1 we examined how the missional church conversation began with trinitarian roots, as expressed in the development of the *missio Dei* concept in mid-twentieth-century ecumenical missiology. This perspective shifted the focus and basis for mission from the church to the wider sending movement of God in the economy of salvation. David Bosch summarizes this view in his description of the 1952 Willingen conference: "The classical doctrine on the *missio Dei* as God the Father sending the Son, and God the Father and the Son sending the Spirit was expanded to include yet another 'movement': Father, Son, and Holy Spirit sending the church into the world."[1] Lesslie Newbigin draws from this same perspective in formulating his trinitarian missiology.[2]

One of the key questions for the missional conversation is *how* such a sending movement is to be conceived. Chapter 3 makes clear that there is significant ambiguity in the recent missional literature regarding the question of agency. We need to consider carefully to what extent the Triune God is directly involved in the church's sending, as well as how this is imagined to take place. Some voices are deeply trinitarian in their imagination, while others stress the role of human agency and initiative in performing tasks commanded by God. This results in the life and movement of Father, Son, and Spirit in the world receding into the background. If the Trinity is at the heart of the missional view of God and the church, it is fitting that we begin by unpacking the contemporary trinitarian renaissance and some of its implications for the missional conversation.

### Toward a Fuller Trinitarian Vision

Chapter 4 of *Missional Church* acknowledges the new wave of trinitarian theology emerging in the late twentieth century from Western theologians such as Colin Gunton, Jürgen Moltmann, and Catherine Mowry LaCugna. The

---

1. Bosch, *Transforming Mission*, 390.
2. See especially Lesslie Newbigin, *The Open Secret: An Introduction to the Theology of Mission* (Grand Rapids: Eerdmans, 1978).

author of that chapter, however, notes that "what is not yet fully developed in these fresh approaches to trinitarian doctrines is the missional implications for ecclesiology."[3] Rich trinitarian ecclesiologies began to appear in the last decades of the twentieth century from such authors as John Zizioulas and Miroslav Volf, yet these works did not deal explicitly with mission. For instance, Volf's *After Our Likeness*, perhaps the most prominent contemporary Protestant trinitarian ecclesiology, does not take up the question of mission directly.[4] Unfortunately, ecclesiology and missiology have largely been treated separately within the rich resurgence of trinitarian thought. This separation is likely a legacy of the earlier "church and mission/missions" dichotomized view. It is critical that these be connected, as the missional church conversation has sought to do, so that the wealth of new insights into the Trinity can bear fruit for a more fully developed missional ecclesiology.

The doctrine of the Trinity, as various contemporary authors have demonstrated, has had a complicated history in Western theology.[5] The standard reading of the history of the doctrine points to a tendency within the West, from Tertullian on, to emphasize the single divine substance of God and to treat the personhood within the Trinity secondarily. God is imagined primarily as a single divine essence, and the distinctions of Father, Son, and Spirit follow from this. In contrast, the Eastern tradition is seen as beginning with the relationality of the three divine persons, whose unity is found in the source or origin of the Father, as well as in their *perichoresis*, or mutual indwelling. The Western tradition's stress on the divine "supreme substance," or God as a single "absolute subject,"[6] presents a problem. It has rightly been blamed for a gradual diminishment of the functioning of trinitarian doctrine in the life of the church from the Reformation through the modern period. The Trinity has come to be regarded more as a mathematical puzzle than as a way of describing how the Bible narrates God's involvement in the world.[7]

This historical synopsis oversimplifies a long and complex history.[8] But it is readily apparent that the receding of the Trinity from the Western theological

3. Guder, *Missional Church*, 82.

4. Miroslav Volf, *After Our Likeness: The Church as the Image of the Trinity* (Grand Rapids: Eerdmans, 1998), 7. Volf explicitly states that mission is beyond the scope of the book.

5. See Moltmann, *Trinity and the Kingdom*; Stanley J. Grenz, *Rediscovering the Triune God: The Trinity in Contemporary Theology* (Minneapolis: Fortress, 2004); Catherine Mowry LaCugna, *God for Us: The Trinity and Christian Life* (San Francisco: HarperSanFrancisco, 1991).

6. See Moltmann, *Trinity and the Kingdom*, 10–16.

7. For a fuller exposition of this narrative, see Grenz, *Rediscovering the Triune God*.

8. For a treatment that challenges the standard narrative, see Mark Husbands, "The Trinity Is Not Our Social Program," in *Trinitarian Theology for the Church*, ed. Daniel J. Treier and David Lauber (Downers Grove, IL: IVP Academic, 2009), 120–41.

imagination in the modern era had serious consequences, some of which remain with us. Theologians, for example, have linked this underfunctioning of the doctrine to: (1) patriarchal and dominating patterns of social and ecclesial life and leadership; (2) the problematic legacies of colonial missions; and (3) the rise of modern atheism.[9] This is because losing the Trinity means losing the primary Christian way of envisioning God's active presence and engagement with the world, not only in the past but also in the present and the future.

The relationships between the Father, the Son, and the Spirit came to refer in the Western tradition largely to God's inner life (the so-called immanent Trinity). Thus the church ended up with a functionally monistic way of imagining God's engagement with the world. Father, Son, and Spirit are viewed as acting individually toward the world, as evidenced in *Missional Church*. This view fostered individualistic understandings of the human person, monarchical forms of leadership, and a kind of methodological atheism in which God is not seen to be actively at work in the life of the church and the world.

Irenaeus referred to the Son and the Spirit as God's hands at work in the world.[10] When we lose the Trinity, we lose our way of conceiving of God's missionary presence in creation. Without the Son and the Spirit, God becomes a distant, aloof, detached creator (as in deism); a controlling, dictatorial monarch without compassion for his creatures; or an abstract, impersonal force. Modernity tended to render the Trinity superfluous, and, along the way, removed a sense of God's dynamic immediacy and personal presence from the cosmos. Theologians across Christian traditions have recently given the Trinity increased attention, but the extent to which the doctrine functions in shaping the theological imagination of local churches today remains an open question. The missional conversation represents a vital exception to this, although the overview of literature in chapter 3 suggests that a functionally monistic imagination of God still lingers today in some places in the missional conversation. In particular, it is striking how little the Eastern tradition's more social, relational conception of the Trinity appears in the missional literature.

The recovery of the Trinity as discussed in chapter 1 was initiated by Barth and Karl Rahner in the twentieth century and extended by such theologians as Wolfhart Pannenberg, Jürgen Moltmann, Catherine LaCugna, Elizabeth

9. For a sampling, see Moltmann, *Trinity and the Kingdom*; Elizabeth A. Johnson, *She Who Is: The Mystery of God in Feminist Theological Discourse* (New York: Crossroad, 1992); Gary M. Simpson, "No Trinity, No Mission: The Apostolic Difference of Revisioning the Trinity," *Word & World* 15, no. 3 (1998): 264–71.

10. *Against Heresies* 4.20.1, in Robert M. Grant, ed., *Irenaeus of Lyons*, Early Church Fathers (New York: Routledge, 1997), 150.

Johnson, Leonardo Boff, Robert Jenson, and Colin Gunton. These theologians have sought to reverse the modern West's eclipse of the Trinity by stressing the doctrine's profound relevance for human life and church practices in the world. The Trinity, unfortunately, became something of an add-on in Western theology (unlike in the Eastern tradition), but it is now being reasserted increasingly as the framework within which other doctrines are to be explored and explained.

One major facet of this trinitarian renewal is the fresh attention being given to the relationality of God. This represents a crucial complement to the sending emphasis so characteristic of the West.[11] Theologians such as John Zizioulas have argued that the Cappadocian fathers (Gregory of Nyssa, Gregory of Nazianzus, and Basil of Caesarea) made a revolutionary move against the backdrop of Greek philosophy by asserting that relational personhood is constitutive of being—an inherent aspect of its essence. In this view, God's very being is not an abstract divine substance characterized by certain attributes, but rather it is profoundly personal. There is no personal identity without relationality.[12]

The Orthodox tradition, in particular, has stressed the generative, outward-reaching love (*ekstasis*) and communion (*koinonia*) of the three persons. The Trinity is seen as a community whose orientation is outward, and whose shared love spills over beyond itself. Moreover, the concept of *perichoresis*, or the mutual indwelling/interpenetration of the three persons in a dynamic, circulating movement, has offered rich analogies for human interdependence and relational community.[13] In this trinitarian perspective, to be a person is to participate in others' lives, to have an identity shaped by other persons, rather than to be an isolated individual. The use of this understanding of Trinity is clearly evident in the *Mission-Shaped Church* document of the Fresh Expressions movement in the Church of England.[14] Interestingly, the themes of communion (*koinonia*) and *perichoresis* are present in the thought of some Western theologians, including Barth, but these elements have not been emphasized within the missional conversation.[15]

---

11. See John D. Zizioulas, *Communion and Otherness: Further Studies in Personhood and the Church* (New York: T&T Clark, 2007); Stanley J. Grenz, *The Social God and the Relational Self: A Trinitarian Theology of the Imago Dei* (Louisville: Westminster John Knox, 2001).

12. John D. Zizioulas, *Being as Communion: Studies in Personhood and the Church* (Crestwood, NY: St. Vladimir's Seminary Press, 1985), 41.

13. See Jürgen Moltmann, "Perichoresis: An Old Magic Word for a New Trinitarian Theology," in *Trinity, Community and Power: Mapping Trajectories in Wesleyan Theology*, ed. M. Douglas Meeks (Nashville: Kingswood Books, 2000), 111–25; Colin E. Gunton, *The Promise of Trinitarian Theology*, 2nd ed. (Edinburgh: T&T Clark, 1997).

14. Archbishops' Council 2004, *Mission-Shaped Church*.

15. See Karl Barth, *Church Dogmatics*, trans. Thomas F. Torrance and Geoffrey W. Bromiley (New York: Scribner, 1936), IV/3.

### Limitations of the "Sending" View of the Trinity

The use of the Western trinitarian emphasis on God's *sending* (from Barth and Newbigin) in the initial missional church conversation brought a helpful reconception of the church as a sent community that witnesses to God's reign in Christ through the power of the Spirit. Recovering this dynamic movement for engagement with a post-Christian culture continues to be pivotal for churches still enmeshed in the norms of a functional Christendom. Yet this emphasis has significant limitations and liabilities if it is not integrated with insights about the church as a social community in the image of the Triune God.

As noted in chapter 3, a certain tendency toward functional modalism can appear in this conception, which isolates the works of the three persons of the Trinity from one another. This leads, in turn, to more individualistic conceptions of the Father, Son, and Spirit, downplaying their relationality. It is easy to move from this to a kind of Christomonism focused solely on an individual's relationship with Jesus that fails to attend both to the other persons of the Trinity and to the wider fabric of human community. In the Discovering and the Utilizing branches of the missional conversation, this tendency appears in some instances under the guise of an incarnational approach to mission. Jesus's identity as the Son of the Father and the one who is anointed and led by the Spirit can fade from view. This can foster a view of mission as the isolated actions of individual Christians or individual churches on behalf of God, rather than the participation of the church in the Triune God's life and movement within all creation. We will explore incarnational mission from a more thoroughly trinitarian perspective below.

Moreover, the sending movement from Father to Son to Spirit to church to world can result in making the church primarily an instrument and rendering the world a mere "target" of mission. Thus we often find language in the church about "target audiences" for the gospel, or the social justice equivalent in which people can be seen primarily as objects of benevolence or service. *Missional Church*, following Newbigin, carefully asserts a fuller view, noting that the church is a "sign," "foretaste," "agent," and "instrument" of the reign of God.[16] But one of the tendencies in contemporary popular ecclesiology has been to stress the instrumental and to eclipse the representational dimension. In an instrumental view, the church primarily exists to *do* something; the character of its *being* is neglected. What remains is a purposive ecclesiology in which the wider framework of God's trinitarian agency recedes. Its eschatological dimension, or the way in which the church embodies the future toward which God is drawing all humanity, is unfortunately underemphasized. The church exists merely

16. Guder, *Missional Church*, 97–102.

to accomplish something on behalf of God.[17] It is then not *God* who is doing something through the church but the *church* that bears the primary responsibility.

This kind of thinking, as noted in chapter 3, surfaces in the missional conversation in particular in the Discovering branch, which tends to view the Great Commission as the primary rationale for mission. Mission is something we as the church do because God told us to. It also appears in the stress on mission as imitation of Christ, which emerges in both the Discovering and the Utilizing branches. It is easy, in this pattern, for the integrity and vocation of the church as a reconciled community filled with the Spirit—as the body of Christ—to be diminished.

Missional ecclesiology is also a *representational* ecclesiology. Barth describes the church as "the provisional representation of the whole world of humanity justified in [Christ]."[18] Newbigin uses the term "hermeneutic of the gospel" to describe how the church as a concrete community provides the interpretive key to God's wider purposes for humanity.[19] Reducing the church to a merely instrumental or purposive entity eclipses its vocation as a community of promise for the wider world.

The Eastern emphasis on relationality enriches the representational view of the Trinity and stands in contrast to the instrumental understanding of the Trinity. Here we find that the church is created in the image of the Trinity and serves as a (provisional, limited, and fallen, yet Spirit-filled) representation of the new humanity in Christ—a view that points toward a key insight, namely, as noted by those who have embraced and developed the social doctrine of the Trinity, that *to be* is *to belong* in community. We are defined by our relationships. Ecclesiology—and mission—involves partaking in a shared, interdependent, common life as the body of Christ in which difference is not cause for division.[20]

The church is not a collection of individuals who choose to associate primarily to have their spiritual needs met or do some good in the world. Rather, the church is a community of mutual participation in God's own life and the life of the world—a participation characterized by openness to others. Just as the Trinity's interdependent, communal life is generative and outward reaching in love, so too must the church's life be focused toward others and the world. This is clear in Jesus's prayer in John 17:21b–23: "As you, Father, are in me and I am in you, may they also be in us, so that the world may believe

17. The most popular example of this kind of instrumental ecclesiology is Rick Warren, *The Purpose-Driven Church* (Grand Rapids: Zondervan, 1995). See Van Gelder, *Ministry of the Missional Church*, 73–84.

18. Barth, *Church Dogmatics*, IV/1, 643.

19. Newbigin, *Gospel in a Pluralist Society*, 222–33.

20. See Zizioulas, *Communion and Otherness*, 1–12.

that you have sent me. The glory that you have given me I have given them, so that they may be one, as we are one, I in them and you in me, that they may become completely one, so that the world may know that you have sent me and have loved them even as you have loved me."

One of the key points made in the trinitarian renewal since Rahner is that speculating on God's trinitarian life apart from the economy of salvation is misguided: the Trinity we know in salvation history is also the so-called immanent Trinity (discussed as Rahner's Rule in chapter 1).[21] While we want to insist upon an eschatological reserve of mystery in the divine life, God in Godself is also God for us.[22] Relational trinitarian theology gives us a vision of God as a dynamic community of mutuality, openness, difference, and love that makes space for others to participate. These qualities define the image of God in which we are created.

One of the major paradigm shifts that has come from the new focus on a relational Trinity is the shift from an image of God (*imago Dei*) conception based on isolated individuals, to a relational, communal view—the image of the Trinity (*imago Trinitatis*).[23] That is, we are coming to understand that God's character is defined more by the quality of relational life within the trinitarian community than by certain abstract attributes (such as the classical concepts taken from Greek philosophy of omniscience, omnipotence, immutability, impassibility, etc.). This approach fundamentally changes how we view what it means to be human. Humans are not pale imitations of God's eternal rationality and power but rather find their identity in participating communally in the divine community's life and love as well as in one another's lives. Such a view provides a much richer basis for engaging relationally in mission than the focus on imitating Jesus that recurs in the Discovering and the Utilizing branches of the missional conversation.

There is, moreover, reciprocity within the life of God. Robert Jenson traces the lingering influence of pagan philosophy on the doctrine of the Trinity, which runs against the grain of the scriptural narrative of God's actions in salvation history. He notes that in the classical formulations of Father begetting Son and breathing the Spirit, the relations of origin all go in one direction. The Father is active, the Son and the Spirit passive. The Father is unaffected by the Son and the Spirit. He writes, "Therein unbaptized Hellenism's celebration of beginning over ending, of persistence over openness, of security over

---

21. "The 'economic' Trinity is the 'immanent' Trinity and the 'immanent' Trinity is the 'economic' Trinity" (Rahner, *Trinity*, 22).
22. See LaCugna, *God for Us*.
23. See Grenz, *Social God and Relational Self*; Volf, *After Our Likeness*; Zizioulas, *Being as Communion*.

freedom, maintains itself even within the doctrine of the trinity."[24] In other words, conceiving of the relationality of the Trinity in terms of unidirectional sending, which has been the tendency within the Western *sending* theology, leads ultimately to a closed view of God.

Jenson's insight here has serious consequences for a missional ecclesiology. If God is viewed as unaffected by the world, aloof and simply sending from afar, then a church that patterns itself on this understanding will also tend to isolate itself from the world. What is lost is the profound openness and reciprocity not only of God's inner-trinitarian life but also of God's interactive relationship with the world. One wonders whether this kind of thinking implicitly informs sectarian understandings of the church, where the church seeks to hold itself apart from the world, rather than maintaining a distinctive identity while participating deeply in the life of the world. Mission in such a paradigm, in applying this understanding of God, is also understood unidirectionally. The church goes out in mission and at the same time seeks to avoid being changed by the world along the way. This pattern surfaces fairly regularly in the Discovering and the Utilizing branches of the missional conversation, where there is often little imagination for how the church can learn from the world.

The biblical narrative, however, suggests a much more deeply reciprocal understanding of the Trinity and God's relationship with the world. This is classically defined in terms of *perichoresis*, and it is played out most poignantly in the passion of God. The incarnation, crucifixion, and resurrection must be viewed from within a trinitarian perspective. Jürgen Moltmann develops this theme at length, asserting that the passion of Jesus affects the Father and the Spirit as well: "The Son suffers dying, the Father suffers the death of the Son. The grief of the Father here is just as important as the death of the Son."[25] God's own inner life is affected by the world, which means that the actions of humanity affect the inner life of God. The mission implications become clearer if the church sees its own life not as an *imitation* of the Trinity but as a *participation* in the life and mission of the Trinity.

### From Imitation to Participation

Chapter 2 noted that the mid-twentieth-century missiological conversation about *missio Dei* was ambiguous concerning the relationships between God,

24. Robert W. Jenson, *Unbaptized God: The Basic Flaw in Ecumenical Theology* (Minneapolis: Fortress, 1992), 139. See also Gary M. Simpson, "A Reformation Is a Terrible Thing to Waste," in *The Missional Church in Context*, ed. Craig Van Gelder (Grand Rapids: Eerdmans, 2007), 80–82.

25. Jürgen Moltmann, *The Crucified God: The Cross of Christ as the Foundation and Criticism of Christian Theology* (Minneapolis: Fortress, 1993), 243. See also his *Trinity and the Kingdom*, 75–83.

world, and church. *Missio Dei* was mapped out such that several different possibilities of interpretation emerged, each with significant consequences for mission and the church. We expressed the two specialized views of *missio Dei* and the reign of God as follows: the church embodies the reign of God and the church witnesses to the reign of God. Alongside these views, two generalized secular views were also identified: God's mission as secular history and God's mission in the midst of secular history. It is important to note that all these approaches are based to some extent on the Western, linear conception of the Trinity. This is problematic for the church in a postcolonial age, when there is a renewed call for reciprocity, mutual openness, and a more dynamic understanding of God's relationship with the world in which the church's essential vocation is retained.[26] We believe the answer to the conundrum of how to relate the continuing works of God in the world and church is found in the integrated view, discussed above in chapter 2: the church participates in God's continuing creation and redemptive mission.

Participation, grounded in a new appreciation for the relationality of God's Triune life, offers a much more helpful framework for conceiving of the relationship between God, world, and church. The theme of participation has received attention in several recent trinitarian works.[27] Drawing on the biblical concepts of *koinonia*, communion, sharing, and fellowship, an understanding of participation describes the *perichoretic* (mutual indwelling) relationality of God's own trinitarian life, as well as God's creative, incarnational, and Spirit-infused relationship with creation.[28] Paul describes this as being "in Christ."[29]

A focus on mere *imitation* of God's life and mission, in contrast, tends to be problematic on several fronts.[30] First, the stress falls on human agency.

26. See Scott Hagley et al., "Toward a Missional Theology of Participation: Ecumenical Reflections on Contributions to Trinity, Mission, and Church," *Missiology* 37, no. 1 (January 2009): 75–87.

27. See David S. Cunningham, *These Three Are One: The Practice of Trinitarian Theology* (Malden, MA: Blackwell, 1998); Paul S. Fiddes, *Participating in God: A Pastoral Doctrine of the Trinity* (Louisville: Westminster John Knox, 2000).

28. It is vital to note that the concept of participation is not being used here in a Platonic sense. For a discussion of the Platonic background to the term and a contrast with imitative approaches, see Fiddes, *Participating in God*, 11–56.

29. See, e.g., Rom. 8:1; 1 Cor. 1:30; 2 Cor. 5:17.

30. Examples of this include Leonardo Boff, who construes the social Trinity primarily as an ideal model for human political and social life. Boff fails to address how such a model can be realized in the midst of human sin. See Leonardo Boff, *Trinity and Society* (Maryknoll, NY: Orbis Books, 1988). For a critique of the social Trinity as a model, see Husbands, "Trinity Is Not Our Social Program." Imitative approaches also include the christological focus of Michael Frost and Alan Hirsch, in which mission is seen primarily as an imitation of the life of Jesus. See Michael Frost and Alan Hirsch, *The Shaping of Things to Come: Innovation and Mission for the 21st-Century Church* (Peabody, MA/Grand Rapids: Hendrickson/Baker Books, 2003).

It is up to us to realize the perfect trinitarian model community or to enact the life of Jesus through our own performance. This fails to attend deeply enough to human sin—both personal and corporate/systemic. Second, God's own trinitarian involvement in the world (which is the basis for the paradigm shift toward a missional ecclesiology) is rendered largely irrelevant. Mission is something humans do, rather than primarily an attribute of God in which humans (and the church) participate.

Several subbranches of the missional conversation in the Discovering and the Utilizing branches have embraced imitation as the primary way of understanding the missional church, as indicated in chapter 3. Often this derives from a renewed focus on Christology or an attempt to recover a primitive experience of the early church. What is often lacking in these approaches is a fully trinitarian understanding of Christ. Christ lies at the heart of the missional church, but Christology cannot be understood apart from Christ's relationship with the Father/Creator or his being anointed, empowered, and led by the Spirit. The missional church must keep all three persons of the Trinity within a balanced and integrated view, for apart from one another, they cannot be understood. Likewise, the church's identity must be shaped not only by Christ but also by attentiveness to the Father and the Spirit.

A participatory understanding opens up a highly reciprocal view of the God-world-church relationship, in which the church shares in the Triune God's own vulnerable engagement with the world. One significant dimension of this is openness to the future that God is bringing forth. Imitation tends to stress what God *has done*. Participation invites us into what God *is doing* and *will continue to do* as God's promises in Christ are brought to fulfillment.[31] We now turn to developing several facets of this participatory view of God and mission.

## Creation, Incarnation, and Passion within the Trinity's Life

### Creation

A more fully developed doctrine of creation can enrich our understanding of missional as well as our framing of a missional ecclesiology. A strain of this thinking can be found in chapters 6 and 7 of *Missional Church* (as we noted in chapter 2), but it was not adequately developed or integrated into the fuller argument. It is striking in much of the subsequent missional church literature how little theological attention is paid to creation. Often there seems to be a

31. Hagley et al., "Toward a Missional Theology of Participation," 85.

deep ambivalence about the God-world relationship. Creation is viewed either as lacking God's presence or as the mere object of missionary work. In either case, it is understood largely as being without God-given worth and agency. Most striking is the lack of imagination of the Spirit's ongoing movement within creation, especially outside the church. A more robustly trinitarian framework invites us into a deeper, more theological view of the world and God's continuing work of creation within it.

Moltmann helpfully traces the intellectual roots of this ambivalence about God's relationship to creation, linking it to a diminishment of the Trinity. "As long as God was thought of as the absolute subject, the world had to be viewed as the object of his creation, preservation, and redemption. . . . Through the monotheism of the absolute subject, God was increasingly stripped of his connection with the world, and the world was increasingly secularized."[32] The missional conversation would be well served by a more nuanced, fully trinitarian doctrine of creation that stresses God's presence through the Spirit. Moltmann writes, "If the Creator is himself present in his creation by virtue of the Spirit, then his relationship to creation must rather be viewed as an intricate web of unilateral, reciprocal, and many-sided relationships."[33] That is, God is relationally involved with creation in a complex and dynamic fashion.

It is less helpful to understand God's relationship to creation, as has traditionally been done, in terms of an analogy of being (*analogia entis*) in which creation exists as an imperfect or weak imitation of God's own attributes and powers. An analogy of relation (*analogia relationis*) approach is much more fruitful, one in which creation has its own integrity and distinctiveness yet is relationally linked with God.[34] God makes space within God's own trinitarian life for creation, and creation participates relationally in that life. Unlike the view of creation as simply a onetime event, a multifaceted view better expresses the multiple ways in which Scripture speaks of creation: creation in the beginning, continual creation, and the consummation of creation in the kingdom of glory—the new creation.[35] In all this, God's creativity is deeply involved in the world's past, present, and future.

It is worth drawing out some implications for the missional conversation. First, the world is a field of God's ongoing activity and presence through the

---

32. Jürgen Moltmann, *God in Creation: A New Theology of Creation and the Spirit of God* (Minneapolis: Fortress, 1993), 1.

33. Ibid., 14.

34. Ibid., 77. Moltmann follows Barth and Bonhoeffer in this respect. See also Grenz, *Social God and Relational Self*, 294–98.

35. Moltmann, *God in Creation*, 206.

Spirit. The movement of the Spirit in creation raises the central missional question that goes back to the *missio Dei* concept in the twentieth century: discerning what God is doing in the world. This cannot be merely an in-house process when creation is understood to be infused with God's presence and activity. A much wider horizon of God's movement in and through so-called secular space, people, and cultures is needed.[36] The church does not have exclusive possession of God's presence and activity. All persons, made in God's image, are born to serve as cocreative creatures with God in the world.

Second, creativity is connected deeply to God. As Moltmann suggests, "The Spirit is the principle of creativity on all levels of matter and life."[37] We will return to the theme of creativity in mission later. Third, there are implications for humanity. Created in the image of the Trinity, humans correspond to the Triune God through their relationality with one another.[38] This relationality points forward to our calling and destiny in Christ. When we participate in Christ, we enter the relational body of believers that is the community of the new creation.[39] Human salvation involves sharing in the community of Christ, which finds its vocation (another way of talking about mission) through taking part in Christ's ministry in the world. Finally, we must always remember that salvation is *in*, *of*, and *for* the world, not *out of* the world. The new creation that is our eschatological promise includes everything God has made. Amid the environmental crises of today, that is a critical promise to keep in mind in considering the church's missional vocation.

Since the created world participates relationally in God's trinitarian life, it is inappropriate to view it as a mere target for mission. God is active and alive within creation. The church must enter into deep reciprocal engagement with the world, while retaining a posture of critical discernment. As 1 John 4:1 states, "Beloved, do not believe every spirit, but test the spirits to see whether they are from God." A tendency in much of the Western missiological literature is to utilize an instrumental view of mission and the church. Here the focus falls on strategies and methods for making converts, growing congregations, or delivering religious goods, services, or aid.

This approach is usually a reflection either of a Western *sending* trinitarian logic that fails to adequately account for God's active involvement in creation or of the absence of a trinitarian imagination altogether. The missional church

---

36. See Hagley et al., "Toward a Missional Theology of Participation," 85–86. On the theme of reciprocity, see Lamin O. Sanneh, *Translating the Message: The Missionary Impact on Culture* (Maryknoll, NY: Orbis Books, 1989).

37. Moltmann, *God in Creation*, 100.

38. Ibid., 216.

39. Ibid., 226.

movement arose precisely to raise deeper questions about the ecclesiological and missiological identity of the church in relation to the world. Viewing God and creation through a participatory lens provides the grounds on which such a reversion to strategies and methods can be resisted.[40]

### Incarnation

Incarnation has become a major theme in current missional church literature, especially among many of those identified in the Discovering and the Utilizing branches in chapter 3. It functions within these sources primarily as a way to talk about the church's contextualization within changing cultures. Much of the literature espousing this view tends to stress the church's ethical embodiment of kingdom practices. In some ways, this is a fruitful impulse, yet it is worth unpacking the incarnation from a slightly different angle. Nowhere is the theme of reciprocity in relationships more evident than in the incarnation. Incarnation is God's ultimate missional participation in human life. The Word was made flesh in Jesus, and the church as the body of Christ must continue to be enfleshed in every human culture and moment in mission. Yet the church's incarnate ministry is not merely an imitation of what Jesus did; it is a participation in a much larger movement in which God is the primary actor.

One of Christianity's richest ways of understanding this truth is highlighted in the doctrine of the communication of attributes (*communicatio idiomatum*, also known as the "happy exchange"). This doctrine is particularly developed within Lutheran theology.[41] In 2 Corinthians 5:21, Paul writes, "For our sake he made him to be sin who knew no sin, so that in him we might become the righteousness of God." The incarnation is a profound, concrete act of God's participatory presence. God enters into and takes upon himself our sinfulness and shares with us his righteousness.

This *entering into* is in fact an *emptying into* by God in order to raise up humanity, as the kenosis hymn in Philippians 2 expresses so powerfully.[42] Christ pours his power and privilege into us, forsaking his greater status to become dependent upon humanity, so that we might be free. Dietrich Bonhoeffer interpreted this doctrine of the communication of attributes in terms of an act of *bearing* humanity: "God is a God who bears."[43] God's lordship is not

---

40. See Hagley et al., "Toward a Missional Theology of Participation," 86.

41. See Martin Luther, "On the Councils and the Church" (1539), in *Luther's Works*, vol. 41, edited by Eric W. Gritsch (Philadelphia: Fortress, 1966), 93–106.

42. See David Frederickson, "Congregations, Democracy, and the Action of God in Philippians 1–2," in *Testing the Spirits*, ed. Patrick R. Keifert (Grand Rapids: Eerdmans, 2009), 48–66.

43. Dietrich Bonhoeffer, *The Cost of Discipleship* (New York: Touchstone, 1995), 92. See Simpson, "Reformation Is a Terrible Thing to Waste," 70–74.

an aloof freedom unaffected by humanity but rather a cruciform lordship that reconciles by sacrificially entering into the life of the other. God gives up the freedom of not being under restraint or condition in order to be free *for* us in Christ and, in so doing, to make us truly free. For Martin Luther and Bonhoeffer, God makes Godself available to us in the concrete particularity of the cross, and in Word and sacrament, under conditions of vulnerability and physicality. God becomes present to us in the humility of the crucified one and in the humble elements of bread and wine.

This realization suggests an incarnational approach to missional church in which relational identification with the neighbor leads us into concrete acts of solidarity and accompaniment. If God loves us in Christ, so that God identifies with us relationally in a posture of humility, then we are to share this same love with our neighbors. The corollary of God's bearing humanity in Christ is the church's bearing the burdens of its neighbors as it participates deeply in the life and struggle of the community into which it is sent and within which it lives. A relational conception of the Trinity and mission, grounded in the paradigm of participation and the doctrine of the incarnation, understands such an engagement as profoundly reciprocal.[44] The church is free in Christ not *from* the world but *for* the world.[45]

### Passion

The missional church is a *passionate* church—a church that feels, listens, and acts deeply in sympathy with its neighbors in the world. Mission is rooted in the Spirit's moving the church to compassionate love for its neighbors—a love that "suffers with" (*cum-passio*). Moses discovered in Exodus 3 that God hears the cry of the oppressed and, therefore, calls people to be agents of God's redeeming power to help deliver them from that oppression. Moses's broken heart for the Israelites is also God's broken heart for them. Moses's eventual mission is a participation in God's passionate response of liberation (unlike Moses's initial, retributive response, the killing of the Egyptian taskmaster).

The missional church cannot participate in God's passion for the world without drawing close to its neighbors. This means surrendering a posture of control, distance, and mere benevolence in order to enter closely into relational community. The legacies of Christendom and colonialism, along with modernity's stress on human agency, programs, and activities, have fostered

44. It is important to note here that in Christology, *communicatio idiomatum* has traditionally functioned as an equivalent of *perichoresis*. See Moltmann, "Perichoresis," 113–14.

45. See Simpson, "Reformation Is a Terrible Thing to Waste." For a rich discussion of freedom *for* rather than *from*, see Moltmann, *Trinity and the Kingdom*.

approaches to mission that tend to keep the church apart from and unaffected by those in need. It is easier to do something *on behalf* of our neighbors than to enter fully into their reality. A great deal of what has been understood as mission activity within the modern church is, as a result, indirect. It lacks the opportunity to develop significant relational ties with the neighbor. By contrast, the missional church discovers God's compassionate love for all humanity by participating in the life of the neighbor, not expecting the neighbor to participate in the church's life on the church's terms.

The risk in this kind of "embrace" of the neighbor (especially the neighbor who is a diverse other, or even an "enemy") is the way of the cross.[46] The cross stands at the heart of the reign of God and God's missionary life with the world as the most profound moment of missionary compassion, identification, and vulnerability. The victory of the cross has been won. Yet, as Paul repeatedly stresses, participation "in Christ" is also a sharing in the way of the cross. "I have been crucified with Christ; and it is no longer I who live, but it is Christ who lives in me. And the life I now live in the flesh I live by faith in the Son of God, who loved me and gave himself for me" (Gal. 2:19–20). Attention to the cross points us toward the larger framework of what God was doing in Christ and offers the church a wider imagination for how it might share in God's mission.

### Reconciliation

A postcolonial missional ecclesiology must be grounded in the cruciform mission of the Triune God. Some churches in the West still (often unintentionally) cling to patterns of imperial authority, social privilege, and assumed centrality. Yet the era of Christendom is over, even as forms of economic and cultural imperialism persist amid globalization. Churches that have inherited the legacy of Christendom and colonialism must adopt a different posture in today's polycentric world. Difference is newly omnipresent in many communities. Conflicts erupt daily in our world along national, ethnic, economic, religious, and cultural lines. The need for reconciliation in our world—and within the church itself—is profound.

At the heart of God's missional response to this reality is the cross. The cross calls us to decenter our identities so that in Christ we might be reconciled with the neighbor.[47] In the space opened up by the cross, God acts to overcome the enmity, hostility, division, and violence of human sin. We find our calling

---

46. See Miroslav Volf, *Exclusion and Embrace: A Theological Exploration of Identity, Otherness, and Reconciliation* (Nashville: Abingdon, 1996).
47. Ibid., 69–71.

as ambassadors in this reconciliation in which we are freed to view ourselves and our neighbors as participants in a new humanity in Christ:

> So if anyone is in Christ, there is a new creation: everything old has passed away; see, everything has become new! All this is from God, who reconciled us to himself through Christ, and has given us the ministry of reconciliation; that is, in Christ God was reconciling the world to himself, not counting their trespasses against them, and entrusting the message of reconciliation to us. So we are ambassadors for Christ, since God is making his appeal through us; we entreat you on behalf of Christ, be reconciled to God. (2 Cor. 5:17–20)

A cruciform approach to mission that is a participation in God's passionate movement of reconciliation goes a long way toward addressing the crisis of authority in mission after colonialism.

## The Spirit within the Trinity

We participate in the Triune God's creative and reconciling mission through the power of the Spirit. Pneumatology, the doctrine of the Holy Spirit, represents a significant dimension of the missional conversation that also invites further development. This is particularly the case against the backdrop of the explosion in world Christianity, global Pentecostalism, and the increasing openness to spirituality among those in secularized Western cultures. Western theology since the Reformation has tended to focus on Christology, particularly given the functional eclipse of the Trinity. The Spirit is now beginning to receive long-overdue attention within the context of the trinitarian renewal.

One of the most promising approaches to pneumatology for the missional conversation is Michael Welker's work on a biblical theology of the Spirit.[48] Welker stresses the public, political, and communal character of the Spirit's work within the biblical narrative: "The Spirit of God was originally experienced as a power that overcomes the internal disintegration of the people and its political powerlessness in the face of external threats."[49] When God's people are lost in moments of disorganization and crisis, as was often the case in Judges, the Spirit unifics and empowers them: "The Spirit causes the people of Israel to come out of a situation of insecurity, fear, paralysis, and mere complaint."[50] Within human communities, the Spirit creates a "force field" of unity, in which creaturely differences are retained but unjust divisions are

---

48. Michael Welker, *God the Spirit* (Minneapolis: Fortress, 1994).
49. Ibid., 108.
50. Ibid., 56.

removed.[51] Perhaps most pointedly for mission, it is through the pouring out of the Spirit that God brings about an explosive, multilingual, multicultural, public testimony to Godself.[52]

Craig Van Gelder similarly develops a biblical approach to the Spirit in light of a missional ecclesiology in *The Essence of the Church* and *The Ministry of the Missional Church*. He argues that being aware of the role of the Spirit is the key to understanding the active participation of the church in God's world. Van Gelder notes how the biblical emphasis concerning the Spirit of God focuses on the Spirit's work in raising up leadership, restoring community, and establishing practices so that all life can flourish. This same ministry of the Spirit occurs across the whole of the biblical record: Old Testament and Israel, the Gospels and Jesus, and the New Testament letters and the churches. Churches today exercise their responsibility for this same approach by engaging in communal discernment of the Spirit's leading in their ministry context even as they seek to bring God's redemptive reign to bear within that context in light of biblical teaching.

We are witnessing remarkable signs today of the Spirit's movement within the church around the world. Perhaps the most striking is the phenomenal growth of Pentecostal and charismatic churches and movements that highlight the Spirit's agency and gifts. The expectant attention these churches bring to the Spirit's work is something from which other Christian traditions might learn. This is especially the case in relation to the dramatic rise of world Christianity in the global South within cultures that were never fully secularized or Westernized. Here there is a ready openness to embodied experiences of the Spirit. Christianity is now predominantly a non-Western religion, and the Spirit is alive and well within the global church.[53] The trend toward secularization in the modern West is also in many places giving way, especially among postmodern generations, to a new receptivity to spirituality. Globally, there is a dramatic resurgence of religious engagement.[54]

These developments point toward the vibrant role of the Spirit in the missional church in cultivating a Spirit-shaped imagination. Focusing primarily on Christology in the missional conversation has tended to lead the church toward a *backward*-oriented vision, one that emphasizes imitating what Christ has done in the past. We can lose our sense of what God is doing in the present

51. Ibid., 228.
52. Ibid., 235.
53. See Lamin O. Sanneh, *Whose Religion Is Christianity? The Gospel beyond the West* (Grand Rapids: Eerdmans, 2003).
54. See Peter L. Berger, *The Desecularization of the World: Resurgent Religion and World Politics* (Grand Rapids: Eerdmans, 1999).

and will do in the future. The Spirit is the primary way in which God acts in the world in the present. Living within God's trinitarian life means continual discernment of the Spirit's movement. The missional church is a community led by the Spirit.[55] It is a community that constantly looks for signs of the Spirit's leading in its own life and in the surrounding neighborhood. Its communal imagination must be pregnant with anticipation of the Spirit.

This is a struggle, however, for churches hampered by the legacy of modernity. As we described in the introduction, ideas and beliefs (theological or otherwise) are mediated through practicing communities. Charles Taylor has identified what he calls the "social imaginary" of a culture. He describes a social imaginary as "the ways in which [people] imagine their social existence, how they fit together with others, how things go on between them and their fellows, the expectations which are normally met, and the deeper normative notions which underlie these expectations."[56] The social imaginary of the modern West, he argues, has largely been one in which God's presence is removed from ordinary life. The sense of God's agency and immanence within the world receded during this period and was exchanged for what Taylor calls "excarnation."[57]

Through a complex historical development, people in the modern West have come to see God primarily as the author of moral laws to which humanity should adhere. This approach allows humanity to function more or less without God's involvement or grace. Instead of there being sacramental moments, people, objects, or events that are charged with divine presence (as in premodern Europe), time and space have become secularized—regular, measurable, and predictable. Time is measured by mechanical clocks. There is no longer a sense of waiting expectantly on God to speak or act. Human agency becomes the central focus in a vacated universe.

Taylor's rich narration of this process bears fuller attention than can be given here, but the implications for mission are striking. The church in the West has come to operate largely within a secular social imaginary, in which mission is a predictable, manageable, executable human effort following divine laws, commandments, and principles. This is a social imaginary largely devoid of imagination for the Triune God's disruptive, graceful, provocative power and agency. We have traced in the discussion above how some strains of the missional conversation revert to a primary stress on human agency. This is an indication of the lingering impact of the modern social imaginary on

55. Van Gelder, *Ministry of the Missional Church.*
56. Taylor, *Secular Age*, 171.
57. Ibid., 288.

the church. What is required in Westernized contexts today is a retrieval of a biblical imagination for the Spirit's presence and power in our midst. This recovery must be in relation to the world around us and not simply within the interiorized hearts and minds of individuals.

One of the ways in which the Spirit works in creation, as noted above, is by animating or inspiring creativity.[58] Creativity in mission is a hallmark of vibrant contextualization of the gospel and of the church's vitality in witness. Many traditional churches, struggling with the aftermath of secularization and functional Christendom, seem to lack the passion and energy for creativity in their common life or in their engagement with neighbors. Many innovative churches functioning in a more instrumental mode can be highly creative in seeking to be "culturally relevant," yet the presence and agency of God in that creativity are often underimagined. Recontextualizing the church for new generations becomes one more task left up to us by God.

A robust missional pneumatology opens up key theological foundations for participating creatively and imaginatively in the Spirit's work of innovation and renewal. We are not on our own in constructing forms of church life and mission that will speak to people. Rather, we are called into a process of communal discernment and creative experimentation grounded in the Word of God as our imaginations for God's world are shaped by the Spirit in our own communities and in conversation with our neighbors.[59] The Bible clearly presents God as constantly moving to disrupt settled patterns when they are unjust, oppressive, or complacent. God's Spirit raises up anointed leaders as catalysts of shared vision and momentum. The Spirit pushes or pulls disciples of Jesus into unfamiliar territory to encounter God across cultural barriers and social lines.[60] This places the spiritual discipline of discernment at the heart of missional church practice, a theme that we will explore in more detail below.

## Rethinking Humanity in Light of the Trinity and Postmodernity

Enriching our doctrine of the Trinity with a fuller appreciation for the relationality of the divine life, as noted above, has implications for theological anthropology—our understanding of humanity. Consistent with the stress on

58. Moltmann, *God in Creation*, 100.
59. For a discussion of the leadership implications of the social Trinity and socially embodied imagination and discernment, see Jannie Swart, "Christian Leadership as Communion Imagination in the Public Networking of Organizational Companionship," *Journal of Religious Leadership* 7, no. 2 (Fall 2008): 87–115.
60. The story of Peter and Cornelius is a prime example. See Van Gelder, *Ministry of the Missional Church*, 155–59.

the single divine substance within Western trinitarian thought, the doctrine of humanity (the *imago Dei*) in much of Western theological history has been construed in substantialist terms. Here certain attributes or capabilities are lodged within the person.[61] The tendency is to see the self primarily as an individual thinking subject whose approach to mission is guided by imitation or performance. In this case, it is up to us to enact Jesus's love or lifestyle on our own. This view tends to underappreciate the wider web of relationality and power in which we participate through the Spirit.

The retrieval of the social Trinity invites us to a renewed understanding of humanity. Here, an understanding of "person" concerns relationality or communal embeddedness more so than it concerns conceiving of individuals as being isolated or apart from community.[62] For Stanley Grenz, as for others such as Gunton and Zizioulas who develop this theme, "the image of God does not lie in the individual per se but in the relationality of persons in community."[63] The image of God is not a static set of individual attributes or a fixed nature, but rather an eschatological reality that shapes the church's identity and mission. "In short, the indwelling Spirit leads and empowers the church to fulfill its divinely mandated calling to be a sacrament of trinitarian communion, a temporal, visible sign of the eternal, dynamic life of the triune God."[64] The church represents through its way of being community together a limited and provisional but powerful glimpse of what it means to be human in God's image. In this manner, the church as a communion of persons sharing an interdependent, reciprocal life of mutuality, reconciled in Christ and united by the Spirit, shows forth something of God's own nature to the world.

### Relationality and Mission

This understanding of personhood in communion also has implications for how the church conceives of its missional practice. Ecclesial being—participating with a new identity in the body of Christ—is something that happens fundamentally *between*, between us and the Triune God, between us and others in the fellowship of faith, and between us and our neighbors in the world. This relationality and betweenness are the spaces within which mission occurs. Mission is not the transmission of a particular set of properties, ideas, goods, or concepts to people, but rather the entering into relational webs

61. Grenz, *Social God and Relational Self*, 17.
62. Ibid.
63. Ibid., 305. See also Gunton, *Promise of Trinitarian Theology*; and Zizioulas, *Being as Communion*.
64. Grenz, *Social God and Relational Self*, 336.

that transform us even as we engage in shaping others. The agency involved is God's, ours, and our neighbor's.

A grassroots practice known as "dwelling in the world," developed by churches in South Africa, speaks to this reality. In this exercise, church members are invited to think back to a time in the previous week when an opportunity arose for them to share the peace of Christ with someone (this draws on Luke 10:1–12, where the seventy are sent to share the peace). People are encouraged to revisit those relationships imaginatively and consider what God might be doing in them and what God might want to do. What are the conversations, gestures, and actions that might be taken up going forward? By taking seriously the ordinary daily relationships within which Christians live and work as spaces for mission, the practice of dwelling in the world stresses both the relational character of mission and the betweenness of God's movement in the world.

### Identity in Late-Modern/Postmodern Culture

Identity has become a highly problematic and fluid thing within late-modern and postmodern cultures. As Zygmunt Bauman observes, "'Identity' is revealed to us only as something to be invented rather than discovered; as a target of an effort, 'an objective'; as something one still needs to build from scratch or to choose from alternative offers and then to struggle for."[65] While identities were once acquired by birth into stable communities, for late-modern or postmodern people today they are the product of endless work and anxiety.

Underneath this constant work of identity construction and maintenance lies profound ontological insecurity—the question of where the foundation of one's very existence lies. Anthony Giddens describes how this constant threat of meaninglessness is assuaged by the controlled nature of day-to-day activities within closed systems. "Mastery . . . substitutes for morality; to be able to control one's life circumstances, colonize the future with some degree of success and live within the parameters of internally referential systems can, in many circumstances, allow the social and natural framework of things to seem a secure grounding for life activities."[66]

Against this backdrop, it is vital for the missional church to offer an alternative view of humanity. It must be a view that recognizes the fluid and socially embedded character of personhood in pointing toward relationships of communion and love, through the Spirit, rather than the cultivation of lifestyles that offer false security by seeking to isolate us from others. To be

65. Zygmunt Bauman, *Identity* (Malden, MA: Polity Press, 2004), 16.
66. Anthony Giddens, *Modernity and Self-Identity* (Stanford, CA: Stanford University Press, 1991), 202.

a Christian is to be given an ecclesial identity that is dynamic and relational, defined intersubjectively, but freed through participation in Christ to share in the lives of others with open hearts and hands.

## Conclusion

This chapter has attempted to extend the missional conversation by bringing renewed attention to core theological commitments. We have identified places where new perspectives and theological insights can enrich the various branches of the discussion. We have highlighted but a few of the theological concepts that invite further exploration as the missional church conversation unfolds in the twenty-first century. Each locus identified above calls for deeper engagement, both through incorporating voices from various strands of the Christian tradition and through teasing out the implications for ecclesial life and leadership. As the missional conversation continues to expand, there remains an open-ended opportunity for additional contributions from other perspectives in the Christian world. This chapter has only begun to suggest some of the promising streams of new energy and insight as the conversation continues to unfold. We now shift in the following two chapters to unpacking two key dimensions of the missional conversation that warrant sustained attention: the areas of culture and congregational life and practice.

# 5

## Missional Engagement with Culture in a Globalized World

The first part of this book chronicled the ambiguity in the missional conversation regarding the relationship between God, the world, and the church. To resolve the conundrum growing out of this ambiguity, chapter 4 proposed using a framework of *participation* rooted in a renewed trinitarian theology. It is now time to unpack further the question of culture. In doing so, we continue the deep commitment in the missional church conversation to attend to context: the specific situations within which the church embodies an incarnate gospel in mission. The question of culture has been central to this conversation, from Lesslie Newbigin's attempts to define a missionary engagement with Western culture to the early chapters of *Missional Church* and beyond. This chapter describes the growing complexity of culture and context within the twenty-first-century world and its implications for the missional church. Along the way, we also chart some of the provocative avenues that missional theology opens for understanding the church's relationship to God's world.

### Twenty-First-Century Cultural Complexity

The concept of culture is a highly contested one with a long and complicated history.[1] It is employed with multiple meanings in the missional conversation

1. For a summary of this history, see William A. Dyrness, *The Earth Is God's: A Theology of American Culture* (Maryknoll, NY: Orbis Books, 1997), 62–66; Kathryn Tanner, *Theories of Culture: A New Agenda for Theology* (Minneapolis: Fortress, 1997).

today, where some authors are more attentive to this history than others. As Harvie Conn noted some years ago, evangelicals have tended to lack a developed theology of culture.[2] They often display concern about the relativistic assumptions of the modern anthropological notion of culture; therefore, some evangelical discourse has tended to assume that culture is something "out there" apart from the church. Culture is seen as a target for theology or mission.[3] This is evident even in some recent missional literature, where being missional is understood as our responsibility to participate in the culture of the surrounding society—as if it were possible for the church *not* to participate in culture.[4]

The English term "culture" has Latin roots that describe the organic process of growth, as in the care and tending of crops or animals. In the modern Enlightenment, culture came to be understood in *developmental* terms. A "cultured" person was one who was well educated, whose intellectual and aesthetic faculties had been developed and refined. Culture in this sense came to be associated with social elitism. Western culture was seen as the most advanced, especially at its highest social levels, and other peoples needed to become "civilized" by being educated in Western traditions and patterns of thought and life.

Only in the last century was this elitist, developmental understanding of culture displaced by a significant alternative. The modern anthropological notion of culture emerged in the 1920s primarily in American circles. It tends to view culture as a cohesive, internally coherent, stable, geographically defined way of life shared by a people group.[5] Rather than viewing Western "high culture" as true culture and all other ways of life as "uncivilized," modern anthropologists began to insist on the uniqueness and equality of cultures.

The great twentieth-century anthropologist Clifford Geertz built upon this tradition by understanding culture symbolically as "webs of significance" created by people to make meaning. These webs of significance are also socially determinative in shaping behavior.[6] That is, culture expresses meaning and values within a human community even while it shapes the participants in that community by determining how they act and see the world. In this view, various people groups inhabit different symbolic worlds.

One important theological approach that draws from Geertz's symbolic view of culture, as well as Ludwig Wittgenstein's philosophy of language,

2. Harvie Conn, *Eternal Word and Changing Worlds* (Grand Rapids: Zondervan, 1984).

3. For an evangelical mapping of the question of Christianity and culture, see Charles H. Kraft, *Christianity in Culture*, 2nd ed. (Maryknoll, NY: Orbis Books, 2005).

4. See, e.g., Ed Stetzer, *Planting Missional Churches: Planting a Church That's Biblically Sound and Reaching People in Culture* (Nashville: Broadman & Holman, 2006).

5. Tanner, *Theories of Culture*, 25–37.

6. Clifford Geertz, *The Interpretation of Cultures: Selected Essays* (New York: Basic Books, 1973), 5.

is postliberal theology. This approach remains a key influence today within the missional church conversation. Postliberal ecclesiology, as articulated most prominently in George Lindbeck's 1984 book, *The Nature of Doctrine*, construes the church as a cultural community of its own.[7] Christianity for Lindbeck involves not so much adherence to certain abstract propositions, or a space where individuals express their spiritual experiences, as it involves constituting an alternative community with its own cultural "grammar" that shapes the imagination, behavior, and thought of its members. Newcomers are apprenticed into this symbolic thought world, with its own language of categories and patterns of life.

This line of thinking influenced Stanley Hauerwas (Lindbeck's student), whose thought is often referenced in the missional conversation, particularly by people utilizing an Anabaptist perspective. We explore Hauerwas's legacy more fully in the section "Beyond the Christian Colony" below. Many of the ways in which culture is understood to function in missiological and church discussion retain the assumptions of the modern anthropological view. "Culture" is defined in discrete, relatively stable, and consistent terms. Missionary engagement proceeds from this basis. A popular example would be the kind of cultural profiling found in Rick Warren's *Purpose-Driven Church* in the form of "Saddleback Sam," who is "targeted" for evangelistic outreach.[8]

The modern anthropological notion of culture, however, has come under increasing critique in recent years. The assumptions of internal consistency and consensus within cultures have been seriously questioned as postmodernism has brought greater attention to power dynamics, conflict, and fragmentation. Modern anthropological ideas of culture tend not to take into account the historical processes of cultural production, which can be quite fluid, indeterminate, and contested. In today's world, cultures can no longer be regarded as sharply bounded, self-contained units.[9] We have entered a vastly more complicated era of hybridity—the mixing and fusing of cultures—especially within the context of globalization.

### Cultural Diversity and Hybridity in a Networked World

We live in a world of macrocultures and microcultures characterized by multiple levels of interpenetration and reflexivity. People's identities, perspectives, and ways of life are defined simultaneously by numerous threads of

7. George A. Lindbeck, *The Nature of Doctrine: Religion and Theology in a Postliberal Age* (Philadelphia: Westminster, 1984).

8. Warren, *Purpose-Driven Church*, 169–72.

9. Tanner, *Theories of Culture*, 38–58.

cultural influences. Cultural innovations and developments that begin in one part of the world often spread rapidly to others, morphing along the way before returning to affect the culture in which they first emerged. This leads to a heightened sense of cultural difference. Robert Schreiter notes that boundaries today are increasingly not boundaries of territory but boundaries of difference: "The compression of time, the world of cyberspace, and the movement of peoples mean that people are now participating in different realities at the same time—there is multiple belonging."[10]

Within the U.S. context, as in many societies, cultural and religious pluralism increasingly defines the twenty-first-century landscape.[11] The neighbors in most U.S. communities (even many isolated rural communities) adhere to a plethora of faiths or no faith at all. They embody multiple cultural and religious perspectives and experiences. Missional engagement with people in a globalized world must take seriously the nuances of myriad subcultures and layers of difference, including between generations.

One implication of globalization has been a striking deterritorialization of culture. Locality today is rendered more complex because people live in both spatial and virtual neighborhoods.[12] Arjun Appadurai suggests that the best analogy for thinking of culture in today's world is chaos theory.[13] Order in the paradigm of chaos theory is often difficult to discern amid so much complexity and fluidity. Global migration and technology in late modernity have unmoored cultural identity from many of the historical patterns and localities that have shaped it over generations. Kathryn Tanner suggests that cultural identity has become "a hybrid, relational affair, something that lives between as much as within cultures."[14] We live in a messy, fluid, and ever-shifting cultural world, a world that is vastly more complex and conflicted than the one experienced by previous generations.

One new paradigm for this kind of fluid, relational production of cultural identity is the network. As Manuel Castells writes, "Networks constitute the new social morphology of our societies, and the diffusion of networking logic substantially modifies the operation and outcomes in processes of production, experience, power, and culture."[15] In this sense, the internet represents the

10. Robert J. Schreiter, *The New Catholicity: Theology between the Global and the Local* (Maryknoll, NY: Orbis Books, 1997), 26.

11. See Diana L. Eck, *A New Religious America* (New York: HarperCollins, 2001).

12. Arjun Appadurai, *Modernity at Large: Cultural Dimensions of Globalization* (Minneapolis: University of Minnesota Press, 1996), 178, 194–95.

13. Ibid., 46.

14. Tanner, *Theories of Culture*, 57–58.

15. Manuel Castells, *The Rise of the Network Society*, 2nd ed. (Malden, MA: Blackwell, 2000), 500.

dominant cultural metaphor of the twenty-first-century world—decentralized, highly participatory, fluid, self-organizing, geographically dispersed.

We are seeing a shift away from what Yochai Benkler calls the "industrial information economy" of the twentieth century, in which high production-value mass-media cultural products were distributed widely (globally in many cases) by a few producers. An example of such a twentieth-century media product would be Hollywood movies disseminated around the world. What is now emerging as an alternative means of production is a "network information economy" characterized by large-scale cooperative efforts—"peer production of information, knowledge, and culture."[16] The internet and other networked media offer the promise of a new kind of cultural commons, where participant-producers collaborate without any single agent having control over the outcome. This emerging culture is profoundly dynamic and unsettled. People are depending less on embedded, unmediated, stable, and primarily local social relations. Instead, we see the rise of networked individuals who switch networks through crossing social boundaries and weaving their own web of instrumental, relatively fluid relationships.[17]

What does all this mean for the missional church's engagement with culture? To begin, it is no longer possible to speak of "U.S. culture" or "British culture" or "Ethiopian culture" in a monolithic manner. The church's missionary relationship to culture must take seriously the complex, multiple, and overlapping cultural webs, networks, and streams in which people participate in any given locale. This calls for paying careful attention to traditional forms of cultural knowledge and identity and to the variety of contemporary media flows that shape people's attitudes, perspectives, and imaginations. These flows are now often self-selective, ad hoc, and coproduced by participants, as exemplified by blogs or social networking sites like Facebook. People can choose to receive their news from sources whose worldview and assumptions they already share. A new kind of self-reinforcing cultural tribalism is emerging.

## The Missional Church and Geography

A key turn in the missional church conversation has been its shift toward focusing mission on every congregation's immediate context rather than on some distant community. This remains a pivotal impulse. Yet the geographical focus of the missional church on particular places in which churches are located must be complemented by consideration of the nongeographical character

16. Yochai Benkler, *The Wealth of Networks: How Social Production Transforms Markets and Freedom* (New Haven: Yale University Press, 2006), 3–5.
17. Ibid., 362.

of community life today. The question, who is my neighbor? is now much more complex. It is not enough merely to focus on an immediate geographic neighborhood. If one does, one will likely discover that the neighbors' tightest relational networks may span hundreds or thousands of miles. Building relationships with neighbors and participating in their lives and living spaces must engage virtual, as well as physical, forms of community.

It is fascinating to observe the recent rise of various forms of neighborhood-based house churches and new monastic communities that seek to establish roots in specific geographical neighborhoods for the sake of incarnational ministry.[18] This development can be understood as a counterreaction to the cultural trends of globalization, mobility, and displacement identified above. In particular, members of younger generations who have grown up without the kind of stable, local relationships that their parents and grandparents enjoyed (or found suffocating and tried to escape) often find themselves hungering for an intimate experience of local community. Yet even for these Christians who intentionally cultivate missional relationships on the local level, being part of a community means also participating in a much wider web of connections maintained through Facebook, Twitter, email, and blogs.

The classic Christendom pattern of the geographical parish must be rethought for churches in the West that are inheritors of the state church traditions from Europe (Roman Catholic and mainline denominations in particular). On the one hand, the parish concept points toward a particular locale as a focus for missional participation—not just as an area from which merely to draw the members of one's denomination but as a focused mission field. On the other hand, the natural flows of community life are often no longer primarily neighborhood based. The Church of England has recognized this in its publication *Mission-Shaped Church*, calling for a mixed economy of "network" and "neighborhood" churches[19] (see the Extending branch discussion in chapter 3).

Yet there are provocative spiritual possibilities in the very complexity and disruptions of today's cultural environment. Robert Schreiter considers the very moments of change to be openings for spiritual discernment: "For it is in the experience of moving from one place to another, of cobbling together new identities out of the old ones, of negotiating multiple identities and logics that insight into where God is at work in a globalized culture will be found."[20] The church as a pilgrim people is called to indwell those spaces of intersection

18. See Jonathan Wilson-Hartgrove, *New Monasticism: What It Has to Say to Today's Church* (Grand Rapids: Brazos, 2008).
19. Archbishops' Council 2004, *Mission-Shaped Church*.
20. Schreiter, *New Catholicity*, 59.

and change, meeting people amid the flux of dislocation and identity seeking that is the norm for a globalized, postmodern world. This calling invites the church out of closed, settled forms of community life into flexible, adaptive, relational encounters.

### Reversals of Global Mission

One of the more provocative developments in recent years is the missionary impact on Europe and North America by immigrants from the growing churches of the global South. These pilgrims-in-mission embody the reflexivity of globalization. Just as the gospel was brought to the Southern Hemisphere during the period of colonial mission, ambassadors from those cultures are now following the flows of migration north (whether for economic opportunity, as refugees, or for other reasons). Many are bringing with them an intentional missionary posture toward the cultures of the West. Their congregations and social networks are the crucibles for a new kind of globalized missionary and cultural encounter.

These Christians from Africa, Asia, and Latin America recognize the secular character of the societies in which they are finding their new homes. They often seek very directly to reach native-born members of these societies with the gospel. Jehu Hanciles has documented this trend with African migrants in the United States in particular. He notes, "Far from being a one-directional, single, unified phenomenon, the processes of globalization are multidirectional, inherently paradoxical, and incorporate movement and countermovement."[21] What is so fascinating in this encounter is that the cultural forms of Christianity being brought to the United States, Canada, and Europe are largely non-Western forms. Hanciles further observes, "The new immigrant Christian communities are effectively 'de-Europeanizing' American Christianity."[22] The most problematic legacy of Christendom was Christianity's overaccommodation to Western culture (to the point of becoming what Hanciles calls a "territorial and tribal faith"). It can be a dramatic experience for Westerners to encounter the power of the gospel freed from that Western cultural baggage. Some European and U.S. churches are purposely calling missionaries from Africa and elsewhere to help revitalize their own communities and catalyze fresh encounters with gospel and culture. It is indeed a wondrously strange and paradoxical world for mission today—a stirring reminder that the *missio Dei* is far beyond the church's control.

21. Jehu Hanciles, *Beyond Christendom: Globalization, African Migration, and the Transformation of the West* (Maryknoll, NY: Orbis Books, 2008), 2.
22. Ibid., 7.

## God's Mission and Hospitality

Hospitality has been a theme of mission that has received increased attention in recent years. Christine Pohl has traced how the practice of hospitality lies deep within biblical tradition and church history.[23] Its neglect in the modern Western church begs to be remedied, for hospitality is often the space where we encounter the "other," the stranger who brings a blessing (Heb. 13:2).[24] Churches with an attractional posture toward mission have long sought to be hospitable to seekers and other visitors who might attend worship. Much of the missional church literature, especially in the Discovering and the Utilizing branches, has recently critiqued the attractional emphasis in favor of an incarnational approach to the world. Incarnation is a fruitful lens to utilize, especially when the depth of participation and reciprocity in the incarnation is kept in view. In the incarnation, God, the great host of the universe, comes to rely on the world's hospitality.

One of the seminal texts for the missional conversation, the sending of the seventy in Luke 10:1–12, takes hospitality in this provocative direction.[25] Jesus appoints seventy disciples to go ahead of him into what are most likely Samaritan villages, across religious and cultural barriers. Recognizing that "I am sending you out like lambs into the midst of wolves" (an acknowledgment of the hostilities that prevailed between Jews and Samaritans at that time), Jesus does a remarkable thing. He commands the seventy to rely on the hospitality of the Samaritan villagers for their well-being. "Carry no purse, no bag, no sandals, and greet no one on the road. Whatever house you enter, first say, 'Peace to this house!'" (vv. 4–5). The disciples were to enter deeply into the lives of the Samaritans on the terms of the Samaritans' culture. Hospitality in mission here is reversed—not offering hospitality *to* the stranger but seeking the hospitality *of* the stranger, with all the vulnerability that implies.

When you consider how intimate the living quarters of first-century Palestinian houses were, the story becomes all the more remarkable. The disciples are to eat what is set before them (even if the food is not kosher), staying in the same house so as to build relationships with those people. Their ministry in God's mission is one of bringing the peace between peoples that had long been estranged. They heal the sick and proclaim the inception of the kingdom

---

23. Christine D. Pohl, *Making Room: Recovering Hospitality as a Christian Tradition* (Grand Rapids: Eerdmans, 1999).

24. See Stephanie Spellers, *Radical Welcome: Embracing God, the Other and the Spirit of Transformation* (New York: Church Publishing, 2006).

25. This text has become particularly influential in the missional church through its use around the world in the Partnership for Missional Church process of the Church Innovations Institute. See Keifert, *We Are Here Now.*

of God—a reality demonstrated by their very presence and posture. It is only when a village refuses the offer of peace that the judgment is pronounced—and it is a harsh one. The stakes are high, for Jesus points out that such a rejection is a refusal to participate in the kingdom.

What might this story say to us about the missional church's posture toward culture and the world? Relying on the hospitality of the community to which you have been sent—especially in the radically vulnerable way that Jesus commands the disciples to do—changes the terms of the missionary encounter. The one to whom you are sent is offering gifts to you—the gifts of safety, food (with all the cultural distinctiveness embedded there), protection, and an opportunity to enter into her or his way of life. You are dependent upon that person, household, or community. Whatever you offer in the way of sharing the peace, healing, or proclaiming the good news of the kingdom is shared in a relationship of reciprocity, mutuality, and vulnerability.

This is a vivid example of the kind of transformative, participatory encounter that a robust trinitarian theology of the *missio Dei* evokes. God is active in the relationships between disciple and host. The encounter goes both ways between host and guest. God provides for the church's well-being through the stranger in the world, just as the stranger and the church are mutually transformed in the engagement.

### Reciprocity

The themes of reciprocity, mutuality, and vulnerability were explored in chapter 4 in relation to the Trinity and incarnation. These themes also shape the missional church's engagement with culture and the world. To view the world as a place of hospitality (as in Luke 10) is to recognize the gifts that lie within it to be shared—gifts that inform and enrich our own experience and understanding of the gospel. It invites us to cultivate open, receptive imaginations for how God is at work in people's lives and cultures.

The principle of reciprocity, or mutual transformation, in the missionary encounter has been unpacked most vividly by the missiologist Lamin Sanneh. His work offers important insights for the missional conversation in considering engagement with culture and the world. Sanneh argues that Christianity from its origins was always being translated out of its original culture into another culture. This move in the New Testament churches relativized the Jewish cultural roots of the faith, which also worked to destigmatize gentile cultures.[26] He writes that "cross-cultural experience helped to check the tendency toward

26. Sanneh, *Translating the Message*, 1.

the divinization of one cultural stream by promoting all cultures as essentially equal in the scale of divine providence."[27] In this process of translation, the authentic values of a particular culture are strengthened, while the cultural elements that are weak and conflict with the gospel are displaced.

As the gospel spread within African cultures through missionary encounters, it was in the places where the local vernacular culture was strongest that Christianity tended to take hold most vigorously.[28] A process of reciprocity took place in which the missionaries' own culture was challenged and called into question by new Christians as they learned to read the Scriptures in their own tongue. New insights into the faith were disclosed through this process of translation. The missionaries' understandings of Christianity were often modified by the perspectives and values of the cultures with which they had contact as the faith took root in this fresh soil.[29] Cross-cultural missionary encounters are mutually transformational, for the gospel is always embedded in particular cultural forms even as it is not captive to any one cultural form.

A promising insight from the process of cultural reciprocity in mission is the awareness that the missional church must cultivate an intentionally mutual and open, yet critical, engagement with culture. Just as the gospel is always culturally embedded, so too is the church. Today this usually means submersion in multiple cultures simultaneously, and here again the framework of participation is helpful. The gospel is not merely a possession to be passed from one person to another, a kernel that exists in whatever cultural husk is at hand, but rather a living event in, between, and beyond us that changes both parties involved in the encounter. God's incarnational participation in human culture is not just a model for how the church is to incarnate the gospel in our moment (a set of methods or rules to follow); rather, it points to God's ongoing participation in human life and culture. Missionary encounters on the front lines of today's complex cultural environment bear the promise of fresh perspectives, insights, and illumination into the gospel, precisely because God is participating there long before we arrive.

The key to this transformation process is the Word of God as it is illuminated by the Spirit of God. As Sanneh narrates in African mission history, it was the Scriptures that played the central role in empowering new Christians to challenge the cultural accommodation and presuppositions of the missionaries. Reading the Scriptures with people in relation to their particular context can be a freeing experience for those sent in mission as well as for

27. Ibid., 51.
28. Ibid., 182.
29. Ibid., 172–73.

those who are new to the faith. The Spirit works in and among us in these encounters. From this perspective, we should anticipate learning something about the gospel from the cultures of others. The Word and the Spirit provide the critical elements that challenge syncretism and accommodation, which are always dangers, in the cross-cultural encounter. Yet the Word and the Spirit also make possible the reciprocity that opens us for renewal.

## Enriching Creation and Culture in the Missional Conversation

The first generation of missional church authors focused the church's attention on Western culture, recognizing rightly that the West had become one of the world's great mission fields. They sought to draw lines of distinction between the values and commitments of the gospel, on the one hand, and those of late-modern Western culture, on the other. What was less developed in that literature—and much of the "missional" literature that followed—was an explication of how creation and culture could be understood theologically, or in relation to God. This reflects to some extent the conundrum of how to interpret the *missio Dei* that is discussed in part 1 of this book.

There is a deep ambivalence within evangelical thought in particular about creation and culture, as evidenced in much of the Discovering and the Utilizing branches of the missional conversation. William Dyrness traces this to the two predominant ways of approaching theology today: the propositional and the narrative.[30] The propositional approach, which dominated Western theology from the Enlightenment into the early twentieth century, understood theology as "sure knowledge inwardly grasped." Theology in this view consists of correct doctrinal formulations held in the mind of the believer. The biblical theology movement in the first half of the twentieth century brought deep challenges to the propositional approach with a new stress on the "narrative of God's actions in history." This second approach deeply informs the theological roots of the missional conversation, as evidenced in the thought of such figures as Barth and Newbigin. In the latter decades of the twentieth century, the focus on story was expanded and rendered more complex, through fresh attention to the hermeneutics of difference and the need to include many stories. This led to theology being done from specific cultural locations.

Yet neither the propositional nor the narrative approaches are able to engage sufficiently with the realities of creation and culture. Dyrness writes, "The language we have inherited to speak of God and the world has not been adequate to express this continuing relationship of God to the earth

30. Dyrness, *Earth Is God's*, 1–8.

and its peoples."[31] The propositional approach tends toward static, abstract teachings that do not express the dynamic presence of God in relationship to creation. The narrative approach stresses temporality (an awareness of the dimension of time lacking in the propositional view) yet fails to adequately describe the spatial and visible dimensions of God's life in and with the world. How is God at work in the cosmos? Where can we see God's work or presence? Dyrness's critique provides a helpful explanation for some of the ambivalence in the missional conversation about how to comprehend creation and culture in relation to God. The reign of God is a vital biblical theme, yet it tends not to address creation and culture directly, focusing more on redemption and consummation. This is particularly the case when the reign of God is identified with the church, as has been the tendency in some streams of the missional literature (see especially several subbranches in the Utilizing branch).

Although it is beyond the scope of this chapter to develop the fuller dimensions of a theology of creation and culture, we have highlighted some resources and avenues that might be explored to enrich the missional conversation in its understanding of the God-world relationship. It is important to remember that culture is part of creation. Culture in all its diversity, as such, is infused with the promise of God's creative presence and the Spirit, and at the same time liable to distortion through human sin. The missional church should not overly romanticize culture. It is nevertheless incumbent upon us for theological reasons to discern attentively the movement and wisdom of God within human cultures.

The Trinity is the key to engaging theologically with creation and culture. In deep trinitarian collaboration, God creates the world and all that is in it, calls a people (Israel) to show forth God's vision for human community, enters fully into human culture in the incarnation to redeem humanity, and actively moves to renew, inspire, rebuke, reconcile, and bring creation to its fulfillment. The world is by no means godforsaken, but rather charged with God's presence and movement and redeemed at the greatest cost: the cross.

### Traditional Theological Frames for Creation and Culture

Rich theological resources within the Christian tradition speak to an understanding of God's relationship to creation and culture. One of the most exciting developments in today's growing global church is the emergence of powerful theological insights about creation and culture from non-Western

31. Ibid., xiv.

perspectives.[32] Yet even within churches in Western contexts, it is striking how neglected their own traditions' deep conversations about creation and culture often are in today's missional conversation. Among those resources are the concepts of general revelation, the natural law tradition, divine sovereignty, the idea of common grace, and Luther's doctrine of the two kingdoms.

Several of these theological concepts can be traced far back in the history of Christian thought, evident in such places in Scripture as Romans 1, where creation is seen as a book of wisdom that can be read by all. The *logos* concept in Greek thought, which is taken up and transformed in the New Testament, speaks to God's creative agency in all things: the Word "was in the beginning with God. All things came into being through him, and without him not one thing came into being" (John 1:2–3). The Wisdom literature in the Bible also testifies to God's instructive movement within human culture and society.

In the theology of the magisterial reformers such as Luther and Calvin, creation itself is understood in evocative terms as a location of divine self-disclosure and grace. Calvin sees the universe as a book, a theater, or a mirror; God appears "in the garment of creation."[33] Calvin writes, "Wherever you cast your eyes, there is no spot in the universe wherein you cannot discern at least some sparks of his glory. You cannot in one glance survey the most vast and beautiful system of the universe, in its wide expanse, without being completely overwhelmed by the boundless force of its brightness."[34] Calvin understands human competence in art and science as a gift of the Spirit: "It is no wonder, then, that the knowledge of all that is most excellent in human life is said to be communicated to us through the Spirit of God."[35] Moreover, God's providential sovereignty over creation involves active governance, a deep level of participation. For Christ to be Lord of all means that all areas of human life fall under his rule.

Calvin was quick to assert that humanity's capacities were profoundly marred by sin, but he also offered the concept of common grace. This concept involves God inspiring and bestowing, even in the midst of sin, the good impulses in humanity, whether in culture, morality, or religion. Richard Mouw traces this principle through Calvinist thought as a way to engage questions of church and culture today. Mouw writes, "We cannot give up on the im-

32. See Sanneh, *Whose Religion Is Christianity?* and Philip Jenkins, *The New Faces of Christianity: Believing the Bible in the Global South* (New York: Oxford University Press, 2006).

33. See Paul S. Chung, *The Spirit of God Transforming Life: The Reformation and the Theology of the Holy Spirit* (New York: Palgrave Macmillan, 2009), 26.

34. John Calvin, *Institutes of the Christian Religion*, ed. John Thomas McNeill, trans. Ford Lewis Battles (Philadelphia: Westminster, 1960), 1.5.1, 52.

35. Ibid., 1.2.16, 275.

portant task—which the theologians of common grace have correctly urged upon us—of actively working to discern God's complex designs in the midst of our deeply wounded world."[36]

Luther's theology of the two kingdoms of law and gospel provides an expansive framework for attending to God's activity in the world and the church.[37] God's left-hand kingdom, the realm of the law, includes the providential ordering of creation and human life in society, which creates and preserves life. God's right-hand kingdom of grace complements this with the saving action of God in Christ, without which we are condemned under the law as those who cannot fulfill God's creation design in our fallen state. The two kingdoms work hand in hand. This allows for an expansive way to envision God's creative and saving movements working together.

In Roman Catholic theology, Vatican II brought a new openness to understanding God's relationship with human cultures. *Ad Gentes*, the decree on the church's missionary nature, asserts that

> whatever truth and grace are to be found among the nations, as a sort of secret presence of God, He frees from all taint of evil and restores to Christ its maker, who overthrows the devil's domain and wards off the manifold malice of vice. And so, whatever good is found to be sown in the hearts and minds of men, or in the rites and cultures peculiar to various peoples, not only is not lost, but is healed, uplifted, and perfected for the glory of God, the shame of the demon, and the bliss of men. Thus, missionary activity tends toward eschatological fullness.[38]

This idea of fulfillment, based in the classic Thomistic framework of grace perfecting nature, affirms the goodness of human cultures while also recognizing the need for purification and transformation through the gospel. Roman Catholic missiologist Louis Luzbetak develops a model of inculturation in which the primary agents involved in incarnating the gospel are the local Christian community and the Holy Spirit. In his approach, proclaiming the kingdom of God is central, and the ultimate goal is mutual enrichment, or reciprocity, that benefits the local community and the universal church.[39]

These streams are but a sampling of ways in which Christians, particularly in the West, have wrestled theologically with the relationship between God

36. Richard J. Mouw, *He Shines in All That's Fair: Culture and Common Grace* (Grand Rapids: Eerdmans, 2001), 50.

37. See Ulrich Duchrow, *Two Kingdoms: The Use and Misuse of a Lutheran Theological Concept* (Geneva: Lutheran World Federation Department of Studies, 1977).

38. Flannery, *Documents of Vatican II*, 823.

39. Louis J. Luzbetak, *The Church and Cultures: New Perspectives in Missiological Anthropology* (Maryknoll, NY: Orbis Books, 1988), 70.

and human cultures. The dramatic rise of world Christianity has reminded us how contextual all theology is, including the classic theological formulations of the West. The missional conversation can be served not only by recovering these voices from within the Western traditions but also by learning from new voices and insights from Christians in other cultures. Given the Christendom framework within which much Western theology was developed, emerging African, Asian, and Latin American theologies may speak even more fruitfully to the missional church because they are being developed within an explicitly missionary context.

### Toward a Missional Theology of Creation and Culture

The logic of missional theology, particularly as developed in chapter 4, invites us to revisit the question of creation and culture within a missional trinitarian framework. Missional theology begs for a robust understanding of creation and culture existing within the life of the Trinity and as integral to God's missionary ends of bringing the whole cosmos to fulfillment. Culture as an integral aspect of creation cannot be seen in a manner disengaged from a missional perspective.

Recognizing this connection is essential because the world participates in God's missional life, and God participates in the world's ongoing life. As we have noted in several places, one of the great conundrums of twentieth-century missiology has been the way in which the relationship between God, world, and church is conceived. We have proposed participation as the key to resolving this dilemma. Yet participation must be focused explicitly on the incarnation if it is to be a helpful category. Christ is the ultimate key to discerning the participation of God in the world and of the world in God as the one in whom that participation is fully realized. Incarnation is the meeting point of God and humanity, the two natures of Christ coexisting, in the classic Chalcedonian formulation, "without confusion, without division, and without separation."[40] In Christ we see the new humanity, fully immersed in creation and human culture, while at the same time undistorted by sin and estrangement.

If the church is to live incarnationally as the body of Christ, its own missional vocation involves a simultaneous participation in culture/world and God's redeeming activity, so that the world can see and experience provisionally but powerfully the new humanity that God is bringing forth through the Spirit. In the sacraments the relationship between God and world becomes visible in the church's midst for the sake of all people. Through the water of baptism we are

40. "Definition of Chalcedon, 451," in *Documents of the Christian Church*, ed. Henry Bettenson (Oxford: Oxford University Press, 1963), 51.

reborn and enter into God's community of promise. We share the bread and wine at Christ's table as signs of the whole creation transformed in the power of the Spirit. These concrete realities offer a tangible answer to the question of God's participation in the world and our participation in God. It is particularly in the sacraments that we see ourselves and the world renewed, pointing back to Christ's life, deep into our present reality, and forward to our promised future.

## The Missional Church in Public

It has been frequently noted in the missional conversation that the early church chose to describe the Christian community not as a private cult but rather as an *ekklesia*, a called-out public assembly. The gospel has been notably captive to modern Western culture in the privatization of faith and the relegation of Christianity (and other religions too, for that matter) to matters of individual spiritual conscience and morality.[41] Christianity's role in modernity was to make better moral individuals. Unfortunately, Jesus's announcement of the coming reign of God, which calls into question the ways of life of all societies, was often muted. Newbigin in particular has offered a vigorous critique of this assumption: "The Church, therefore, as the bearer of the gospel, inhabits a plausibility structure which is at variance with, and which calls into question, those that govern all human cultures without exception."[42]

One of the major contributions of the missional conversation has been to reclaim the public character of the gospel in a pluralist age. Yet what precisely constitutes this public role of the church deserves further scrutiny. As noted in chapters 2 and 3, the book *Missional Church* and the missional conversation do not always cohere on this question. The Anabaptist voices tend toward construing the church as an alternative community that lives its witness in sharp distinction from the world. Reformed voices have stressed the church's witness and proclamation within a broader framework for God's activity in human culture and society. Additional streams that have entered the conversation offer the promise of enriching and expanding it.

It is worth exploring the historical role of congregations in American public life. Martin Marty notes how in the early period churches often served as the primary center for community assembly (thus the "meetinghouses" in colonial New England, for instance).[43] In the nineteenth century and later,

41. Newbigin, *Foolishness to the Greeks*, 18–19.
42. Newbigin, *Gospel in a Pluralist Society*, 9.
43. Martin Marty, "Public and Private: Congregation as Meeting Place," in *American Congregations*, ed. James P. Wind and James W. Lewis (Chicago: University of Chicago Press, 1994), 152–53.

many congregations became increasingly privatized through their focus on individual salvation or on their own internal activities and programs.[44] The rise of contemporary megachurches, with their attempts to offer comprehensive programming for all ages, represents a further outworking of this logic.

American congregations entered a new phase of involvement with public life with the social activism of many liberal congregations in the 1960s and 1970s and with the rise of the Religious Right in the 1980s. Yet both of these approaches hold deep Christendom assumptions about the church's ability to reform society in its image (however contested that image might be). The missional church conversation has sought to avoid these postures by taking seriously the pluralistic nature of contemporary Western society. Newbigin helpfully distinguishes between the "fact of plurality," the sociological reality of many religions and no religion in Western societies, and the "ideology of pluralism," the modern Western cultural assumption that no religion is permitted to make ultimate truth claims in public.[45] What, then, should the church's public posture be?

### Beyond the Christian Colony

One answer to this question has been articulated by Stanley Hauerwas and William Willimon in *Resident Aliens*.[46] Their answer has been highly influential within the missional conversation. They argue for understanding the church as a "Christian colony," a new polis focused on living the gospel of Jesus with integrity over against a world that follows other gods. Participating in the Christian community means being apprenticed into patterns of life and practice that distinguish this community from all others in society. Hauerwas and Willimon's rejection of the terms of Christendom and their attempt to recover the distinctiveness of Christian life are invaluable contributions. Indeed, the recovery and deepening of practices of communal discipleship is at the heart of missional renewal, and they deserve credit for focusing the church's attention there.

What is less clear in their proposal is the missional dimension of the church's engagement with the world. Hauerwas and Willimon write, "We argue that the political task of Christians is to be the church rather than to transform

44. The latter of these forms of privatization is described trenchantly by Gibson Winter in *The Suburban Captivity of the Churches: An Analysis of Protestant Responsibility in the Expanding Metropolis* (Garden City, NY: Doubleday, 1961).

45. Newbigin, *Gospel in a Pluralist Society*, 14.

46. Stanley Hauerwas and William H. Willimon, *Resident Aliens: Life in the Christian Colony* (Nashville: Abingdon, 1989).

the world."[47] This argument invites the question of why these things need to be mutually exclusive. Certainly, if Christians fail to be the church, their attempts to transform the world will hardly be a witness to the gospel. Yet the connection between God, church, and world is underdeveloped in this more sectarian approach to ecclesiology.[48] According to Hauerwas and Willimon, Christians are to embody the ethics of Jesus before a watching world, which then can see the gospel in the integrity of lived witness. Yet how precisely does this watching take place?

The idea that the church can sustain itself as a discrete culture reflecting Christian values, isolating itself from the competing values of the secular world, is a problematic premise. This is particularly the case in light of the hybrid, fluid, reflexive nature of culture today. It is hard to envision the church as a separate colony when the members of congregations also participate deeply and simultaneously in the complex cultural forces that shape identity in our world. In practice, these forces inevitably exercise significant influence on the cultural and social imaginations of Christians. The theology of culture undergirding Hauerwas and Willimon's proposal, which is deeply indebted to postliberalism, does not adequately describe the complexity of the contemporary globalized cultural environment.

Most significantly from the perspective of missional theology, the horizon for the Triune God's active involvement in creation and culture can recede from view in the "Christian colony" approach. On one level, Hauerwas and Willimon are right to assert that it is not Christians who are primarily charged with transforming the world. That is *God's* mission, in which the church finds its vocation as partner and participant. Yet *being the church* from a missional perspective means that Christians share in the Triune God's creative, redemptive, and reconciling movement within human societies, communities, and cultures. The Christian church must be very intentional about its own patterns of life, seeking faithfulness to Christ in the power of the Spirit in all that it is and does. This very faithfulness is a call to engagement with the world on multiple levels, not because the world is a space lacking God's presence and activity, but because it is the primary sphere of God's missional movement. While we affirm Hauerwas and Willimon's call to develop the distinctiveness of Christian community, we also must insist on that community's deep participation in the surrounding society.

47. Ibid., 38.
48. For the critique of *Resident Aliens* as sectarian, see James Gustafson, "The Sectarian Temptation: Reflections on Theology, the Church, and the University," *Proceedings of the Catholic Theological Society* 40 (1985): 83–94. Hauerwas responds in *Christian Existence Today: Essays on Church, World, and Living in Between* (Grand Rapids: Baker Academic, 1995), 1–24.

The Spirit is critical to this sense of renewed participation, something that is suggested in chapter 6 of *Missional Church*. That chapter focused on congregational practices, but these were not developed consistently within that book. Without such a robust pneumatology, the stress tends to fall on our responsibility to imitate Christ through our own performative efforts. The next chapter will take up the question of spiritual formation and practices in greater depth, but it is worth noting here how central the Spirit must be in conceiving this from the perspective of missional theology.

George Hunsberger addresses the question of the missional church's public calling by first affirming the emphasis, as proposed by Hauerwas, Willimon, and John H. Yoder, on Christian identity as lived practice. But he complements this with a Reformed stress on the church's missional witness to the coming reign of God.[49] This Reformed construal is at work in Newbigin's idea of the congregation as a "hermeneutic of the gospel."[50]

Hunsberger suggests several themes that should guide the public theologizing of the missional church. First, he commends a *spirit of companionship*: the principle of walking with others in the world in a posture of identification, rather than standing over against them. Hunsberger reminds us that the church is a combination of both gospel and culture, and Christians share a great deal with those outside the church.[51] Second, the church must be *humble in its truth telling*. While Christians can be bold in the confidence of the gospel, "we know in part, and all our knowing is qualified by the limitations of one vantage point and the distortions of human sin."[52] Third, Christians must accept and affirm *particularity in discourse*. They must own the personal character of Christian knowledge; "to hold the posture of those who speak from the place where our own commitments and visions have been formed around this good news of God is to be both more honest and more able to invite others to exhibit similar honesty."[53] Fourth, Christians must have *courage in public action*; that is, they must embody in their own lives the change they would advocate in society.[54] Finally, they must keep an *eye on the horizon*—a view toward God's promised future, which is where hope is found.[55]

49. George R. Hunsberger, "The Missional Voice and Posture of Public Theologizing," *Missiology* 34, no. 1 (January 2006): 15–28.

50. Newbigin, *Gospel in a Pluralist Society*, 222–33.

51. Hunsberger, "Missional Voice and Posture," 21–22.

52. Ibid., 22.

53. Ibid., 24.

54. Ibid., 25.

55. Ibid., 26–27.

## Congregations as Public Participants

These Anabaptist and Reformed approaches are enriched by interaction with various theological and theoretical streams as well as by insights from the sociology of congregations. As Martin Marty observes, congregations today often function as "publics" within a larger public context—not as separate colonies in isolation, but rather as public gatherings of people whose activities often engage directly with the wider society.[56] There is a public shape to the life of many congregations, not only in their own public gatherings but in their participation and partnership with other institutions and organizations within the surrounding community. The black church is perhaps the most notable instance in American Christianity of the church functioning as a public with a powerful impact on and role in the wider community. Marty's description of congregations as publics invites an imagination for how the church can function as a space for community gathering where issues of concern to the wider world are engaged.

One key question for Christian communities today is how to pursue their prophetic vocation within society apart from the framework of Christendom. The church in Christendom typically controlled or had significant access to the institutions of society and the common good through its position at the center. That is no longer the case. The framework of missional participation again offers a fruitful imagination.

The Lutheran theologian Gary Simpson suggests that congregations need to exist at the intersection of public and private life, where they can serve as public moral companions in civil society.[57] Thus congregations should see themselves as participants in God's wider work in the world and society. This takes place not only through the church but also beyond it in such civil society organizations as social service institutions and charities. Congregations need to partner, collaborate, and participate in what God is doing in the world. What is particularly unique about congregations is their capacity to engage in communicative reasoning and deliberation on behalf of the common good—to be spaces where the questions of human flourishing in a given community are brought for critical discussion that leads to action.[58]

This expanded imagination for the collaborative role of the church amid other institutions within civil society suggests the church's unique capacity to

56. Marty, "Public and Private," 160.
57. Gary M. Simpson, *Critical Social Theory: Prophetic Reason, Civil Society, and Christian Imagination* (Minneapolis: Fortress, 2002). Simpson draws from the Frankfurt School of critical theorists, Paul Tillich's idea of congregations exercising prophetic reasoning, and Jürgen Habermas's theory of communicative action to explore how congregations can become spaces for engaging questions of public and prophetic concern to local communities and the world.
58. Ibid., 144–45.

be a place of moral discernment, seeking God's wisdom for living life. This is not just the private moral discernment of individuals but rather the moral discernment of communities on behalf of the common good. Robert Putnam and Lewis Feldstein feature churches in their recent research on American institutions that build social capital by bringing people together across lines of social difference to develop relationships and share common life.[59] This is a promising dimension for missional engagement with God's world.

## Conclusion

Missional theology offers an expanded framework for understanding creation and culture as existing within the Triune God's dynamic movement. It is critical that the integral role of the church in regard to God's purposes never be neglected or eclipsed in this larger framework. The church is the communal body bearing God's promises in Christ. No other community plays that unique role. At the same time, a robust, participatory understanding of the *missio Dei* rules out any restriction of God's activity, wisdom, and presence to the church alone. The church possesses the interpretive focus for comprehending that wider movement through the Word and the Spirit. The church offers to the world a sacramental promise of the world's future as the body of Christ, both in its rejection of the distortions, sins, and abuses of creation and culture and in its affirmation of the signs of abundant life.

59. Robert D. Putnam and Lewis Feldstein, *Better Together: Restoring the American Community* (New York: Simon & Schuster, 2003).

# 6

## Missional Practices of Church Life and Leadership

What does missional church look like in practice? This has been a common question raised by many as they struggle to envision what the paradigm shift from being a "church with a mission" to being a missional church signifies for the life of congregations and church systems. Chapter 3 noted how the Engaging branch of the conversation has taken up this question. In this chapter, we offer a contribution to understanding how the concrete patterns of the church's life, leadership, and organization might be reframed from a missional point of view. We proceed by specifically building on the theological foundations laid in chapters 4 and 5. The logic of missional theology offers promising possibilities for matters such as congregational practices, leadership, structures, the starting of new congregations, and the renewal of existing ones.

### Missional Imagination

Missional church is, on a deep level, about theological *imagination*—a different way to see and experience life in the church and the world. We have noted at several points in this book how differing theological assumptions have introduced diversity into the interpretation of missional church. In our view, missional imagination is fundamentally about seeing the church and the world in light of the Triune God's presence and activity. Jesus repeatedly stresses new ways of seeing in his encounters with various people in the Gospels. Discerning the presence and possibility of the reign of God in our midst involves a fresh perspective illuminated by the Spirit.

Our understanding of the concept of imagination in the West is still deeply shaped by nineteenth-century Romanticism, which viewed it as the productive, self-expressive faculty of artistic individuals. What was lost in this view was both the communal dimension of imagination (referred to in chapter 4 as the "social imaginary") and the theological dimension, that is, the way in which God's Spirit operates in our imaginations to inform, expand, illuminate, and transform us. From the perspective of missional theology, imagination is not the property of autonomous individuals. Rather, it is one of the ways in which the Holy Spirit moves within and among us to lead us into God's missional activity in the world. What follows in this chapter touches on this crucial dimension of missional imagination, which must be attentively cultivated as missional theology is embodied and practiced.

## Missional Practices of Discipleship

Discipleship is following Christ into participation in God's mission in the world in the power of the Spirit. This means that it lies at the heart of the missional turn. Since missional church is fundamentally about identity—about *being* the church—developing and deepening the Christian identity of every disciple must be at the forefront of the church's focus. The church cannot witness credibly to or participate effectively in God's mission without faithful discipleship. Christian identity in Christendom was assumed to be transmitted primarily through the broader culture. One learned how to be a good Christian by being a good citizen as well as a faithful family member. Today the culture can no longer be assumed to contribute constructively to Christian formation, and few families are equipped to do so. Thus Christian identity must be cultivated intentionally, patiently, and comprehensively by congregations and other Christian communities. Practices of discipleship are primarily a communal reality, given the trinitarian understanding of the *imago Dei* offered above. Unfortunately, late-modern culture has tended to de-emphasize the communal dimension of discipleship in favor of focusing on the individual.

One of the more fruitful developments in contemporary theology is the renewed attention to practices that shape Christian life, imagination, and discipleship.[1] Most of the literature that is focused on practices, however, has not assumed a specific missional theological perspective. The impulse reflected in these writings is nevertheless a helpful one for holistically engaging Christian formation and mission. This impulse recognizes that the Christian faith is expressed not only in doctrinal formulations but also in concrete acts. It understands that our beliefs and imaginations are shaped through patterns of behavior over time and that these patterns are grounded in and passed down by communities into which we are apprenticed. Chapters 5 and 6 of *Missional Church* sought to describe patterns of congregational practice—such as peacemaking, worship, healing, hospitality, and discernment—that are integral to the church's participation in God's mission. In addition, the GOCN publication *Treasure in Clay Jars* identified eight "patterns in missional faithfulness" to serve as indicators of a missional church.[2] Other books in the Engaging branch have also tried to give definition to missional congregational practices.

We have stressed above, however, that it is important to resist the common tendency to reduce missional church to a set of rules to follow, discrete characteristics, or summary principles. There is no model for what a missional church looks like. Rather, missional church needs to be defined by the church's dynamic participation in the Triune God's movement in the world. There is thus no how-to list or set of defining characteristics for the missional church, an approach often pursued in some of the current literature as noted in chapter 3. It takes on different expressions at different times and places. Missional church is a habit of mind and heart, a posture of openness and discernment, and a faithful attentiveness both to the Spirit's presence and to the world that God so loves. Recognizing and seeking the leadership of the Spirit in the church's communal life and practice is the key. This was helpfully emphasized in chapter 6 of *Missional Church*, but unfortunately it was largely missing in much of the literature that followed. The tendency to reduce missional to a set of lists and attributes often appears in that literature (especially in the Discovering and the Utilizing branches described in chapter 3).

Missional theology, understood through the framework of the church's participation in the Triune God's creative, redemptive, and reconciling movement in the world, invites us to recognize the missionary character of Christian practices. Practices must be understood not simply as things we do to grow

1. See Miroslav Volf and Dorothy C. Bass, *Practicing Theology: Beliefs and Practices in Christian Life* (Grand Rapids: Eerdmans, 2002), 70; Dorothy C. Bass, *Practicing Our Faith: A Way of Life for a Searching People* (San Francisco: Jossey-Bass, 1997); Diana Butler Bass, *The Practicing Congregation: Imagining a New Old Church* (Herndon, VA: Alban Institute, 2004).

2. Barrett et al., *Treasure in Clay Jars*. See the discussion of the Engaging branch in chapter 3 above.

spiritually but rather as concrete ways in which our participation in God's mission is embodied in relation to our neighbor. For instance, the Christian practice of prayer—a central one, as most would agree—can take on a powerful missionary dimension when done with attentiveness to the world. Reggie McNeal offers an example of how one congregation attempted this:

> Each member of the staff at one church was instructed to go to a coffee shop, sit on a park bench, or stand in a mall parking lot and pray a simple prayer: "Lord, help me to see what you see." They were to listen for an hour to the voice of God and then reconvene to share what they had heard. This simple outing radically changed their outlook as they realized that what was in the heart of God was much bigger than typical church concerns. They began to see broken families, homeless people, at-risk children, stressed teenagers—all people they were not engaging with their church ministry.[3]

When this attentiveness is grounded in an imagination for God's presence and movement in the world, our eyes are opened with compassion. We connect with God's passionate care for all creation.[4]

The missionary dimension of practices such as service and hospitality might seem more obvious, but a robust trinitarian missional theology opens up their reciprocal, mutually transformative potential. When we enter into participation in the ministry of Christ with our neighbor, we expect to meet Christ in the stranger and to experience the Spirit's movement between us and those whom we serve or welcome. We are sharing in a bigger movement that may lead us into surprising and unexpected places. Mother Teresa of Calcutta would sometimes ask those serving alongside her as she cared for the poor and dying, "Do you see Christ in them yet?"[5] This was not a pious platitude but rather a profound spiritual insight into what happens when we follow Christ into identification with the poor. God is there, the passionate God who suffers with the lost and downtrodden, whose Spirit breaks down walls of division and creates new community where one might least expect it.

For this reason, spiritual formation or Christian discipleship, from a missional view, cannot be merely an in-house affair. We must engage the curriculum of the world as we expect to encounter God's presence in the neighbor or stranger. Congregations must make space for deep engagement with the biblical narrative in direct relationship to an engagement with the world. We

---

3. McNeal, *Missional Renaissance*, 70.

4. See Trevor Hudson, *A Mile in My Shoes: Cultivating Compassion* (Nashville: Upper Room, 2005).

5. This story was shared by a ministry colleague who spent several weeks with Mother Teresa in Calcutta.

are formed spiritually as faithful disciples through immersion not only in a vibrant, practicing community where we learn from mature mentors in the faith, but also through coming to recognize the signs of the Triune God's movement in the lives of our neighbors and our world.

### Dwelling in the Word

One fruitful practice for shaping the imagination of congregations in mission is known as "dwelling in the Word" (not to be confused with the practice of dwelling in the *world*, referenced in chapter 4). Dwelling in the Word is a way to read Scripture in community that was adapted from Gospel Based Discipleship, a practice of Native American Episcopalians in Minnesota.[6] In dwelling in the Word, a short passage of Scripture is read aloud, while people are encouraged to listen to where their imagination was *caught* in the text. Participants then pair up and listen to each other by attending carefully to what the other person heard and thus allowing them to speak freely. In the larger group sharing, people are invited to share not what they heard but what their partner heard.

This process does several key things. First, it avoids the expert-driven approach to Scripture that prevails in many congregations, where the pastor or some other person with formal theological training is expected to interpret on behalf of the people. Instead, it is assumed in dwelling in the Word that God speaks through the Word to each and every one. Second, it focuses on the imagination, recognizing the power of the Word to inform, enliven, and renew our vision for God's activity in the biblical narrative and in our world. The Bible is treated not as a rule book or a tool box but as a living story. Third, it develops the capacity of congregations to listen to one another attentively while listening to the Word, which is foundational for learning to listen to the neighbor in mission.[7]

### Missional Discernment

Listening attentively to the Word, to one another, and to the world is central to participating in God's mission. This listening must be accompanied by discernment—the Christian practice of attending to God's call for Christian communities corporately and for each of us personally. Missional churches

6. See Keifert, *We Are Here Now*, 68–71.
7. See Pat Taylor Ellison, "Word-Dwelling, Deep Listening, and Faith-Based Moral Conversation in Congregations: A Nested Vision for Learning New Habits," in *Testing the Spirits: How Theology Informs the Study of Congregations*, ed. Patrick Keifert (Grand Rapids: Eerdmans, 2009), 91–108.

ask the question, what is God up to in the world? That question must be approached from a posture of deep humility, however, given the realities of human sinfulness and the limitations of our knowledge. The church can easily distort its discernment toward selfish ends or fail to see God's surprising presence and activity, especially in the lives of people on the margins. As noted previously, the New Testament contains numerous moments of reciprocity in which disciples of Jesus are transformed by encounters with previously shunned strangers—the Samaritan villagers in Luke 10, for instance, or Cornelius in Acts 10. Discernment must be grounded in the Word of God, in attentive prayer and listening to the Holy Spirit, in community, and especially in relationship with the neighbor.

Unlike some ways in which discernment has classically been practiced, missional discernment must take seriously the participation of those outside the church. One striking instance of this comes from South Africa, where an all-white, Afrikaans-speaking Dutch Reformed megachurch sought to become multiracial and multiethnic in the years after apartheid ended. The leaders of the church realized that they couldn't figure out how to do this on their own, so they built relationships with local black leaders, even going so far as to invite a few of those leaders to serve on the church board without requiring them to become members. Their journey taught them that they could not discern how to move into a new future with their neighbors without having those neighbors at the table.

### Missional Worship

In Romans 12:1, Paul encourages his readers to "present your bodies as a living sacrifice, holy and acceptable to God, which is your spiritual worship." This holistic way of thinking about worship, as offering our whole lives sacrificially to God, gives us a helpful lens for comprehending worship in a missional perspective. Worship is not merely a gathering of private individuals seeking an intimate experience of the divine; rather, it is a public work (*leiturgia*) in which we participate with God.[8] God calls us to live our whole lives doxologically—in worshipful praise and to the glory of our Creator. This dimension of our life is brought to focused attention and celebration in community in our practice of corporate worship.

Worship is not merely an instrumental opportunity to present the gospel to seekers, to teach believers, or to administer sacraments; rather, it is the public practice in which we show forth who we are in and with God. In Word and sacrament, we are nourished and renewed in order to be sent forth in service

8. See Patrick Keifert, *Welcoming the Stranger: A Public Theology of Worship and Evangelism* (Minneapolis: Fortress, 1992).

and mission, to live lives of sacrificial witness to God. The gathering movement of worship is complemented by a sending movement into the world. In the Eucharist, we experience a foretaste of the communion that is our destiny as God's redeemed people.[9] The Spirit, in this communion, reconciles diverse people into participation in a new community of love, sharing, and reciprocity at Christ's table. Our relational personhood as humanity created in the image of the Trinity comes into focus in that feast.

Worship must invite participants into an *experience* of the Spirit in community in light of the ongoing creativity of the Spirit in the life of the church and beyond. This will take countless forms, but the public, experiential character of worship in the missional church is vital. Worship is one area of the church's life in which vibrant and creative contextualization of the gospel must take place. This is especially so given the dynamic, hybrid, globalized nature of culture in the twenty-first century. Worship must embody the multiple microcultures present in most locales among various generations and populations. The Church of England's framework of a "mixed economy" of expressions of church is a helpful way to describe the multiple forms of church life, worship, and organization required to engage the multiplicity of cultures in a given place.[10]

### Mission in Daily Life

Mission is not simply an occasional activity or a program of the church; rather, it defines the church's core identity, where all disciples are called to be missionaries in their spheres of life. This holistic understanding of missional vocation begs for further development.[11] How is it that ordinary Christians can authentically imagine and enter into participation in God's mission in their workplaces, homes, neighborhoods, and world? If mission isn't something that specialists ("missionaries") do on behalf of most ordinary Christians or that takes place a few times a year ("mission trips"), how can it be comprehended within daily life? How can congregations form and equip their members for such missional witness?

These are challenging questions to answer, especially given the significant gap many lay Christians perceive between what they experience at church and what they have to face in their daily lives.[12] The classical response has been to

---

9. See Zizioulas, *Being as Communion*.

10. Archbishops' Council 2004, *Mission-Shaped Church*.

11. See Darrell L. Guder, "Work and Witness from the Perspective of Missional Church Theology," *Word & World* 25, no. 4 (Fall 2005): 424–32.

12. See Robert Banks, *Redeeming the Routines: Bringing Theology to Life* (Grand Rapids: Baker Academic, 1993).

focus on principles of correct ethical behavior. Certainly this must be affirmed. But missional theology will not let us stop there. Instead, congregations are charged with assisting their disciples in active, daily discernment of God's movement in the "secular" spaces in which they spend the great majority of their days. This is an invitation for church leaders to take far more seriously the realities of the world in which Christians struggle to live faithfully each day. It is a call to recognize that those spaces are pregnant with missional possibility and to learn alongside those Christians how to discern and witness to the signs of God's inbreaking reign. This means developing a robust theological imagination for the Spirit's presence and movement. It means cultivating a posture of *wonder* among all of God's people for God's presence and works within and around us, especially in the lives of our neighbors.

### Discovering Missional Identity through Practice

The practices we have identified above are just a few of the dimensions of congregational life that must be addressed from a missional perspective. The list is by no means exhaustive. Missional theology invites us to recognize the integral role of the neighbor, the stranger, and the wider world in the congregation's life and imagination. Not only must space be made for the stranger or the neighbor to participate in the church's life but the church must also *discover* its missional identity in its participation in the life of God in the neighborhood and the world. Our attention must be focused outward in discernment as the church learns how to sacrificially give itself away in ministry to the community.

Reggie McNeal observes that in most churches today, the indicators of success or effectiveness are skewed inward, toward the attractional, programmatic, and institutional factors of Christendom, rather than outward toward participation in God's mission.[13] In the eyes of many church leaders and denominational or judicatory systems, what matters is attendance at worship, dollars in the offering plate, the number of people coming to church programs, and the size of the church's organizational footprint (including real estate).[14] How might we reframe our evaluation in a missional direction, refocusing budgets, facilities, staff time, activities, worship, and other elements of congregational life outward, upon the world? Although some may find attempts to quantify

13. McNeal, *Missional Renaissance*.
14. It is worth noting that perhaps the most prominent megachurch in America, Willow Creek Community Church in South Barrington, Illinois, has discovered that participation in its church programs and activities does not correlate with spiritual growth among its membership. See Greg Hawkins and Cally Parkinson, *Reveal* (South Barrington, IL: Willow Creek Association, 2007).

missional participation (such as McNeal's) less than fully helpful, missional church invites us to redefine what we value and how we assess it.

## Participatory Missional Leadership

Leadership in Christian churches in the West has for centuries been deeply shaped by Christendom assumptions. Ministry was reserved primarily for the clergy who taught, cared for, and administered settled flocks, often as a hierarchical class set apart from or above the rest of the congregation. These clergy were often understood to represent Christ to the congregation, rather than the whole congregation representing Christ to the world in the power of the Spirit. *Missional Church* describes the dominant historical paradigms of church leadership in Christendom as priest (medieval), pedagogue (Reformation), and professional (modern era, with subvariants of counselor, technician, and entrepreneur).[15] With the collapse of functional Christendom, the role and nature of leadership in Christian communities are being fundamentally reevaluated. A new paradigm is emerging to replace the professional model: that of the participatory leader.

Participatory leadership for the missional church is grounded in the premise that the church finds its identity in participation in God's mission in the world, and that it is primarily the Holy Spirit who leads Christian communities. In the previous paradigms of priest, pedagogue, or professional, authority was understood to be concentrated in individuals who held office or who possessed certain professional skills and certifications. However, emerging understandings of leadership recognize that it is understood best not as a fixed set of individual roles or attributes but as a process of relational influence.[16] This interpretation fits with the relational understanding of personhood explored in chapter 4 in light of the Trinity. Participatory leadership assumes that authority is distributed among the community by God, both in the form of spiritual gifts and in the presence of the Spirit. Leadership is one of the gifts of the Spirit (see Rom. 12:8), but its function is not to control, dictate, or monopolize the church's ministry. It is rather to cultivate and steward the faithful participation of the whole community and its gifts in God's mission.

Cultivation—a metaphor drawn from farming and gardening—is a pivotal way to envision missional leadership.[17] It reminds us that we can plant, water, and seek to provide good light and air, but it is God who gives the

15. Guder, *Missional Church*, 190–98.
16. See Peter Guy Northouse, *Leadership: Theory and Practice*, 4th ed. (Thousand Oaks, CA: Sage, 2007).
17. Roxburgh and Romanuk, *Missional Leader*.

growth. Settled flocks cannot be assumed to exist after Christendom, and even if they do, they must be led deeper into discipleship and engagement with their contexts in the world. Leaders must intentionally cultivate authentic Christian community. They must not seek primarily to satisfy the hungers of spiritual consumers (as in the professional paradigm) but rather to create the conditions under which people can come together in shared life to discover their participation in God's mission. This means the facilitation of spaces of communal belonging, sharing, and practice. Christian leaders must not only be proficient in the practices of discipleship themselves but they must also engage intentionally in developing those practices in the people around them.

Participatory leadership is sense-making leadership.[18] Leaders are responsible not for monopolizing theological discourse in the congregation but for leading and equipping people in the practice of theological imagination for interpreting the Word and making sense of their daily lives in the world. It is the people who primarily enact this work of interpretation and discernment within a Christian imagination for God's movement and presence within and around them. This takes place in light of the processes of meaning making and identity construction in late modernity that were described in chapter 4. People need help with this interpretation and discernment if it is to be faithful, and this work must take place in community. Participatory leaders attentively create spaces for this work, spaces of listening and dialogue, of engagement with Scripture and theological tradition, of encounter with the world. The function of leadership is to equip, empower, and facilitate this process, leading people deeper into Christian tradition and deeper into the world in mission.

Moving from the settled, maintenance paradigm of Christendom leadership to missional leadership for a new apostolic age calls for revisiting one of Jesus's own deep leadership commitments: leadership multiplication. In the missional church, leadership must be multiplied intentionally in order to steward well the gifts God has given the community while also opening the ministry of the community as wide as possible in mission. One of the key assumptions of a Spirit-filled understanding of ministry in the missional church is that ministry is fundamentally uncontrollable. God's mission through the congregation cannot be tightly regulated and managed by leaders. Rather, the Spirit is constantly working to expand, deepen, provoke, and enrich that ministry. The cultivation and multiplication of leaders is necessary for the growth of the church's participation in God's mission.

---

18. See Scott Cormode, *Making Spiritual Sense: Christian Leaders as Spiritual Interpreters* (Nashville: Abingdon, 2006); and Karl E. Weick, *Sensemaking in Organizations* (Thousand Oaks, CA: Sage, 1995).

The shift from solo leadership models to team-based leadership is becoming increasingly established in the church as well as in other organizations in society. The team approach to leadership is particularly pronounced for emerging churches that are living intentionally within postmodern culture. Eddie Gibbs and Ryan Bolger describe this as "leading as a body."[19] The decentering of leadership from solo clergy to polycentric teams not only reflects a renewed emphasis on the variety of spiritual gifts within the community and the emergence of a more participatory culture in postmodernity, but it also invites a more thoroughly trinitarian imagination for the church as created in the Trinity's image.[20]

At the heart of our faith is a divine leadership community: the Trinity. Each person of the Trinity shares deeply in the others' life and work, which leads to each person's identity being shaped in relationship to the others. Authority flows between, among, and out from all three in complementary ways. The logic of trinitarian missional theology points toward a communal, collaborative leadership paradigm in which different persons together employ their God-given gifts to steward, shepherd, and influence the community toward deeper participation in what God is doing in the world. A missional church cultivated in the Trinity's image will recognize that authority and leadership are dynamic, fluid, distributed realities grounded in the Holy Spirit's presence and gifts. Authority and leadership tended to be hoarded in the Christendom maintenance paradigm of the church's life. In a missional paradigm, these gifts are meant to be shared and given away.

## Reframing Church Organization for Mission

The organizational forms the church has inherited are shaped largely by the assumptions of very different eras. A great many local congregations, judicatories, and denominations are still organized for functional Christendom, not for being missional churches. If mission is part of their structural DNA at all, it tends to be mission *somewhere else*. Chapter 1 traced how most denominations were first organized in the nineteenth century to do mission overseas or across the frontier, not to engage missionally in their own immediate contexts.[21]

19. Eddie Gibbs and Ryan K. Bolger, *Emerging Churches: Creating Christian Community in Postmodern Cultures* (Grand Rapids: Baker Academic, 2005), 191–215.

20. See Dwight Zscheile, "The Trinity, Leadership and Power," *Journal of Religious Leadership* 6, no. 2 (Fall 2007): 43–63.

21. See also Russell E. Richey, "Denominations and Denominationalism: An American Morphology," in *Reimagining Denominationalism: Interpretive Essays*, ed. Robert Bruce Mullin and Russell E. Richey (New York: Oxford University Press, 1994), 74–98.

Bringing a missional imagination to the structure and organization of the church's life invites deep reenvisioning.

The first impulse to address the challenges facing the church within late modernity is often a move toward strategic reorganization. Yet it is crucial to keep the church's missional identity at the forefront, followed by its purpose, so that organization flows from the church's missionary nature and purpose. As we have earlier argued, the church *is*; the church *does what it is*; the church *organizes what it does*.[22] What then does a missional identity suggest for reframing church organization?

Due to the contextual nature of the church's participation in God's mission in its local time and place, church organization will, of necessity, vary widely. The Christendom organizational paradigms of parish, diocese, and state church tended to reinforce a standardized model of local church, staffed by a solo clergyperson. This was complemented in medieval Catholicism by monastic orders, which carried out much of the missionary work through their more flexible structures. The corporate bureaucratic paradigm of the industrial age in the modern era in the West fostered greater levels of standardization, both in the "franchise" approach to denominational church planting in the 1950s and 1960s and in the accompanying standardization of clergy training and credentialing. Late modernity brought the packaging and distribution of church models and programs from Willow Creek, Saddleback, and other leading megachurches through their training networks.

The erosion of functional Christendom and the advent of postmodernity have revealed the limitations of these approaches in the face of an increasingly complex and differentiated cultural situation. No single size fits all, and postmodern generations tend to be highly suspicious of prepackaged versions of church.[23] There is now an opportunity to participate in a powerful new era of missional innovation, experimentation, and diversification regarding how church is organized. Church organization must emerge organically from the Spirit's work in local contexts as congregations and other forms of Christian community are gathered, renewed, and sent. This transformation begins with attending to the missional Triune God's movement in our midst and in the world.

We increasingly live in a participatory age in the twenty-first century.[24] This is evident in the shift from traditional, centralized forms of authority to de-

22. Van Gelder, *Essence of the Church*.
23. See Neil Cole, *Organic Church* (San Francisco: Jossey-Bass, 2005); and Tim Keel, *Intuitive Leadership* (Grand Rapids: Baker Books, 2007).
24. See Peter Reason and Hilary Bradbury, "Inquiry and Participation in Search of a World Worthy of Human Aspiration," in *Handbook of Action Research*, ed. Peter Reason and Hilary Bradbury, concise paperback ed. (Thousand Oaks, CA: Sage, 2006), 1–14.

centralized, emergent patterns of leadership. This applies directly to church organization. From a missional point of view, organization must help to create the highest degree of participation on the part of church members in God's mission in their time and place. Church organization in Christendom tended to focus inward on the care, education, and discipline of church members. The church in a missional era must organize outward while providing for the deepening of Christian community.

It is vital to keep at the forefront of our imaginations the creative power of the Spirit in shaping church organization. Biblically, it is the Spirit who guides the early church's process of discerning how to organize its common life. It is the Spirit who leads the church into engagement across lines of social and cultural difference. The creativity of the Spirit animates and renews forms of church organization as part of God's dynamic and ongoing creation. Reframing church organization for mission points us toward one of the bedrock foci of the missional church: discerning the movement of the Spirit. That is always a dynamic process.

This means a much more flexible and open posture on the part of church leaders. This is especially the case for those in judicatory or denominational roles, as local churches innovate in partnership with the Holy Spirit to engage more deeply in mission. We can expect fewer standardized organizational models and, instead, much greater diversification. As noted above, a mixed economy of churches representing multiple organizational expressions coexisting in the same communities will be the norm, not the exception. As in other moments of profound reorientation and change in church history, the Spirit's creative ordering and reordering of the church's life emerge in the midst of apparent chaos.

### Missional Denominations, Connectional Structures, and Ministries of Mobility

What might this creative reordering look like for connectional structures like denominations and judicatories? As described in chapter 3, one subbranch of the Engaging branch of the missional conversation has worked within judicatory organizations to leverage change at the congregational level. The shift toward a missional posture brings a welcome opportunity to recontextualize these structures for a post–functional Christendom in a postbureaucratic age. Many denominations and judicatories still reflect the organizational assumptions of industrial bureaucracies in their (1) centralization of authority, communication, and resources; (2) regulatory approach to controlling and managing ministry; and (3) rigidity. The stresses on these systems are rising and in many cases have reached crisis levels, as grassroots support has eroded in many cases and shrinking funding has mandated repeated retrenchments.

It is an opportune time to overhaul denominational and connectional structures for a missional era within an emerging networked information economy. Rather than organizing primarily for the purpose of doing mission *away* from local churches, a missional denomination or connectional structure exists to support and enhance mission *through* local churches. Rather than extracting resources from those churches into a central mission budget that is redistributed by those at the top, missional connectional structures might function better as networks of local congregations and other forms of Christian ministry collaborating in mission. Resources may still circulate in redistribution, but this would take place through networks on a largely voluntary, rather than compulsory, basis. This approach corresponds both to a renewed imagination for the relational Trinity in whose image we are created and to the Spirit's flow among and beyond us.

The shift toward the grass roots in mission has been documented for some time now by research within church systems.[25] Local churches in the twenty-first century consider the grass roots to be the primary place of missional engagement. At the same time, many want to partner and collaborate in mission rather than go it alone. Thus there is still a need for connectional structures, but the emphasis shifts from governance and control to empowerment, encouragement, and mutual sharing.

We can expect to see connectional and denominational structures that have much lighter organizational footprints, leaner staffs, greater mutual communication flows, and more flexible patterns of ministry. Missional expertise can no longer be assumed to exist primarily at the top of a hierarchical structure (as in a bureaucracy). Rather, a missional understanding of the Spirit's work among all of God's people and the highly contextual nature of the missional church suggest that expertise lies primarily at the grass roots. This changes the role and function of connectional structures significantly. Reconceived as networks that facilitate missional collaboration, these structures may be renewed for a new apostolic era.[26]

One way to reenvision these structures is in terms of ministries of mobility. At various points in history, ministries of mobility have coexisted alongside

25. For one example, see William L. Sachs, Thomas P. Holland, and the Episcopal Church Foundation, *Restoring the Ties That Bind: The Grassroots Transformation of the Episcopal Church* (New York: Church Publishing, 2003). See also Richey, "Denominations and Denominationalism."

26. See Dwight Zscheile, "Social Networking and Church Systems," *Word & World* 30, no. 3 (Summer 2010): 247–55.

local churches.[27] Perhaps the most vivid biblical example is Paul's apostolic ministry, which operated across multiple local churches in mission. In the medieval period, traveling monastic and missionary orders were responsible for evangelizing much of Europe. In the modern era, Protestants used mission societies to take the gospel around the world. While in Christendom (and its later variant, functional Christendom), judicatories and other regional and national connectional structures (including state churches and denominations) focused largely on governance, today's new apostolic context invites a shift in posture. Judicatories, denominations, and other connectional structures can discover a new missional identity as ministries of mobility as they link local churches in mission within their areas and beyond.

## Missional Church Planting

It is often observed that starting new congregations with a missional imagination and posture is easier than reorienting existing ones. This is so in part because the process of planting a new church is inherently missiological and open ended.[28] Leaders of new congregations must ask the key missional questions of identity and purpose that existing congregations often take for granted. These congregations must engage with those outside their doors in order to grow and thrive. How might missional theology inform the starting of new churches?

To begin with, new congregations must be understood within the Spirit's formative work. The church is always both *forming* and *reforming*.[29] That is, the Spirit creates new expressions of ministry in different times and places, while at the same time renewing and transforming existing ministries. The creation of new congregations is an integral aspect of the Spirit's movement in the world in history, which points us again toward the key theme of discernment. Within missional theology, it is vital to recognize the Spirit's primary agency in bringing new churches to life.

At the same time, missional theology suggests that new congregations do not come into being merely to service the existing members of a denomination who happen to live within a particular area. Rather, the Spirit gives birth to new churches to witness to God's coming reign in Christ. The church is called, gathered, deepened, and sent to be a sign, a foretaste, and a witness to God's

27. See Van Gelder, *Essence of the Church*, 169–72.
28. Darrell L. Guder, "Leadership in New Congregations: New-Church Development from the Perspective of Missional Theology," in *Extraordinary Leaders in Extraordinary Times: Unadorned Clay Pot Messengers*, ed. H. Stanley Wood (Grand Rapids: Eerdmans, 2006), 1–29.
29. Van Gelder, *Ministry of the Missional Church*, 54.

reign for all humanity. It exists to participate in the Triune God's mission in a particular time and place. Church planting offers abundant opportunities to fulfill this vocation creatively and innovatively without some of the constraints that existing churches have. Church plants are free to recontextualize the gospel anew within cultural spaces that have been neglected by the established church. The fluid nature of new churches allows for high levels of participation and change—key dimensions of the missional church.

Moreover, new missional congregations have an imagination for the church's public vocation in society.[30] That is, the missional church is not about attracting spiritual consumers and seeking to meet their private needs. Rather, missional churches serve as a vital public presence, both through their own gathered life, in which the challenges affecting the common good of the surrounding community are engaged for deliberation and action, and in their diaconal service to the neediest neighbors. They refuse to accept the dichotomies of public and private by which modernity bifurcated and reduced the gospel. Instead, they embrace a holistic understanding of God's reign, which touches every aspect of human life and culture, both personal and social.

In a missional era, many of the assumptions underlying current practices of church planting by denominations and judicatories will need to be reexamined. For instance, in many church systems, a new congregation becomes officially "legitimate" only when it comes to resemble the functional Christendom model of church—a congregation that can support a full-time pastor and a building. Prevailing models of church planting leadership often draw more from business entrepreneurship and institution building than from the practices of cultivating communities of discipleship, discernment, and witness as outlined above. The institutional character of new congregations may, in some cases, need to be intentionally underplayed in order for robust missional communities to be formed and sent to engage populations that have been excluded from the institutional church.

New missional congregations keep at the forefront of their minds and hearts the question of how they can give the gospel as well as their gifts to the community. They resist the tendency to make their own institutional stability and survival the primary end. Rather, they recognize that their primary end—indeed, the very reason for their existence—is participation in the Triune God's mission in the world. This does not mean that new missional congregations will not take institutional form. On the contrary, institutional expressions of church can be used powerfully by God in mis-

---

30. See Mary Sue Dreier, ed., *Created and Led by the Spirit: Planting Missional Congregations* (Grand Rapids: Eerdmans, forthcoming).

sion, and organizations that are sustainable over time typically adopt some institutional form. Organizational and institutional expressions of the church must serve its dynamic vocation of witness and service to the neighbor. The creation and multiplication of new congregations is integral to the future of the missional church.

## Renewing Congregations for Mission

For the many churches that already exist, however, it is vital to attend carefully to the possibilities of their missional transformation. Missional theology—informed by key insights from organizational theory about how change actually takes place in human communities—suggests a different approach to renewing congregations than is often employed. The fundamental emphasis in renewal efforts, in many instances, is strategic or programmatic. That is, congregations that are not engaging their surrounding community well are encouraged to do a better job of marketing or offering more relevant and enticing programs to attract more people. The assumption is often that the world is a target for the church's mission. Widely used church renewal programs such as Natural Church Development assess the deficiencies of congregations, with the premise that correcting those deficiencies will bring health and vitality.[31]

Missional theology begins from a different starting point: the Triune God's mission in the world. Beginning with a focus on the church's identity and purpose as found in participation in God's mission leads in different, deeper directions. To begin with, the horizon for church renewal is not just attracting more people into the congregation or even church "health" as defined by certain lists or criteria. It is God's coming reign, as embodied and proclaimed by Christ and manifested partially in the here and now through the presence of the Spirit. There is a decidedly *theological* focus to missional church renewal that is often lacking in other approaches.

Thus discernment of the Spirit is central. Most modern attempts at church renewal are based more in planning than in discernment, which reflects the secular modern social imaginary discussed in chapter 4. Planning is not unimportant, and it has its place. But the central challenge is one of listening to the Spirit in order to comprehend a church's particular missional vocation and the missional vocations of all its members. This can take place only through intentional spiritual practices and in relationship with the neighbor in the world. Discerning the Spirit's leadership renders missional renewal

31. Christian A. Schwarz, *Natural Church Development: A Guide to Eight Essential Qualities of Healthy Churches*, 4th ed. (St. Charles, IL: ChurchSmart Resources, 2000).

processes more open ended and uncontrollable. It is not so much a matter of developing a strategic plan, mission statement, or action steps as it is a matter of cultivating a congregation's capacity to live and witness as disciples. This task is harder to quantify but nonetheless requires great intentionality and discipline.

One subbranch of the Engaging branch of the conversation has fruitfully taken up the question of the missional renewal of church systems.[32] One of the key insights about missional change recognized in that literature is the importance of a "diffusion of innovations" approach to change, rather than a "gap" approach. In classic modernist planning, organizations tend to proceed by identifying what is lacking in their life against the backdrop of an aspirational future. Then they try to get members of the organization to close this "gap" through various strategic methods or incentives. In churches, the gap approach often leads to poor outcomes. First, the process of identifying the deficiencies within a church's life has the effect of blaming and shaming the congregation. Second, the aspirational future is typically developed and articulated primarily by a small set of leaders, not by the congregation's membership more widely, and thus isn't grounded deeply in the grass roots. Finally, it is very difficult to move church members across such a gap without the kind of coercive methods that can be employed by nonvoluntary organizations such as businesses. Many such strategic-planning approaches end up failing to engage the membership in the kind of deep culture change necessary for missional transformation.

The diffusion of innovations approach, in contrast, draws on decades of worldwide research on how changes actually spread through human communities.[33] Diffusion research recognizes that change typically spreads through social networks by a process of trial and experimentation. Key influencers within those social networks are integral to the spread of change and innovation. People tend to fall into different categories in their readiness to embrace change—from the innovators, who are impatient to embody the future, to the laggards, who resist it as long as possible. The key to lasting change is extensive participation by as many people as possible, where they are able over time to try out the new way of being church without risk of shame for failing.

What is significant about this approach from the perspective of missional theology is that the outcomes are not predetermined. The ordinary members of a congregation are invited to discern and live into a missional future under

32. See Keifert, *We Are Here Now*; and Roxburgh and Romanuk, *Missional Leader*.
33. See Everett M. Rogers, *Diffusion of Innovations*, 5th ed. (New York: Free Press, 2003).

the leadership of the Spirit through a diffusion process of trial and experimentation. A committee is not responsible for articulating an aspirational vision from on high, but rather the vision will emerge from the bottom up. When it becomes clear, the leadership can articulate and narrate it, but by that time it is already owned and embodied by the people.[34]

The importance of trial and experimentation must not be underestimated. Missional church is not a model, a standardized program, or a strategy that can be applied to churches with a predetermined result. Therefore, what missional transformation looks like in each congregation will tend to be somewhat unique. The key is for ordinary church members to develop their capacity to listen to God's Word in community, to listen to the Spirit, and to listen to their neighbors in love. These are in some respects very simple things, relative to the complex strategies, programs, and fixes on which many churches spend their energy today. Yet the impact is dramatic when local disciples begin to experience themselves as participants in God's greater movement in the world.

## Conclusion

We began part 2 of this book with the assertion that theology matters; our ways of conceiving of God and the world inevitably shape patterns of life and practice. Readers hoping to discover in this chapter a set of plans for quickly becoming a missional church will inevitably be disappointed. Missional church is not a prescribed set of things to do or a packaged vision for what church should look like, but rather a particular perspective on the church's theological identity.

That identity has numerous implications for how we approach the pressing questions of church life and leadership. It beckons us deeper into our theological imaginations for God's presence and movement in the world. It raises the bar for discipleship and spiritual formation within intentionally cultivated Christian communities. It reorients church leadership toward guiding disciples into participation in mission. It expands and diversifies patterns of church organization for the sake of mission. It informs the expectant planting of new churches through the creativity of the Spirit. It suggests deeper and more experiential approaches to church renewal. Following the logic of missional

34. See Dave Daubert, "Vision-Discerning vs. Vision-Casting: How Shared Vision Can Raise Up Communities of Leaders Rather than Mere Leaders of Communities," in *The Missional Church and Leadership Formation: Helping Congregations Develop Leadership Capacity*, ed. Craig Van Gelder (Grand Rapids: Eerdmans, 2009), 147–71.

theology will take each church somewhere different due to the diversity of contexts, cultures, and gifts present in our world today. This very openness and particularity testifies to core missional ideas: the diversity and integrity of God's creation, the transformational embrace of local cultures in the incarnation, and the ongoing agency of the Spirit in the world.

# Epilogue

## Reviewing Our Purpose

Our overall purpose in writing this book was to place the missional church conversation in perspective in relation to four things. First, we sought to clarify the emergence of the term "missional." We did this by exploring the popularization of the term in the 1998 book *Missional Church*; we also discussed the seemingly inherent elasticity of this term. The significant cluster of biblical and theological concepts that were embedded in its use in that book was examined in detail, concepts that were referenced as a "missiological consensus." We also observed how the writing team that produced *Missional Church* appeared to fall short of adequately incorporating these various biblical and theological concepts into an integrated argument, and we noted how this has contributed to diverse interpretations of what it means to be missional.

Second, we identified the extensive usage of the term "missional" today, noting how it is being employed across many diverse faith traditions within the church, where the widespread production of missional literature is found in both print publications and Web sources. We provided a mapping of this diverse literature into four primary branches and ten subbranches by utilizing the hermeneutic of theological imagination in relation to agency in church life. The key question we asked in constructing this mapping was, To what extent are we simply dealing with human agency, and to what extent is God's agency operative, and discernible, within human choices?

Third, we examined how recent biblical and theological developments are continuing to enrich an understanding of missional as it relates to divine

167

agency. The theological proposal of participation was employed to develop a more integrated understanding of how God continues to work in the world as well as through the church. The theological proposal of relationality was utilized to develop a more substantive understanding of how the church relates to the world even as believers relate to one another and to the neighbor or the stranger.

Finally, we considered how these recent biblical and theological developments might be brought into conversation with various branches and sub-branches of the current missional conversation. Our intent throughout was to be invitational and constructive toward everyone engaged in the missional conversation as we continue together to discern how we might more fully participate in God's mission.

### Considering the Opportunity before Us

One of the more important insights coalescing within the missional conversation is the recognition that the church increasingly finds itself within a dramatically changed context. Although we do not believe that this development represents the most basic meaning of missional, we do concur that it is a very important dimension of the missional conversation. A variety of terms are used to discuss this shift, such as "postmodern," "post-Christendom," "globalized world," "information age," and "network society." We believe this shared insight among so many in the diverse missional conversation about our changed and changing context provides a fruitful opportunity for bringing many contributors within the different branches into mutual conversations. There is much to learn from one another. We want to encourage the pursuit of such conversations in light of two important considerations.

First, we believe, as we have attempted to demonstrate throughout this book, that important biblical and theological insights embedded within diverse faith traditions must be reconsidered from a missional perspective, even as these insights are discussed with those from other faith traditions. We would further encourage participants in such conversations to carefully consider how recent biblical and theological developments as explored in this book might inform their own faith traditions. The practice of engaging in such conversations theologically can be framed by bringing the theme of participation to bear (see chapter 4).

Second, we know that the missional conversation has taken root in many locations around the world, even though we have not explicitly pursued the mapping of such in this book. We have tried to carefully examine our own context since that is our particular social location. But clearly, there are diverse global voices that must be included in mutual conversation for the missional church to understand and engage more deeply what God is doing in the world today. A way to frame the pursuit of such conversations theologically is to bring the themes of relationality and reciprocity to bear (see chapter 5).

## To the Glory of God for the Sake of the World

The missional church conversation has unleashed a great deal of energy and hopefulness among churches stuck in patterns of church life that have become disconnected from a changing world. Leaders weary of trying the latest strategy or technique, burdened by the impossible expectations of entertaining and satisfying fickle spiritual consumers, and staggering under the weight of collapsing church institutions are waking up to a new sense of possibility as they explore what it means to rediscover their identities within God's larger mission. The horizon of imagination is expanding.

On some level, the elasticity of missional that we have traced in this book corresponds to the wideness of God's own life and the richness of cultures and perspectives in God's church and world. Our hope is that the expanding missional conversation may continue to go deeper and grow more expansive as it incorporates more theological and church traditions, contexts, and diverse voices. The Spirit is doing something powerful in the missional conversation. May the Spirit lead us all into deeper engagement and participation in the Triune God's life and the life of God's world.

# Bibliography

Ammons, Edsel Albert. "Congregational Linkage for Missional Ministry: Examination of the Endeavor of Two Urban Churches to Create a New Form of Faithful Witness." DMin thesis, Chicago Theological Seminary, 1975.

Anderson, Ray S. *An Emergent Theology for Emerging Churches*. Downers Grove, IL: IVP Books, 2006.

Appadurai, Arjun. *Modernity at Large: Cultural Dimensions of Globalization*. Minneapolis: University of Minnesota Press, 1996.

Archbishops' Council 2004. *Mission-Shaped Church: Church Planting and Fresh Expressions of Church in a Changing Context*. London: Church Publishing House, 2004.

Bailey, John M., ed. *Pursuing the Mission of God in Church Planting: The Missional Church in North America*. Alpharetta, GA: North American Mission Board of the Southern Baptist Convention, 2007.

Banks, Robert. *Redeeming the Routines: Bringing Theology to Life*. Grand Rapids: Baker Academic, 1993.

Barrett, Lois Y., et al. *Treasure in Clay Jars: Patterns in Missional Faithfulness*. Grand Rapids: Eerdmans, 2004.

Barth, Karl. *Church Dogmatics*. Vol. 4. Translated by Thomas F. Torrance and Geoffrey W. Bromiley. New York: Scribner, 1936.

———. *Theologische Fragen und Antworten*. Zollikon: Evangelischer Verlag, 1957.

Bass, Diana Butler. *The Practicing Congregation: Imagining a New Old Church*. Herndon, VA: Alban Institute, 2004.

Bass, Dorothy C. *Practicing Our Faith: A Way of Life for a Searching People*. San Francisco: Jossey-Bass, 1997.

Bassham, Rodger C. *Mission Theology 1948–1975: Years of Worldwide Creative Tension, Ecumenical, Evangelical, and Roman Catholic.* Pasadena, CA: William Carey Library, 1979.

Bauman, Zygmunt. *Identity.* Malden, MA: Polity Press, 2004.

Belcher, Jim. *Deep Church: A Third Way beyond Emerging and Traditional.* Downers Grove, IL: IVP Books, 2009.

Benkler, Yochai. *The Wealth of Networks: How Social Production Transforms Markets and Freedom.* New Haven: Yale University Press, 2006.

Berger, Peter L. *The Desecularization of the World: Resurgent Religion and World Politics.* Grand Rapids: Eerdmans, 1999.

Bergquist, Linda, and Allan Karr. *Church Turned Inside Out: A Guide for Designers, Refiners, and Re-Aligners.* San Francisco: Jossey-Bass, 2010.

Bettenson, Henry, ed. *Documents of the Christian Church.* Oxford: Oxford University Press, 1963.

Bevans, Stephen. *Models of Contextual Theology.* Rev. ed. Maryknoll, NY: Orbis Books, 2002.

Bickers, Dennis. *Intentional Ministry in a Not-So-Mega Church: Becoming a Missional Community.* Kansas City, MO: Beacon Hill, 2009.

Billings, Todd. "What Makes a Church Missional?" *Christianity Today* (March 2008), http://www.christianitytoday.com/ct/2008/march/16.56.html.

Blauw, Johannas. *The Missionary Nature of the Church: A Survey of the Biblical Theology of Mission.* New York: McGraw-Hill, 1962.

Boff, Leonardo. *Trinity and Society.* Maryknoll, NY: Orbis Books, 1988.

Bonhoeffer, Dietrich. *The Cost of Discipleship.* New York: Touchstone, 1995.

Bosch, David J. *Transforming Mission: Paradigm Shifts in Theology of Mission.* Maryknoll, NY: Orbis Books, 1991.

Bourne, C. E. *The Heroes of African Discovery and Adventure, from the Death of Livingstone to the Year 1882.* London: W. S. Sonnenschein, 1883.

Callahan, Kennon L. *Effective Church Leadership: Building on the Twelve Keys.* San Francisco: Harper & Row, 1990.

———. *Twelve Keys to an Effective Church.* San Francisco: Harper & Row, 1983.

Calvin, John. *Institutes of the Christian Religion.* Vol. 1. Edited by John Thomas McNeill. Translated by Ford Lewis Battles. Philadelphia: Westminster, 1960.

Castells, Manuel. *The Rise of the Network Society.* 2nd ed. Malden, MA: Blackwell, 2000.

Chilcote, Paul W., and Laceye C. Warner. *The Study of Evangelism: Exploring a Missional Practice of the Church.* Grand Rapids: Eerdmans, 2008.

Chung, Paul S. *The Spirit of God Transforming Life: The Reformation and the Theology of the Holy Spirit*. New York: Palgrave Macmillan, 2009.

Cole, Neil. *Organic Church*. San Francisco: Jossey-Bass, 2005.

Conn, Harvie. *Eternal Word and Changing Worlds*. Grand Rapids: Zondervan, 1984.

Cooperative Baptist Fellowship. *It's Time: . . . A Journey toward Missional Faithfulness*. Atlanta: Cooperative Baptist Fellowship, 2005.

Cormode, Scott. *Making Spiritual Sense: Christian Leaders as Spiritual Interpreters*. Nashville: Abingdon, 2006.

Creps, Earl. *Off-Road Disciplines: Spiritual Adventures of Missional Leaders*. San Francisco: Jossey-Bass, 2006.

Cunningham, David S. *These Three Are One: The Practice of Trinitarian Theology*. Malden, MA: Blackwell, 1998.

Dally, John Addison. *Choosing the Kingdom: Missional Preaching for the Household of God*. Herndon, VA: Alban Institute, 2008.

Daubert, Dave. "Vision-Discerning vs. Vision-Casting: How Shared Vision Can Raise Up Communities of Leaders Rather than Mere Leaders of Communities." In *The Missional Church and Leadership Formation: Helping Congregations Develop Leadership Capacity*, edited by Craig Van Gelder, 147–71. Grand Rapids: Eerdmans, 2009.

Dietterich, Inagrace T. *Cultivating Missional Communities*. Eugene, OR: Wipf & Stock, 2006.

Dreier, Mary Sue, ed. *Created and Led by the Spirit: Planting Missional Congregations*. Grand Rapids: Eerdmans, forthcoming.

Driscoll, Mark. *Confessions of a Reformission Rev.: Hard Lessons from an Emerging Missional Church*. Grand Rapids: Zondervan, 2006.

DuBose, Francis. *God Who Sends: A Fresh Quest for Biblical Mission*. Nashville: Broadman, 1983.

Duchrow, Ulrich. *Two Kingdoms: The Use and Misuse of a Lutheran Theological Concept*. Geneva: Lutheran World Federation Department of Studies, 1977.

Dyrness, William A. *The Earth Is God's: A Theology of American Culture*. Maryknoll, NY: Orbis Books, 1997.

Eaker, Mitzi. *Missions Moments 2: 52 Easy-to-Use Missional Messages and Activities for Today's Family*. Birmingham, AL: New Hope, 2008.

Eck, Diana L. *A New Religious America*. New York: HarperCollins, 2001.

Ellison, Pat Taylor. "Word-Dwelling, Deep Listening, and Faith-Based Moral Conversation in Congregations: A Nested Vision for Learning New Habits."

In *Testing the Spirits: How Theology Informs the Study of Congregations*, edited by Patrick Keifert, 91–108. Grand Rapids: Eerdmans, 2009.

Faith and Order. *Baptism, Eucharist, and Ministry*. Geneva: World Council of Churches, 1982.

———. *The Nature and Purpose of the Church*. Geneva: World Council of Churches, 1998.

Fiddes, Paul S. *Participating in God: A Pastoral Doctrine of the Trinity*. Louisville: Westminster John Knox, 2000.

Flannery, Austin P., ed. *Documents of Vatican II*. Grand Rapids: Eerdmans, 1975.

Flett, John. *The Witness of God: The Trinity, Missio Dei, Karl Barth, and the Nature of Christian Community*. Grand Rapids: Eerdmans, 2010.

Frambach, Nate C. P. *Emerging Ministry: Being Church Today*. Minneapolis: Augsburg Fortress, 2007.

Frederickson, David. "Congregations, Democracy, and the Action of God in Philippians 1–2." In *Testing the Spirits*, edited by Patrick R. Keifert, 48–66. Grand Rapids: Eerdmans, 2009.

Frost, Michael, and Alan Hirsch. *ReJesus: A Wild Messiah for a Missional Church*. Peabody, MA/Grand Rapids: Hendrickson/Baker Books, 2009.

———. *The Shaping of Things to Come: Innovation and Mission for the 21st-Century Church*. Peabody, MA/Grand Rapids: Hendrickson/Baker Books, 2003.

Geertz, Clifford. *The Interpretation of Cultures: Selected Essays*. New York: Basic Books, 1973.

Gibbs, Eddie. *ChurchMorph: How Megatrends Are Reshaping Christian Communities*. Grand Rapids: Baker Academic, 2009.

Gibbs, Eddie, and Ryan K. Bolger. *Emerging Churches: Creating Christian Communities in Postmodern Cultures*. Grand Rapids: Baker Academic, 2005.

Giddens, Anthony. *Modernity and Self-Identity*. Stanford, CA: Stanford University Press, 1991.

Goheen, Michael W. "The Missional Church: Ecclesiological Discussion in the Gospel and Our Culture Network in North America." *Missiology* 30, no. 4 (October 2002): 479–90.

"The Gospel and Our Culture." *Missiology: An International Review* 19, no. 4 (October 1991): 391–473.

Grant, Robert M., ed. *Irenaeus of Lyons*. Early Church Fathers. New York: Routledge, 1997.

Grenz, Stanley J. *Rediscovering the Triune God: The Trinity in Contemporary Theology*. Minneapolis: Fortress, 2004.

———. *The Social God and the Relational Self: A Trinitarian Theology of the Imago Dei*. Louisville: Westminster John Knox, 2001.

Guder, Darrell L. *The Continuing Conversion of the Church*. Grand Rapids: Eerdmans, 2000.

———. "Leadership in New Congregations: New-Church Development from the Perspective of Missional Theology." In *Extraordinary Leaders in Extraordinary Times: Unadorned Clay Pot Messengers*, edited by H. Stanley Wood, 1–29. Grand Rapids: Eerdmans, 2006.

———, ed. *Missional Church: A Vision for the Sending of the Church in North America*. Grand Rapids: Eerdmans, 1998.

———. "Work and Witness from the Perspective of Missional Church Theology." *Word & World* 25, no. 4 (Fall 2005): 424–32.

Gunton, Colin E. *The Promise of Trinitarian Theology*. 2nd ed. Edinburgh: T&T Clark, 1997.

Gustafson, James. "The Sectarian Temptation: Reflections on Theology, the Church, and the University." *Proceedings of the Catholic Theological Society* 40 (1985): 83–94.

Hagley, Scott, Mark Love, John Ogren, and Jannie Swart. "Toward a Missional Theology of Participation: Ecumenical Reflections on Contributions to Trinity, Mission, and Church." In *Missiology* 37, no. 1 (January 2009): 75–87.

Hanciles, Jehu. *Beyond Christendom: Globalization, African Migration, and the Transformation of the West*. Maryknoll, NY: Orbis Books, 2008.

Harrington, Todd. *Resonating the Gospel within a Post Christian Culture: Birthing Church within a Church Missional Communities*. La Vergne, TN: Lightning Source, 2008.

Hauerwas, Stanley. *Christian Existence Today: Essays on Church, World, and Living in Between*. Grand Rapids: Baker Academic, 1995.

Hauerwas, Stanley, and William H. Willimon. *Resident Aliens: Life in the Christian Colony*. Nashville: Abingdon, 1989.

Hawkins, Greg, and Cally Parkinson. *Reveal*. South Barrington, IL: Willow Creek Association, 2007.

Hirsch, Alan. *The Forgotten Ways*. Grand Rapids: Brazos, 2006.

Hockendijk, J. C. *The Church Inside Out*. Santa Ana, CA: Westminster, 1967.

Holmes, William Gordon. *The Age of Justinian and Theodora: A History of the Sixth Century AD*. London: G. Bell & Sons, 1912.

Hopkins, Bob, and Freddy Hedley. *Coaching for Missional Leadership*. Sheffield: ACPI Books, 2008.

Hudson, Trevor. *A Mile in My Shoes: Cultivating Compassion*. Nashville: Upper Room, 2005.

Hunsberger, George R. "The Missional Voice and Posture of Public Theologizing." *Missiology* 34, no. 1 (January 2006): 15–28.

Hunsberger, George R., and Craig Van Gelder, eds. *The Church between Gospel and Culture: The Emerging Mission in North America*. Grand Rapids: Eerdmans, 1996.

Husbands, Mark. "The Trinity Is Not Our Social Program." In *Trinitarian Theology for the Church*, edited by Daniel J. Treier and David Lauber, 120–41. Downers Grove, IL: IVP Academic, 2009.

Jenkins, Philip. *The New Faces of Christianity: Believing the Bible in the Global South*. New York: Oxford University Press, 2006.

Jenson, Robert W. *Unbaptized God: The Basic Flaw in Ecumenical Theology*. Minneapolis: Fortress, 1992.

Johnson, Elizabeth A. *She Who Is: The Mystery of God in Feminist Theological Discourse*. New York: Crossroad, 1992.

Kant, Immanuel. *Religion and Rational Theology*. Translated by Allen W. Wood and George Di Giovanni. New York: Cambridge University Press, 1996.

Keel, Tim. *Intuitive Leadership*. Grand Rapids: Baker Books, 2007.

Keifert, Patrick. *We Are Here Now: A Missional Journey of Spiritual Discovery*. Eagle, ID: Allelon, 2006.

———. *Welcoming the Stranger: A Public Theology of Worship and Evangelism*. Minneapolis: Fortress, 1992.

Kimball, Dan. *The Emerging Church: Vintage Christianity for New Generations*. Grand Rapids: Zondervan, 2003.

———. "Missional Misgivings," *Leadership* 29, no. 4 (Fall 2008), http://www.ctlibrary.com/le/2008/fall/14.112.html.

Klaas, Alan C., and Cheryl D. Klaas. *Flexible, Missional Constitution/Bylaws: In One Day, Not Two Years*. Oak Park, IL: Mission Growth, 2000.

Kraft, Charles H. *Christianity in Culture*. 2nd ed. Maryknoll, NY: Orbis Books, 2005.

Küng, Hans. *The Church*. New York: Sheed & Ward, 1967.

LaCugna, Catherine Mowry. *God for Us: The Trinity and Christian Life*. San Francisco: HarperSanFrancisco, 1991.

Ladd, George Eldon. *Gospel of the Kingdom: Scriptural Studies in the Kingdom of God*. Grand Rapids: Eerdmans, 1959.

Lausanne Committee for World Evangelization. "The Local Church in Mission: Becoming a Missional Congregation in the Twenty-First Century Global Context and the Opportunities Offered through Tentmaking Ministry." Lausanne Occasional Paper no. 39, 2005.

Liederbach, Mark, and Alvin L. Reid. *The Convergent Church: Missional Worshippers in an Emerging Culture*. Grand Rapids: Kregel, 2009.

Lindbeck, George A. *The Nature of Doctrine: Religion and Theology in a Post-liberal Age*. Philadelphia: Westminster, 1984.

Lindgren, Alvin J., and Norman Shawchuck. *Management for Your Church*. Nashville: Abingdon, 1977.

Lohfink, Gerhard. *Jesus and Community: The Social Dimension of Christian Faith*. Translated by John P. Galvin. Philadelphia: Fortress, 1984.

Luther, Martin. "On the Councils and the Church," 1539. In *Luther's Works*, vol. 41, edited by Eric W. Gritsch. Philadelphia: Fortress, 1966.

Luzbetak, Louis J. *The Church and Cultures: New Perspectives in Missiological Anthropology*. Maryknoll, NY: Orbis Books, 1988.

MacIntyre, Alasdair C. *After Virtue: A Study in Moral Theory*. Notre Dame, IN: University of Notre Dame Press, 1981.

Mancini, Will. *Church Unique: How Missional Leaders Cast Vision, Capture Culture, and Create Movement*. San Francisco: Jossey-Bass, 2008.

Marty, Martin E. "Public and Private: Congregation as Meeting Place." In *American Congregations*, edited by James P. Wind and James W. Lewis, 133–66. Chicago: University of Chicago Press, 1994.

———. *Righteous Empire: The Protestant Experience in America*. New York: Dial Press, 1970.

McCord, Peter J. *Pope for All Christians? An Inquiry into the Role of Peter in the Modern Church*. New York: Paulist Press, 1976.

McGavran, Donald. "Will Uppsala Betray the Two Billion?" In *Church Growth Bulletin: Institute of Church Growth* 7, no. 6 (July 1971): 149–53.

McLaren, Brian D. *A Generous Orthodoxy: Why I am a missional + evangelical + post/protestant + liberal/conservative + mystical/poetic + biblical + charismatic/contemplative + fundamentalist/Calvinist + Anabaptist/Anglican + Methodist + Catholic + Green + incarnational + depressed-yet-hopeful + emergent + unfinished Christian*. Grand Rapids: Zondervan, 2004.

McNeal, Reggie. *Missional Renaissance: Changing the Scorecard for the Church*. San Francisco: Jossey-Bass, 2009.

———. *The Present Future: Six Tough Questions for the Church*. San Francisco: Jossey-Bass, 2003.

Minatrea, Milfred. *Shaped by God's Heart: The Passion and Practices of Missional Churches*. San Francisco: Jossey-Bass, 2004.

Minear, Paul. *Images of the Church in the New Testament*. Philadelphia: Westminster, 1960.

Moltmann, Jürgen. *The Crucified God: The Cross of Christ as the Foundation and Criticism of Christian Theology*. Minneapolis: Fortress, 1993.

———. *God in Creation: A New Theology of Creation and the Spirit of God*. Minneapolis: Fortress, 1993.

———. "Perichoresis: An Old Magic Word for a New Trinitarian Theology." In *Trinity, Community and Power: Mapping Trajectories in Wesleyan Theology*, edited by M. Douglas Meeks, 111–25. Nashville: Kingswood Books, 2000.

———. *The Trinity and the Kingdom: The Doctrine of God*. Minneapolis: Fortress, 1993.

Montefiore, Hugh, ed. *The Gospel and Contemporary Culture*. London: Cassell Academic, 1992.

Mouw, Richard J. *He Shines in All That's Fair: Culture and Common Grace*. Grand Rapids: Eerdmans, 2001.

Nelson, Gary V. *Borderland Churches: A Congregation's Introduction to Missional Living*. St. Louis: Chalice, 2008.

Nelstrop, Louise, and Martyn Percy, eds. *Evaluating Fresh Expressions: Explorations in Emerging Church*. Norwich, UK: Canterbury Press, 2008.

Newbigin, Lesslie. *Foolishness to the Greeks*. Grand Rapids: Eerdmans, 1986.

———. *The Gospel in a Pluralist Society*. Grand Rapids: Eerdmans, 1989.

———. *The Open Secret: An Introduction to the Theology of Mission*. Grand Rapids: Eerdmans, 1978.

———. *The Other Side of 1984: Questions to the Churches*. Geneva: Consul Oecumenique, 1983.

Northouse, Peter Guy. *Leadership: Theory and Practice*. 4th ed. Thousand Oaks, CA: Sage, 2007.

Page, Frank. *The Nehemiah Factor: 16 Characteristics of a Missional Leader*. Birmingham, AL: New Hope, 2008.

Payne, J. D. *Missional House Churches: Reaching Our Communities with the Gospel*. Colorado Springs: Paternoster, 2008.

Pohl, Christine D. *Making Room: Recovering Hospitality as a Christian Tradition*. Grand Rapids: Eerdmans, 1999.

Powell, Kara E., and Brad M. Griffin. *Deep Justice Journeys: Moving from Mission Trips to Missional Living*. Grand Rapids: Zondervan, 2008.

Power, John C. *Mission Theology Today*. Dublin: Gill & Macmillan, 1970.

Prosser, Bo. *Approaching a Missional Mindset*. Macon, GA: NextSunday Resources, 2008.

Putman, David. *Breaking the Discipleship Code: Becoming a Missional Follower of Jesus*. Nashville: B&H Publishing Group, 2008.

Putnam, Robert D., and Lewis Feldstein. *Better Together: Restoring the American Community*. New York: Simon & Schuster, 2003.

Rahner, Karl. *The Trinity*. Translated by Joseph Donceel. New York: Herder, 1970.

Reason, Peter, and Hilary Bradbury. "Inquiry and Participation in Search of a World Worthy of Human Aspiration." In *Handbook of Action Research*, edited by Peter Reason and Hilary Bradbury, 1–14. Concise paperback ed. Thousand Oaks, CA: Sage, 2006.

Reed, Eric. "New Ownership: Missional Is More than a Trend as Today's Christians Recover an Old Calling." *Leadership Journal* (Winter 2007): 19–22.

Regele, Mike. *Robust Church Development: A Vision for Mobilizing Regional Bodies in Support of Missional Congregations*. Rancho Santa Margarita, CA: Percept Group, 2003.

Richey, Russell E. "Denominations and Denominationalism: An American Morphology." In *Reimagining Denominationalism: Interpretive Essays*, edited by Robert Bruce Mullin and Russell E. Richey, 74–98. New York: Oxford University Press, 1994.

Ridderbos, Herman. *The Coming of the Kingdom*. Phillipsburg, NJ: Presbyterian & Reformed, 1962.

Rogers, Everett M. *Diffusion of Innovations*. 5th ed. New York: Free Press, 2003.

Rohrmayer, Gary. *First Steps for Planting a Missional Church*. St. Charles, IL: ChurchSmart Resources, 2006.

Rouse, Rick, and Craig Van Gelder. *A Field Guide for the Missional Congregation: Embarking on a Journey of Transformation*. Minneapolis: Augsburg Fortress, 2008.

Roxburgh, Alan J., and M. Scott Boren. *Introducing the Missional Church: What It Is, Why It Matters, How to Become One*. Grand Rapids: Baker Books, 2009.

Roxburgh, Alan J., and Fred Romanuk. *The Missional Leader: Equipping Your Church to Reach a Changing World*. San Francisco: Jossey-Bass, 2006.

Rusaw, Rick, and Eric Swanson. *The Externally Focused Church*. Loveland, CO: Group, 2004.

Sachs, William L., Thomas P. Holland, and the Episcopal Church Foundation. *Restoring the Ties That Bind: The Grassroots Transformation of the Episcopal Church*. New York: Church Publishing, 2003.

Sanneh, Lamin O. *Translating the Message: The Missionary Impact on Culture*. Maryknoll, NY: Orbis Books, 1989.

———. *Whose Religion Is Christianity? The Gospel beyond the West*. Grand Rapids: Eerdmans, 2003.

Scherer, James A. *Gospel, Church, and Kingdom: Comparative Studies in World Mission Theology*. Minneapolis: Augsburg, 1987.

Schmit, Clayton J. *Sent and Gathered: A Worship Manual for the Missional Church*. Grand Rapids: Baker Academic, 2009.

Schreiter, Robert J. *The New Catholicity: Theology between the Global and the Local*. Maryknoll, NY: Orbis Books, 1997.

Schwarz, Christian A. *Natural Church Development: A Guide to Eight Essential Qualities of Healthy Churches*. 4th ed. St. Charles, IL: ChurchSmart Resources, 2000.

Schweitzer, Albert. *The Quest of the Historical Jesus: A Critical Study of Its Progress from Reimarus to Wrede*. Translated by W. Montgomery. London: A & C Black, 1910.

Simpson, Gary M. *Critical Social Theory: Prophetic Reason, Civil Society, and Christian Imagination*. Minneapolis: Fortress, 2002.

———. "No Trinity, No Mission: The Apostolic Difference of Revisioning the Trinity." *Word & World* 15, no. 3 (1998): 264–71.

———. "A Reformation Is a Terrible Thing to Waste." In *The Missional Church in Context*, edited by Craig Van Gelder, 65–93. Grand Rapids: Eerdmans, 2007.

Snyder, Howard. *Decoding the Church: Mapping the DNA of Christ's Body*. Grand Rapids: Baker Books, 2002.

Spellers, Stephanie. *Radical Welcome: Embracing God, the Other and the Spirit of Transformation*. New York: Church Publishing, 2006.

Stetzer, Ed. *Planting Missional Churches: Planting a Church That's Biblically Sound and Reaching People in Culture*. Nashville: Broadman & Holman, 2006.

———. *Sent: Living the Missional Nature of the Church*. Nashville: LifeWay, 2008.

Stetzer, Ed, and Philip Nation. *Compelled by Love: The Most Excellent Way to Missional Living*. Birmingham, AL: New Hope, 2008.

Stetzer, Ed, and David Putman. *Breaking the Missional Code: Your Church Can Become a Missionary in Your Community*. Nashville: Broadman & Holman, 2006.

Swart, Jannie. "Christian Leadership as Communion Imagination in the Public Networking of Organizational Companionship." *Journal of Religious Leadership* 7, no. 2 (Fall 2008): 87–115.

Tanner, Kathryn. *Theories of Culture: A New Agenda for Theology.* Minneapolis: Fortress, 1997.

Taylor, Charles. *A Secular Age.* Cambridge, MA: Belknap Press of Harvard University Press, 2007.

Thomas, Norman E., ed. *Classic Texts in Mission and World Christianity.* Maryknoll, NY: Orbis Books, 1995.

Van Engen, Charles. *God's Missionary People: Rethinking the Purpose of the Local Church.* Grand Rapids: Baker Academic, 1991.

Van Gelder, Craig, ed. *Confident Witness—Changing World: Rediscovering the Gospel in North America.* Grand Rapids: Eerdmans, 1999.

———. *The Essence of the Church: A Community Created by the Spirit.* Grand Rapids: Baker Academic, 2000.

———. *The Ministry of the Missional Church: A Community Led by the Spirit.* Grand Rapids: Baker Academic, 2007.

———. *The Missional Church and Denominations: Helping Congregations Develop a Missional Identity.* Grand Rapids: Eerdmans, 2008.

———. *The Missional Church and Leadership Formation: Helping Congregations Develop Leadership Capacity.* Grand Rapids: Eerdmans, 2009.

———. *The Missional Church in Context: Helping Congregations Develop Contextual Ministry.* Grand Rapids: Eerdmans, 2007.

Vicedom, Georg F. *The Mission of God: An Introduction to the Theology of Mission.* St. Louis: Concordia, 1965.

Volf, Miroslav. *After Our Likeness: The Church as the Image of the Trinity.* Grand Rapids: Eerdmans, 1998.

———. *Exclusion and Embrace: A Theological Exploration of Identity, Otherness, and Reconciliation.* Nashville: Abingdon, 1996.

Volf, Miroslav, and Dorothy C. Bass. *Practicing Theology: Beliefs and Practices in Christian Life.* Grand Rapids: Eerdmans, 2002.

Vos, Geerhardus. *Biblical Theology: Old and New Testaments.* 1948. Reprint, Carlisle, PA: Banner of Truth, 1975.

Waresak, Joe. *The Missional Life: Living and Sharing Christ.* Longwood, FL: Xulon, 2008.

Warren, Rick. *The Purpose-Driven Church.* Grand Rapids: Zondervan, 1995.

Weick, Karl E. *Sensemaking in Organizations.* Thousand Oaks, CA: Sage, 1995.

Weiss, Johannes. *Jesus' Proclamation of the Kingdom of God.* Translated by Richard Hyde Hiers and David Larrimore Holland. 1892. Reprint, Philadelphia: Fortress, 1971.

Welker, Michael. *God the Spirit.* Minneapolis: Fortress, 1994.

Wilson-Hartgrove, Jonathan. *New Monasticism: What It Has to Say to Today's Church.* Grand Rapids: Brazos, 2008.

Winders, Barry E. *Finding the Missional Path.* Longwood, FL: Xulon, 2007.

Winter, Gibson. *The Suburban Captivity of the Churches: An Analysis of Protestant Responsibility in the Expanding Metropolis.* Garden City, NY: Doubleday, 1961.

Wiseman, Neil B., ed. *Next Door and Down the Freeway: Developing a Missional Strategy for USA/Canada.* Kansas City, MO: Beacon Hill, 2001.

World Council of Churches. *The Church for Others: Two Reports on the Missionary Structure of the Church.* Geneva: World Council of Churches, 1967.

Zizioulas, John D. *Being as Communion: Studies in Personhood and the Church.* Crestwood, NY: St. Vladimir's Seminary Press, 1985.

———. *Communion and Otherness: Further Studies in Personhood and the Church.* New York: T&T Clark, 2007.

Zscheile, Dwight. "Social Networking and Church Systems." *Word & World* 30, no. 3 (Summer 2010): 247–55.

———. "The Trinity, Leadership and Power." *Journal of Religious Leadership* 6, no. 2 (Fall 2007): 43–63.

# Index

# THE MISSIONAL NETWORK

**Missional Perspective**—TMN frames its work within a biblical and theological missional perspective—God's mission in the world and the church's participation in this mission. Organizational understanding of systems is used to support transformation across church bodies.

. . . . . . . . . . . . . . . . .

A network of leaders across North America and the UK committed to a practical and biblical/theological engagement with the missional conversation in the church.

. . . . . . . . . . . . . . . . .

**Tools and Resources**—TMN assists the church in processes of missional innovation.

**Consulting and Coaching**—TMN supports church systems at all levels. Consulting builds the capacities of church systems to engage in missional transformation. Coaching walks alongside leaders in strengthening their skills and capacities for leading.

**Writing/Publishing**—TMN's team of teachers and practitioners produce books to deepen the missional conversation from a biblical and theological perspective.

**Associates and Partners**—Our team, equipped with a deep understanding of the historical development of denominations, takes seriously the traditions of church systems viewing them as a helpful gift to the larger church.

**w w w . t h e m i s s i o n a l n e t w o r k . c o m**